A Celebration of the Sea

For my mother
IRENE PRENTICE

A Celebration of the Sea

The Decorative Art Collections
of the
National Maritime Museum

Rina Prentice

ISBN 0 11 290531 5

All the chapter head motifs are derived from objects in the collection of the National Maritime Museum:

1. Liverpool delftware ship tile printed by Sadler *c*1758–61.

2. Printed enamel plaque with portrait of Admiral Rodney *c*1782.

3. Lloyds Patriotic Fund Trafalgar vase to Captain James Morris, 1806.

4. *Jemmy's Farewell*, engraving published by Robert Sayer, 1786.

5. Trade sign of an optical instrument maker, dressed in the uniform of a Lieutenant RN, 1787–1812.

6. Sinking of the *Royal George*, watercolour by T Buttersworth, 1800.

7. Yacht *Lillie*, printed on a Wedgwood plate, 1895.

8. Lord Nelson's coat of arms from his personal porcelain service.

Printed in the United Kingdom for HMSO
Dd 293685 C30 9/94 32719

Contents

Chapter

FOREWORD by Hugh Scully

Rarely has a book been more long-awaited than *A Celebration of the Sea*. All those elements that make our maritime heritage so rich and fascinating come together in these pages. The central theme is the extent to which the sea in general, and the Royal Navy in particular, became so integrated with the British character and way of life that it influenced art and design to a degree never seen before or since. It is a theme in which I have always been passionately interested, and the meticulous research which forms such an essential part of this book is not just valuable but irreplaceable. Having spent many an hour foraging through naval bookshops in Plymouth, Portsmouth and Greenwich, in the vain search for such a comprehensive work, I shall treasure this new volume more than most. In many ways it is a history of the relationship between the Royal Navy and the British people, as expressed through popular art. No other country in the world can claim such a unique bond between a branch of military power and the people it exists to protect. This, in turn, helps to explain why British seapower has been so successful and so durable. In so many ways the Royal Navy and the interests of the British people have been synonymous. *A Celebration of the Sea* helps to explain why.

When Horatio Nelson died, a tide of national grief swept across Britain. It soon became fashionable for ladies in society to wear, around their necks, golden lockets containing a few strands of the admiral's hair. Soon afterwards, these small personal mementoes were followed by massive national monuments – Nelson's Column and Trafalgar Square. Nelson's great victories influenced British art and design to an extraordinary degree. The Battle of the Nile so captured the public imagination that Egyptian themes, the Sphinx and pyramids in particular, began to appear on furniture, wall decorations and garden ornaments. In great country houses entire rooms were decorated in the Egyptian style. One of the most prominent buildings in Penzance is the Egyptian House. The Royal Pavilion in Brighton, itself a celebration of the Indian Empire made possible by seapower, houses a superb collection of dolphin furniture, each piece reflecting in an almost subconscious way the extent to which the sea had penetrated the national psyche. Rope-back chairs and scallop shell designs on other furniture and ceramics were all part of the same nostalgia. After Trafalgar, and the death of the great national hero, the mood became more sombre, but the naval influence persisted. A funereal black line, in memory of Nelson, began to appear as a common inlay on furniture, and the 1st Rate ship of the line (closely resembling HMS *Victory*) became a widely used motif on pottery and porcelain design, as well as inspiring countless water-colour and oil paintings.

When making a series of television documentaries to mark the tenth anniversary of the Falklands War in 1992, one of the things I found most extraordinary about the Argentine Navy is that to this day its officers wear a black stripe down their trouser leg in memory of Nelson.

But the Royal Navy's grip on the public imagination extended far beyond a celebration of great naval victories. British seapower was the key to exploration and to empire. The eighteenth and nineteenth centuries had been years in which we had secured a foothold in many parts of the world where no Europeans had ever ventured. That exploration had resulted in a transformation of our way of life. Cabinet makers had traditionally relied on indigenous woods, such as oak, elm, ash, cherry and French walnut. As a result of the era of exploration made possible by seapower, new exotic woods such as ebony, padouk and mahogany began to be widely used. This, in turn, influenced design. The woods from the West Indies and the Far East were harder and more durable, thus allowing a certain quality of delicacy to be achieved without compromising strength. The furniture of Hepplewhite and Sheraton relied heavily on imported timber and exotic woods.

Seapower also meant that trade routes around the world were kept open, and virtually every aspect of our national life was influenced by the results of being a great naval power. On a fundamental level, the drinking of tea, coffee and rum were a direct result of the era of exploration and the growth of empire. Nineteenth century fashion, both for men and women, relied heavily on imported silks and cottons. Garden designers had access to a vast new world of exotic shrubs and plants. More importantly, the Industrial Revolution, which turned us into the greatest trading nation on earth, was only made possible by our total command of the seas. Our ships brought raw materials in and took finished products out to every part of the globe, always under the guardianship of the Naval ensign.

Explore this relationship between the Navy and the people one stage further and you realise that the most durable hero of all was Jack Tar, the ordinary British seaman whose nickname derived from the fact that his waterproof clothing was made from tarred sailcloth. The British sailor of the nineteenth century became a popular romantic figure. Despite the fact that he lived in often appalling conditions and was often pressed into service, rather than volunteering, he became the focus of public attention, and a somewhat glamorous figure. He had usually seen parts of the world others could only dream of, and his day-to-day experiences – in peacetime let alone in war – were enough to fill the public bar of any waterside tavern. Who else could boast that they had fought the French in the Mediterranean, or had been to parts of the world never seen by another European? Imagine the impact of being able to describe the coastline of Australia or the beauty of a Pacific island to someone whose world extended no further than the town or village in which they were born? This glamorous image did Jack Tar no harm whatever in his relations with women, and the most common and recurring themes in decorative subjects on pottery, porcelain and so many prints of the period were the sad parting, the fond farewell and the sailor home from the sea. What makes all this so poignant, when observing from more than one hundred years of hindsight, is that romance and tragedy were so closely interwoven. The fond farewell and the sad parting were very often the last Jack saw of his familiar shore and his wife or lover. When a woman stood on Plymouth Hoe and watched a sail disappear over the horizon she never knew when – if ever – she would see her man again. She might go, day after day, to the same spot to stand and wait for the homecoming. So often she waited in vain. She might keep hope alive for a whole year, or even two, but gradually and painfully the realisation dawned that Jack Tar was lost and gone forever. Perhaps he had been shipwrecked and drowned at sea; perhaps he had been on the end of a devastating broadside from a French or Spanish man o' war; perhaps he had simply found another woman in a new port. She would never know, but artists, designers, painters and writers would draw deeply from that particular well of inspiration, just as twentieth century popular novelists were later to do.

Every year I travel hundreds of miles around the country with my colleagues from BBC Television's *Antiques Roadshow*. They each have their areas of specialist knowledge and I never cease to be amazed by their expertise. They are people with passionate interests in particular areas of art and design. Several are fascinated by the influence of Chinese potters on European ceramics; others enjoy the pre-Raphaelites; Art Nouveau and Art Deco are also much in vogue, and all of us admire some of the beautiful eighteenth and nineteenth century furniture we see. But for me there is one subject that sets the pulse racing more than any other. Whenever I see a piece of Liverpool pottery, or a Sunderland lustre bowl, decorated with the figure of Jack Tar and his *doxie* (a sailor's slang for his woman) I stop and stare and want to know more; when someone brings in a piece of whale's tooth carving (known as scrimshaw) I am immediately fascinated by it. One of my own favourite nineteenth century prints, *The Sailor's Prayer* by Woodward, portrays a Jack Tar figure promising the Almighty to avenge the life of his friend *poor Mat Mizzen* who had been *popped off the Belerephon's bows at the Nile*. The prayer concludes that – if provided with handsome doxies in every port, spared from the guinea man and an empty can – he will go on to serve King George forever.

I know that *A Celebration of the Sea* will provide you with an invaluable guide to the way in which the sea, the sailor and the Royal Navy have permeated our national consciousness and influenced art and design in such a unique way. The great voyages of exploration, the evolution of empire, the challenge of the elements, the hard life of the sailor, the pain of parting, shipwreck, disaster and death at sea, they are all here.

A Celebration of the Sea is, in many ways, a cultural history of our maritime heritage. If you have ever been stirred by the imagery of a ship of the line under full sail you will enjoy this book enormously, since it explains how that ship, and the crew who manned it, sailed into our national identity and found a permanent berth in our maritime heritage.

Hugh Scully
Falmouth, Cornwall
August 1993

Acknowledgements

This book is based on the collections of the National Maritime Museum, and I am very aware of the large debt of gratitude I owe to all my curatorial predecessors. My own twenty-five years in the Museum have shown me that piecing together the sometimes meagre evidence available on particular items in the collection, in order to explain them and put them into historical context, is a long and painstaking process, and one which is by no means complete. The continuing task of cataloguing such a diverse collection has required much assistance from colleagues at Greenwich and other museums, as well as from collectors, dealers and members of the public whose enquiries have frequently contributed important pieces of evidence to help build up a complete picture.

I am grateful to the Trustees and Director of the National Maritime Museum for giving me the opportunity to work on this publication, and for their permission to illustrate so many items from the Museum's collection. First and foremost among my colleagues I must thank Roger Knight, Director of Collections, and Mary Hatwell, Head Curator, for their constant encouragement and enthusiasm for this project, and for reading and commenting on the typescript. I am grateful to John Munday, former Keeper of Antiquities, who also found time to read the text, and offered me helpful suggestions based on his wide knowledge of the Museum's collections.

My colleagues in the Museum are always generous with their help and advice, and I must mention particularly those curators who are responsible for the collections covered by this book: Patricia Blackett Barber, Caroline Roberts and Barbara Tomlinson, as well as Roger Quarm, Chrissie MacLeod, James Taylor and everyone else who has helped me.

I also offer my sincere thanks to the many curators in other museums who have offered advice and allowed me access to their collections. Again, this particular debt goes back over many years, but I would mention particularly Anthony Tibbles and Myra Brown at the Merseyside Maritime Museum, Arthur Credland of the Town Docks Museum, Hull, Andrew Helme of the Nelson Museum, Monmouth, Ray Allen of the Imperial War Museum, Colin White and Lesley Thomas of the Royal Naval Museum, Portsmouth, Rosemary Weinstein of the Museum of London, Philippa Glanville, Michael Archer and Wendy Hefford of the Victoria and Albert Museum, John Curtis and Janine Bailey of Lloyd's Corporation, Nigel Dalziel of Lancaster Maritime Museum, Pat Halfpenny of the City Museum and Art Gallery, Hanley, and Simon Faulkner of the Lynn Museum.

Many collectors, dealers, auctioneers, donors, lenders and others from the antiques world have generously given their time and expertise, especially James Blewitt, John May, Jonathan Horne, Marc Loost, Bob Ridding, Robert Benner, Sim Comfort, Gerard Molyneux and many others.

Finally I should like to thank some of the people who have enabled this book to come into being: David Spence, Head of Publications at the National Maritime Museum has guided its progress from start to finish, while Robert Gardiner and Richard Dorsett have also assisted. I am also grateful to Elizabeth Wiggans for compiling the index, and to Sarah Clout, who has frequently bailed me out of difficulties with my computer. Last, but certainly not least, I must mention the Museum's Photographic Department. Such a book obviously relies heavily on its illustrations, and I am grateful especially to James Stevenson and Tina Chambers for their patience and the endless pains they have taken to produce such high quality photographs of items in the Museum's collection.

Introduction

Since the earliest times ships and the sea have been an integral part of British life, and representations of seagoing vessels and nautical motifs have been a recurring decorative theme. From the ships on medieval town seals, which have entered into our national heraldry, to everyday modern symbols like anchors and compass roses, it is almost impossible to pass a day without being reminded that we are an island race.

Out of this traditional use of maritime motifs as decoration there grew a conscious intention to celebrate particular events by producing objects which portrayed individual ships and their commanders who had come to public notice. The reason for their manufacture may have been to depict a naval battle and commemorate a victory, or it may have been intended as a memorial to a sea disaster or the death of a hero. Sometimes the occasion may have been some more peaceful event, like the launch of a ship or a toast to the success of a vessel outward bound on her first voyage.

The purpose of this book has been to use the National Maritime Museum's unrivalled collection of decorative art objects with nautical associations to explore a number of historical themes. The illustrations are taken from a wide variety of three-dimensional objects, including pottery and porcelain, silver, glass, furniture, heraldic items and sailors' handicrafts. The subjects examined range from the vessels depicted, through naval battles and rewards for victory, to representations of the officers and seamen who served in the ships. Both the Royal Navy and the merchant service are featured, and the far corners of the collections have been tapped to illustrate passenger and exploration voyages, sea disasters, pleasure boating and the decorative use of nautical motifs.

In the eighteenth century, before the days of mass communications, public figures were much less easily recognised from portraits than they are today, and an inscription was often more important in identifying an individual than a correct likeness. At the lower end of the market the manufacturers, who sometimes had little access to reliable sources themselves, could get away with a mere nod in the direction of accuracy. At the same time there were plenty of high quality pieces which accurately reproduced source engravings.

When Thomas Carlisle wrote in 1757 of one of the better commemorative productions of the mid-eighteenth century, the Worcester porcelain mug printed that year by Robert Hancock with a portrait of Frederick, King of Prussia, he described it as: *this hasty Mug. A mug got up for temporary English enthusiasm, and the accidental instruction of posterity.*[1] In this book we shall encounter many of the productions which he described in the same passage as *poor, well-meant China Portraits,* and our voyage will take us from the finest, most expensive and elegant presentation pieces to those cheap and disposable souvenirs which were intended to be used only as long as the subject was fashionable, or at best promoted to a place of honour on the cottage mantelpiece.

There is an inevitable emphasis on later eighteenth and early nineteenth century examples, which not only reflects the present strengths of the collections at Greenwich but is indicative of the peaks in manufacture of this type of commemorative material. Before the middle of the eighteenth century, objects celebrating specific maritime events tended to be specially commissioned items of value, rather than pieces for a popular market. The twentieth century has seen a decline in the production of comparable pieces of maritime interest, although the commemoration of anniversaries of historic events still flourishes. As the millennium approaches, the Museum is taking steps to build up a more representative collection of twentieth century material, including good examples of appropriate modern decorative art objects.

The present collections of the National Maritime Museum are the result of more than fifty years of collecting in the maritime field. The Greenwich Hospital Collection, which had previously been displayed in the Painted Hall of the Hospital, formed the core of the Nelson collections, and included many items of engraved silver associated with the admiral. The acquisition by the Museum of other collections from various branches of the Nelson family ensured that our holdings of this material would be second to none.

In particular, a major collection of relics was donated in 1939 by the Revd Hugh Nelson-Ward and his brother, Admiral Philip Nelson-Ward, the grandsons of Horatia, daughter of Lord Nelson and Lady Hamilton. In 1948 some important relics in possession of the 5th Earl Nelson at Trafalgar House were purchased for the nation and added to the Museum's collection.

The Museum opened to the public in 1937, and a number of generous gifts, bequests, loans and purchases augmented the core collection. The early days of the Museum saw the acquisition of some major collections of relic and commemorative items, representing the lifelong enthusiasm of a number of collectors. John Walter of Norwich had lent his large private accumulation of commemorative items in 1935, consisting of a large number of ceramic pieces as well as glass and *objets d'art*, particularly Nelson souvenirs. These were subsequently purchased by the Museum. Another similar collection, on loan from Sir Henry Sutcliffe Smith since 1946, was also purchased in later years. This included some personal Nelson relics as well as the commemorative pieces.

In acquiring material for the collection nowadays, curators take a more selective approach than in the past, owing to considerations of space and economy, as well as changes in collecting policies. The energetic collectors whose treasures have become a part of the national heritage often aimed to acquire all the minor variations of popular productions. Although we would not usually collect like this today, the existence of such accumulations of material has an interest in itself, and allows us to gain some fascinating insights into the productions and tastes of another era. In writing this book I have felt that the unique opportunity to survey and describe the range and richness of some parts of the collection is so valuable that it outweighs the risk of creating an imbalance in the treatment of the selected themes.

The variation in quality and craftsmanship of the material described here is remarkably wide, and leads us to look closely at why pieces were produced and who purchased or commissioned them. I have also been particularly interested in the use of prints and other illustrative sources for designs on commemorative maritime objects, and have attempted to trace some of these designs across a range of objects of varying quality.

The illustrations are all from the collections of the National Maritime Museum, and the text concentrates on the material at Greenwich, although I have called on comparisons from other collections where it has been necessary. This book is not intended to be a catalogue, but I hope it provides a taste of the rich variety of material available here for visitors, researchers, historians, lovers of antiques, and all who celebrate ships and the sea.

NOTES

1 Thomas Carlyle: *History of Friedrich II of Prussia, called Frederick the Great* (1858–65) Vol 5 p266

CHAPTER 1 A Ship from Cradle to Grave

In *c*1840 Grandpa Ben wrote an illustrated children's book entitled *The History of a Ship from her Cradle to her Grave*. The author began by describing the naming and launch of HMS *Prince of Wales*, supported on a timber cradle as she slid down the launching ways. After a series of entertaining diversions on famous ships and seamanship, he ended his book with a visit to see the same vessel being broken up at Portsmouth. The present chapter takes a similar look at the lifespan of a variety of ships, from their building and launch, through active career, to final breaking up, as represented in pottery, silver and other commemorative objects.

1 Engraved plate from Diderot's *Encyclopédie Méthodique: Marine* Vol IV (1783).

2 Chinese export porcelain punch bowl *c*1785 painted with ships under construction, after engravings in Chapman's *Architectura Navalis* (1768).

3 Two transfer-printed Liverpool creamware jugs, *c*1795.
Left: Ropemaking.
Right: Shipwrights' Arms.

Shipbuilding scenes are among the rarest depictions on ceramics in the eighteenth century. At the National Maritime Museum there is a large Chinese export porcelain punch bowl of *c*1785 which is handpainted with drawings of ships under construction (plate 2). At first glance the effect is bizarre. The half-built ships are part of a river scene, but they balance unsupported at the water's edge. One is still in frame, and another completed but unrigged, and her masts are broken stumps. The background is a typical Chinese river scene, with a grassy river bank, small boats and a thatched hut.

The explanation is that the design is composed of drawings derived from a well-known eighteenth century shipbuilding treatise which have been set into an imaginary Chinese landscape. It does not seem to have occurred to the artist that the combination of technical ship drawings and realistic background would result in an impossible picture. The source for the ship drawings are the engravings in Fredrik Henrik af Chapman's *Architectura Navalis Mercatoria*, first published in Stockholm in 1768. The same engravings were later used to illustrate the shipbuilding section in Diderot's *Encyclopédie Méthodique* of 1783 (plate 1), and this is likely to have been the source from which the decorator of the bowl drew his inspiration.[1] The same engraving of a ship in frame was used as the source for another later Chinese export porcelain punch bowl of *c*1830, which is in the collection of the Winterthur Museum in Delaware.[2]

Two artists are likely to have worked on the Greenwich bowl, one painting the landscape and another copying the engravings of the ketch and merchant vessel. The bowl itself is a handsome piece, with a finely-painted gold trellis border inside the rim. In the bottom of the bowl is an inscription *Success to Mr Barnard's Yard*. This almost certainly refers to the Barnard family of shipbuilders, who were principally associated with yards at Ipswich, Harwich and Deptford. They were contractors to the Navy Board between 1740 and 1813, and built more ships for the Navy than any other merchant builder, as well as building more than fifty ships for the Honourable East India Company.[3]

4 Creamware mug *c*1800 transfer-printed with a sailmaking scene.

Another shipbuilding scene in the Museum is printed on a Liverpool creamware jug of *c*1795. The black transfer scene shows the hull of a ship, as yet unrigged and again with a large ensign, a jack and a pennant, all within a scrolled cartouche. The other side of the jug appropriately depicts the Shipwrights' Arms (plate 3). Within a rococo cartouche is Noah's Ark and a cross charged with a lion passant, supported on one side by a sailor in striped trousers and on the other by a shipwright wielding an axe. The arms are surmounted by a naval crown and surrounded by gun and shot, flags, trident, a worm for a gun, and other nautical trophies. The jug is one of the very few items commemorating the work of the various craftsmen who worked in the dockyards. A Liverpool jug of *c*1780 in the Schreiber Collection at the Victoria & Albert Museum has the Shipwrights' coat of arms with the inscription *Friendly Society of Shipwrights* and the names *James and Mary Corbin*.[4]

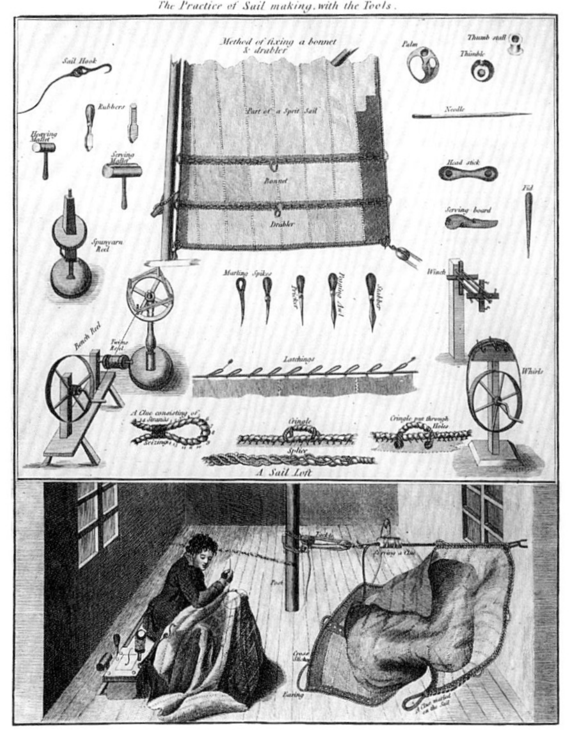

5 Sailmaking engraving from *Elements of Mastmaking, Sailmaking and Rigging* by David Steel, (1794).

Another unusual piece, this time at Greenwich, is a transfer-printed creamware jug decorated with a ropemaking scene (plate 3). The men are shown walking backwards with bundles of hemp around their waists from which they form the rope. Inset in the design is a shield bearing the Ropemakers' Arms, the charges being three coils of rope and a chevron, with another coil as the crest, and the motto *Behold our Support*. On the other side of the jug a figure of Hope leans on an anchor and gestures out to sea. Equally rare is a transfer-engraving on glass depicting the arms of the Friendly Society of Caulkers, instituted on 3rd October 1794. Eighteenth century caulking mallets, caulking irons and other tools feature on the shield and crest, and are held by the supporters, and the Ark also appears on the shield.

A creamware mug, probably made in North East England *c*1800, is inscribed *Success to the Sailmakers* (plate 4). One side is printed with a sailing ship and the motto *Behold our Support*, and the other shows a sailmaker seated at his bench sewing a sail, while two other figures work on a second sail and another stands holding a length of twine. On the back wall of the sail loft and in the foreground are a number of other sailmaking tools and pieces of equipment. The transfer is evidently based on an engraving in David Steel's *Elements of Mastmaking, Sailmaking and Rigging*, first published in 1794, which shows a figure at work in the sail loft (plate 5). The other figures and tools have been added to the print on the mug to enliven the scene. As far as is known, this is the only representation of sailmaking on pottery. We have also heard of another rare piece related to the dockyard trades, a small Liverpool creamware mug transfer-printed with a working scene inscribed *Success to the Coopers,* and at Liverpool Museum of Labour History there is a jug of *c*1790 with the Coopers' Arms.

In the early nineteenth century, when processions took place in the dockyard towns the tradesmen carried various devices and banners relating to their craft. The National Maritime Museum has two large wooden replica axes which the shipwrights used to carry in procession at Plymouth. One, dating from 1820, has the Royal cipher of George III, and the other, from 1830, has William IV's cipher painted in gold on both sides of the wooden blade. Similar processional tools from other towns are known. Liverpool Museum has a standard used in trades processions which is mounted with life-sized replica shipwrights' tools, including an adze, broad axe, hand saw, caulking mallet and caulking irons, all topped by a ship model. A photograph of a Liverpool shipwright shows the standard in use during Queen Victoria's visit in 1886.[5]

Every year the employees of Charles Hill's shipyard at Bristol used to carry gilded wooden models of shipwrights' tools of twice the normal size. A set of caulking tools and mallet on a pole are known, and the Bristol Shipwrights' Company also carried a wooden axe with representations of Noah's Ark on both sides of the yard-long blade.[6]

The launch of a ship has always been an occasion for celebration and traditional ceremony, and it is perhaps strange that there are so few representations of the event in ceramic or precious metal form. There is a dated Liverpool delftware bowl at Greenwich, however, which is painted inside with a charming scene entitled *A Ship and Lanch Thomas Cottle 1752* (colour plate 6). The small vessel, as yet unrigged, is being prepared for launching, and men can be seen on the slipway while others stand on deck apparently raising their hats in a cheer. A simple derrick on deck used for hoisting the masts aboard carries a St George's pennant, and there is also a large red ensign and a jack. These are the flags worn by a naval vessel of the period, but the vessel depicted is not armed. A delftware bowl in the Cecil Higgins Museum in Bedford has something similar. This is a Bristol bowl decorated in blue and *bianco sopra bianco* (white on white) bearing the inscription *John and Susanna Mays 1766.*[7]

The tradition of presenting a piece of plate to the master shipwright at the launching ceremony of a naval vessel goes back at least to the seventeenth century. There is a reference to a gilt cup of wine being drunk at the launch of the *Prince Royal* in 1610, after the ship was named. This ceremony was derived from a fifteenth century Venetian practice, which was usually followed by throwing the cup overboard. On this occasion the cup was given to Phineas Pett, one of the famous shipbuilding family. Half a century later, Samuel Pepys records in his diary for 25th October 1664:

> *So home (in my way taking care of a piece of plate for Mr Chr. Pett, against the lanching* [sic] *of his new great ship tomorrow at Woolwich, which I singly did move to His Royall Highness yesterday, and did obtain it for him, to the value of 20 peeces).*

And next day:

> *At Woolwich, I there up to the King and Duke and they liked the plate well. Here I stayed above with them while the ship was lanched* [sic] . . . *The launching being done, the King and company went down to take barge, And I sent for Mr Pett and put the Flaggon into the Duke's hand, and he, in the presence of the King, did give it, Mr Pett taking it upon his knee.*

Pepys is referring to the *Royal Catherine* built by Christopher Pett, which was launched by the Duke of York, Lord High Admiral. The gilt flagon, weighing 66 ounces, was bought at Backwell's.[8]

The gift was traditionally a bowl or drinking vessel of some type, to enable the King's and Lord Admiral's health to be drunk at the launching. Later this was less strictly adhered to. The value of the gift at that time depended on the rate of the ship. The Museum of London has a large silver-gilt covered cup, with the armorial bearings of James, Duke of York, as Lord High Admiral, and inscribed: *At the launching of his Maties ship ye London June 26 1670 Built at Deptford by Mr Jonas Shish his Maties Mr Shipwright there. Burthen 1338 Tunns Men 750 Guns 94.*[9]

In the Public Record Office there is a document which lists the gifts of plate to master shipwrights between 1708 and 1736. The gifts were engraved, usually with the appropriate Royal Arms, the name of the ship and date of launch. Most of the silver consists of domestic items such as candlesticks, punch bowls, teapots, salvers, plates and even knives and forks and *a cruitt stand*. The list records that in 1712 a pair of candlesticks and snuffers of 34 oz 12 dwt was presented to John Phillips for the launch of the *Feversham*. The value of the candlesticks was £12 and the engraving cost 9 shillings. The next year John Phillips received a salver for the launch of the *Lively*, and a pair of salvers and candlesticks for the launch of the *Strafford*.[10]

The *Feversham* candlesticks (colour plate 7) are now in the collection of the National Maritime Museum. They were made by John Bache of London in 1712, and have baluster stems and faceted octagonal bases. The bases of both candlesticks are engraved with a Royal crown and the inscription: *At launching her Maj'ts ship ye Feversham a 5th Rate 22d July 1712. Burthen 561 Tuns 40 guns 190 men. Built by Mr John Phillips Master Shipwright at Plymouth.* The *Feversham* was ordered on 8th June 1711, and named and launched on 22nd July 1712. She served in the Mediterranean between 1713 and 1715, in the West Indies 1721–2 and again 1728–9, and in June 1730 was taken to pieces at Portsmouth to be rebuilt. She was rebuilt at Blackwall in 1740, and finally sold in 1749.

The other piece of launching plate at Greenwich is a tankard by Thomas Farren of Sweethings Lane, London, hallmarked 1742 (colour plate 7). The baluster-shaped tankard has a scroll handle and is finely engraved with the Hanoverian Royal Arms, above an inscription: *At the launching of his Majests Ship the Captain a 3d Rate of 70 Guns 1230 Tuns ye 14 of April 1743. Built by Mr John Holland at Woolwich.* HMS *Captain* was reduced to 64 guns in 1760, renamed *Buffalo* in 1777, became a storeship, and was broken up in October 1783.

John Holland also received a pair of candlesticks for the launch of the *Bristol*, 4th Rate, at Woolwich in 1746. These came to light some twenty years ago, and a number of other pieces of launching plate are known still to be in existence. These include candlesticks for the launch of the *Triumph*, 74 guns, at Woolwich in 1764 and the *Winchelsea*, 5th Rate, at Sheerness the same year. In 1767 Mr Thomas Bucknale of Portsmouth received a silver dish-cross for the launch of the *Warwick*, 5th Rate. Mr William Gray of Woolwich received a cake basket for the *Prudent*, 64 guns, in 1768, and a salver for the *Intrepid*, 64 guns, in 1770.

Sometimes the presentations were a little more unusual. In 1780 a tea caddy made from the wood of Spanish Armada ships, with a silver plaque engraved for Mr John Hayward of Woolwich, was presented for the launch of the *Salamander* sloop. Another unusual gift was a combined presentation of a tea caddy and salver to Mr Adam Hayes of Deptford for the launch of two ships, the *Otter*, sloop, in 1767 and the *Egmont*, 3rd Rate, in 1768.

In 1801 an Order in Council forbade the taking of rewards by public servants, and the tradition of presenting launching plate was discontinued. It was revived in 1814, however, when the Admiralty directed the Navy Board:

> *to cause a piece of plate of the value of fifty pounds to be accordingly presented to the Master Shipwrights of His Majesty's Yards on their respectively launching a three-decker; and a piece of plate of the value of forty pounds for each two-decker which they may respectively launch.*
>
> *And we further desire and direct you to cause a piece of plate of the before mentioned value to be presented to the Master Shipwrights of His Majesty's Yards for each line of battle ship they may respectively have launched since the discontinuance of this custom.*[11]

We have little evidence of the continuance of the tradition during the nineteenth century. It is interesting, however, that in 1864 a silver casket was presented to mark the completion of the single-screw ship HMS *Achilles*, the first iron-hulled ship to be built by the Admiralty. This piece is now in the National Maritime Museum. A portrait of the four-masted, two-funnelled ship is engraved on the lid of the casket, with her name below, and inside the hinged lid is a presentation inscription: *Presented by Her Majesty's Dock Yard Chatham to Mr E J Reed Esq Secretary of the Institute of Naval Architects for his participation in the Design of the Impregnable Achilles on this Day of Completion 26th November 1864.* This was the vessel being built in 1861 at Chatham Dockyard recorded by Charles Dickens in his *Uncommercial Traveller* series of essays:

> *Ding, Clash, Dong, Bang, Boom, Rattle, Clash, BANG, Clink, Bang, Dong, Bang, Clatter, BANG, BANG, BANG! What on earth is this! This is, or soon will be, the Achilles, iron armour-plated ship. Twelve hundred men are working at her now; twelve hundred men working on stages over her sides, over her bows, over her stern, under her keel, between her decks, down in her hold, within her and without, crawling and creeping into the finest curves of her lines wherever it is possible for men to twist. Twelve hundred hammerers, measurers, caulkers, armourers, forgers, smiths, shipwrights; twelve hundred dingers, clashers, dongers, rattlers, clinkers, bangers, bangers, bangers.*[12]

HMS *Achilles*, 9,820 tons and 380 feet in length was launched on 23rd December 1863 and completed eleven months later. In 1878, under command of Captain Sir William Hewitt, she was one of the squadron of six ships which passed through the Dardanelles to Constantinople to protect British interests during the conflict between Russia and Turkey. In 1882 she reached Alexandria immediately after the bombardment, and in 1902, renamed *Hibernia*, she became the depot ship at Malta. Her name was changed to *Egmont* in 1904, and in 1913 she was towed home. She was renamed *Egremont* in 1916, and was finally sold in 1923.

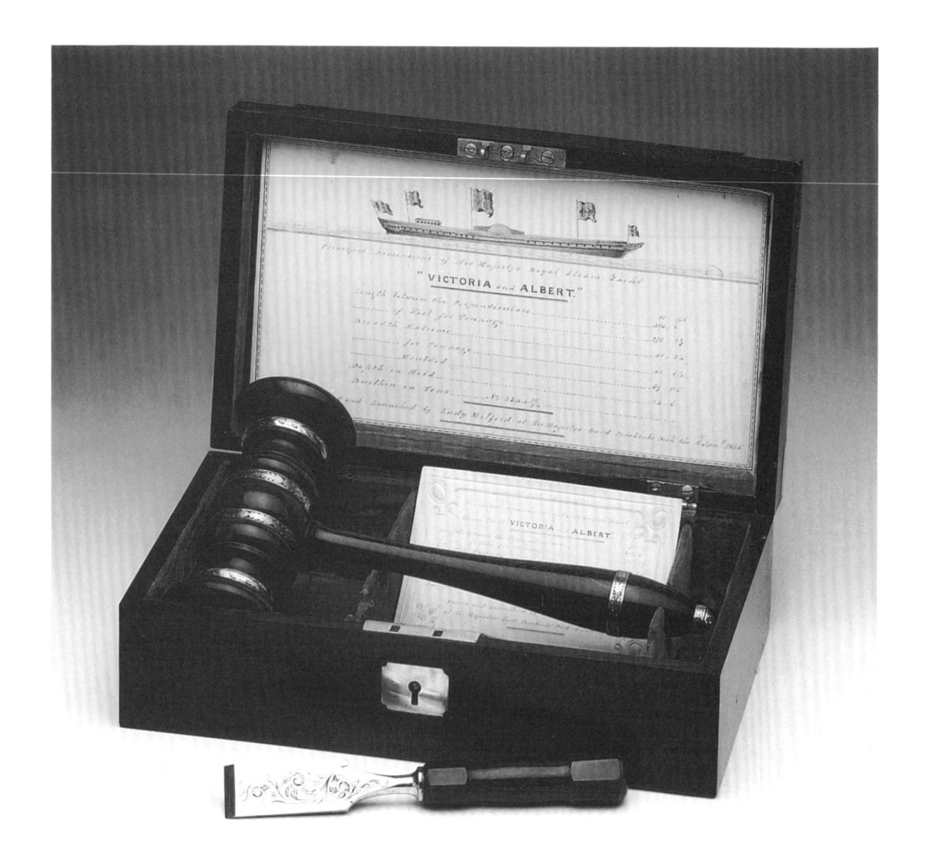

8 Casket presented to Lady Milford at the launch of HM Yacht *Victoria and Albert* at Pembroke in 1855.

In the nineteenth century it was usual to present a launching casket, containing the decorative mallet and chisel used at the launch of a naval ship, to the lady who performed the ceremony. The tools are often highly decorated and mounted in silver, and the boxes containing them varied from a discreet wooden or leather-covered case to an elaborately carved velvet-lined casket.

The earliest example in the collection at Greenwich commemorates the launch of HMS *Royal Albert* in 1854, and is on loan from the Royal Collection. The leather-covered case contains an oak and silver mallet and chisel and a decorative pierced paper sheet printed with the dimensions of the vessel. A silver plaque in the box is inscribed:

> *This mallet and chisel (made from a piece of the Victory's hull) liberated the Dog shores at the launch of the Royal Albert at Woolwich on the 13th May 1854. The ship was named by her Majesty the Queen. The Royal Albert was designed and partly built by the late Oliver Lang Esqre was completed and launched by William McPherson Rice Esqr Master Shipwright.*

The ceremony was illustrated and described in the *Illustrated London News* for 20th May 1854. The hammer and chisel were used to sever a cord to release the dog-shores, the last timber blocks holding the ship on the slip, after the vessel had been named and a bottle shattered against the bow. A gift was usually presented to the sponsor afterwards at a private presentation. The sponsor would later present a gift of silver or a picture to the ship at a separate commissioning ceremony.[13]

Another launching casket with Royal associations is that made for the launch of HM Yacht *Victoria and Albert* – the second of that name – in 1855 (plate 8). She was a wooden paddle-wheel yacht, designed by Mr Oliver W Lang and launched at Pembroke by Lady Milford on 16th January 1855. She was used by Queen Victoria and King Edward VII, and not broken up until 1904. The wooden casket, lined with red velvet, contains an ornamental mallet and chisel in zebra wood and chased silver, with a drawing of the vessel at launching inside the lid, and a list of the principal dimensions of the yacht.

The launching casket of a famous ship, HMS *Condor,* is also at Greenwich. Under the command of Sir Charles Beresford this gunboat attacked Fort Marabout at Alexandria on 11th July 1882 with such success that she earned the signal *Well done Condor* from Admiral Sir Beauchamp Seymour. She was launched in 1876, and the mahogany launching casket contains a mallet and chisel inscribed on the blade *HMS Condor, 8 guns, launched by Miss Annie Moore 28th Decr 1876.* Also in the box is a small wooden shield around which the rope was coiled before being cut at the launching ceremony.

Launching caskets for HMS *Espoir* of 1860, *Bristol* of 1861, *Royal Alfred* of 1864, *Nelson* of 1876 and *Montague* of 1901 are also in the Museum's collection. The latest casket at Greenwich is an oak box made for HMS *Neptune*, a battleship launched at Portsmouth by the Duchess of Albany on 30th September 1909. The lid of the box is carved with Neptune in his chariot drawn by sea-horses and accompanied by a triton. The mallet is carved with roses, thistles and shamrock.

The Illustrated London News of 13th August 1910 illustrates the launching process at that period with a photograph of the bow of HMS *Lion,* as prepared for the ceremony, captioned:

> *Viscountess Childers, having broken the bottle of wine against the vessel, and having named it with the words, I name this ship Lion, God bless the Lion and all who sail in her, took mallet and chisel and cut through the cord which freed a heavy weight on either side of the vessel, the releasing of which displaced the dog-shores.*

Launches were of great public interest, and among the more ephemeral launching souvenirs are verses printed on silk which were sold in the street and the dockyard. A typical example, printed in black on white silk, is headed *Success to his Majesty's Ship Devonshire* below a Royal coat of arms. The ship was launched by Lady Clifford of Chudleigh on 30th April 1904 at Chatham Dockyard. The verses, by Philip Thompson, are set within a decorative border and printed by Parrett and Neves of Chatham. Very similar launching souvenirs were still being produced during World War I. One, for the launch of HMS *Conquest* at Chatham Dockyard in January 1915, has verses by Philip Thompson and was printed by the Thorn Press, Gillingham. Another, for the launch of HMS *Hawkins* at Chatham in 1917, was also printed locally in Gillingham, and has similar verses, one of which ends:

> *How lovely to gaze on the laurel crowned name*
> *Emblazoned in letters of gold:*
> *HAWKINS–Father and Son of immortal fame*
> *Statesmen, and Admirals bold.*

There are a few interesting and unusual objects of earlier date with more general dockyard or harbour scenes. One large patch box at Greenwich has a detailed scene in ivory set under glass in the gold-mounted lid (plate 9). The shipping scene, with a two-decked warship in dock in the foreground, may be Portsmouth, and the box is likely to be by G Stephany and Dresch, Royal carvers in miniature, who worked in Bath and London *c*1793–1800.

Sir Robert Seppings (1767–1840), the famous naval architect, introduced the round stern, among other important innovations in warship design. In 1832 he was presented with a Chinese tortoiseshell snuff box, carved in relief. The box has the stern of a ship depicted on the lid, taken from E W Cooke's etching of the circular stern of HMS *Asia*, 84 guns, one of the ships in the engagement at Navarino, published in his *Fifty Plates of Shipping and Craft* in 1829.

Also at Greenwich is a silver snuff box by Thomas Eley of London, hallmarked 1855, and formed as a ship's hull on the ways, ready for launching (plate 10). The hinged lid is set into the deck, and the hull is engraved with details of planking, ports and stern windows. The lid is inscribed: *Presented to Richard Green Esq the Eminent Shipbuilder of Blackwall as a small Token of Respect and Esteem by the Officers of his Establishment on his Jubilee 5th Decr 1855.*

9 Patch box with a dockyard scene in ivory, likely to be by G Stephany and Dresch *c*1793–1800.

10 Silver snuff box by Thomas Eley, 1855, presented to the shipbuilder Richard Green of Blackwall.

Richard Green (1803–1863) was a member of the famous family partnership which built the Blackwall frigates on the north bank of the Thames a little downriver from Greenwich, and was also responsible for establishing the Sailors' Home, and other charitable activities.

Over the centuries ship portraits have proved to be a popular decoration for pottery and porcelain, glass, silver, jewellery and textiles. Often they are used simply as decorative motifs, but it is even more interesting when the vessel is named and identified sufficiently to enable its history to be traced. This is not always straightforward, for ships were often given the same name, and if the other evidence is scanty it may be impossible to identify the ship with certainty. An inscribed date and the name of the commanding officer is useful, but earlier items often pose problems. The early merchant shipping registers can be confusing, and there is no guarantee that a named ship is a close portrait of the vessel in question. It was very common to decorate pottery with a standard transfer-printed ship portrait and add the name by hand, and it is misleading in such cases to use the illustration to help in identifying the particular vessel. Handpainted ship portraits are more likely to be accurate representations as they were individually commissioned, but even these are unreliable.

Many pottery ship bowls were produced in the eighteenth century but there is little direct evidence regarding reasons for their manufacture. Some were clearly made to celebrate a launch, but others may be related to privateering activities. Privateers were privately owned armed vessels which were licensed by *letters of Marque* to operate against enemy trade in wartime by attacking their merchant ships. A single vessel was normally depicted, and the convention was to portray the ship broadside on, with an inscription giving the ship's name and sometimes a date and the master's name. At Greenwich there are several eighteenth century English tin-glazed delftware bowls handpainted with merchant sailing vessels of various rigs. The earliest dated bowl is the 1752 launching scene described on p4. Another early Liverpool bowl is inscribed inside *Success to the Nancy 1756*. The vessel depicted is a brig, painted in blue and wearing a red ensign, jack and red pennant, on a green sea. The exterior has two chinoiserie scenes.

A smaller vessel is shown on another dated bowl of Bristol delftware decorated in *bianco sopra bianco* (colour plate 11). The interior is painted in blue with a cutter under sail rigged with a square topsail and three foresails, a figurehead and tall ensign staff without an ensign. The inscription surrounding the vessel is *God preserve ye Two Brothers 1761,* and a mark on the base reads *W x A 1761.* This bowl is particularly rare in showing a vessel with fore and aft rig, as the handful of other examples are of Liverpool manufacture. Unfortunately it is not possible to identify the particular vessel since *Two Brothers* was a very popular ship's name at this period. The 1764 *Lloyd's Register*, for instance, lists 16 vessels of the name, and the 1768 edition lists 54.

A Liverpool delftware bowl, this time undated, has a portrait of a snow under sail wearing red ensign, Union Jack and pennant, all picked out in red. (The snow was a rig similar to a brig, but with a small trysail mast stepped abaft the mainmast.) A lion figurehead can clearly be seen at the bow, and the details of the blue-painted scene are touched in with yellow. Some of the ship's company are shown carrying out their tasks. The date is *c*1760–70 and an inscription identifies the subject as *The Hadwen, Thos Falcon* (colour plate 11). Unfortunately even this detail does not enable us to trace the vessel, as she does not appear in the registers.

Another delftware bowl of approximately the same date is painted in blue in a markedly different style. It shows a full-rigged ship under sail wearing ensign, jack and swallow-tailed pennant (colour plate 11). The inscription runs *Success to the Emperor,* and the only *Emperor* which appears in the earliest *Lloyd's Registers* is a ship of 200 tons built in 1762 and belonging to Ipswich. After an early Virginia voyage, she seems to have become a Baltic trader voyaging between London and St Petersburg. She was lost in 1781.

A similar toast, *Success to the Beehive*, appears on another Liverpool delftware bowl painted with a brig. She carries the usual flags, picked out in colour, and the members of the crew can be seen on deck. The exterior of the bowl is painted in blue with floral decoration. *Lloyd's Register* of 1776 lists a *Beehive* sloop of 70 tons built at Bideford, North Devon in 1752. In 1776 she was voyaging between Wales and Bristol under Master John Leelittle, and in subsequent years she is listed as voyaging between Guernsey and London with the master named as A Moore.

Greenwich also has one good example of a Liverpool delftware polychrome ship plate of *c*1760 (colour plate 12). The plate is painted in blue with a Baltic galeas (a two-masted vessel) under sail, and the border is decorated with green, yellow and red panels. The rudderhead is clearly carved as a man's head, and the vessel wears an ensign and jack bearing a gold crown over two white crosses on a blue field, which are almost certainly intended to be the flags of Danzig. The actual Danzig ensign of the period was a gold crown over two white crosses on a *red* field. The subject of the plate is identified by the inscription *De Hoffnung, Carl Gustar* [sic] *Dienies. Lloyd's Register* for 1779 shows a vessel named *De Hoffnung*, described as a hoy of 120 tons, built at Danzig in 1762, rebuilt in 1774 and working mainly between Liverpool and Danzig. It is reasonable to assume that her master would have ordered one or more of these plates during one of his voyages to Liverpool. The master of the vessel appears variously in later *Lloyd's Registers* as J Wetron or J Wolfran, and enquiries at the Polish Maritime Museum in Gdansk reveal that in November 1774 damage occurred to a vessel, *Die Hoffnung*, belonging to Jacob Wolffram from Danzig, who is thought to be the same man. Wolffram evidently owned the vessel for some years, at least from 1774–82, but the only clue to the identity of Carl Gustar Dienies whose name appears on the plate is a 1772 reference to a Carl Gustav Dinnies, who owned a store in Danzig where he offered *fresh and cheap oysters*.

It is very rare for a Royal Navy ship to appear on a delftware bowl, but in 1984 an example was sold at an exhibition in London. The Lambeth delftware bowl was painted with a quarter view of a ship inscribed *Success to the Devonshire. John Robinson, Born December 30th 1760, Baptiz'd Jan 7th 1761.*[14] HMS *Devonshire* was a 3rd Rate of 74 guns built at Woolwich Dockyard and launched in 1745, and her service included the expeditions against Martinique and Havannah in 1762. The Royal Navy is also referred to in inscriptions on some of the plain delftware bowls at Greenwich which have no ship portrait. The wording suggests popular toasts which may have been current among the seafaring communities, such as *Success to ye Navy*, which appears on one London bowl of *c*1780. Two similar bowls of the period, made in London and Liverpool, are inscribed respectively *Trade and Navigation* and *Success to the Herring Fishery*.

The collection at Greenwich also has a number of late eighteenth century ship bowls of other types. One particularly distinctive piece, probably from Donyat in North Devon, is decorated in naive style and inscribed *the Elizebeth sloop E. S. 1774*. The body of the bowl is red earthenware, glazed inside with pale yellow mottled green and brown. The wide flat-based bowl is decorated in *sgraffito* (that is, scratched through the glaze) with a small sailing cutter with green sails.

There are several Liverpool creamware bowls handpainted with vessels of various rigs inside, and printed outside with standard Liverpool transfers. Most of the ships are named and some are dated. One interesting example has a painted brig inside outlined in black with touches of colouring and a bright green sea. She wears a large red ensign, jack and red swallow-tailed pennant, and underneath is the inscription: *John Dawson. Success to she that carries me eather by land or sea* (colour plate 11). The exterior of the bowl is printed with four transfers. Two are the scenes of a sailor's farewell and return after Boitard, which are described in more detail on p62, and the other two are views of Neptune with his chariot and sea creatures.

Another creamware punch bowl, finely painted with a ship-rigged vessel named as *The Ship Molly*, has external transfers of Neptune's chariot, a figure of Hope with her anchor, a church and a coastal scene. The ship portrait is coloured with a yellow and black hull, red flags and a green sea, and small figures are shown on deck, including one with a speaking-trumpet (colour plate 11).

One Liverpool ship bowl of *c*1790 is decorated on the interior with a black transfer of a Baltic trader under sail – she has a long swallow-tailed pennant but no ensign, and underneath is identified as *De Tre Sodskende* (The Three Siblings) – and a trophy of naval arms below a green sea. Six similar transfers of nautical trophies are used as decoration round the inner rim, and the outside is decorated with transfers of *Jemmy's Farewell* and *Return*, and scenes of ploughing and drinking.

Another foreign vessel appears on a Wedgwood bowl decorated in Liverpool. The painted interior depicts a two-masted vessel under sail with a large Dutch ensign picked out in colour. The hull is decorated in blue and yellow, with a coloured sea, and a small seaport and sailing boats appear in the background. A translation of the inscription reads: *Prosperity to the Maria & Petronella – of Maassluis – Captain Jan Van der Endt 25th February 1779*. The exterior is transfer-printed with Neptune and tritons, a sailor's farewell, a drinking scene, and the Birth of Venus.

While most of these bowls were specially decorated for the owners or masters, other creamware ship plates of the late eighteenth century were intended for general sale. They seldom represented named vessels, and it was usual for a standard Liverpool transfer of a ship to appear (plate 13). Typical examples of the plates of *c*1790 are transfer-printed in black with a little hand-colouring, and show either a brig or a three-masted ship, with a trophy of naval arms below. Around the shaped border there are usually six floral sprays. Such plates would be intended for domestic or decorative use and would clearly have been of particular interest to seafaring families, but had no specific commemorative purpose. Other examples of transfer-printed Liverpool ship plates showed a merchant vessel within a border of bird vignettes.

Foreign vessels sometimes appear on such plates, and one creamware example at Greenwich is decorated with a merchant ship under sail wearing a Danish ensign and a red pennant. Dutch vessels are also represented. Such examples would clearly have attracted masters of foreign vessels calling at Liverpool, who would have looked for just such a souvenir to take home. Other similar decorative ship plates were made at Newcastle and Swansea. One Swansea example of *c*1815, impressed *Dillwyn & Co*, is of white earthenware transfer-printed in black with a brig under sail and nautical trophies below. A rather more specific reference appears on a creamware plate made by

13 Transfer-printed creamware plates. Left: Merchant brig by Phillips & Co. of Sunderland *c*1820. Right: Typical Liverpool ship plate *c*1790.

14 Tin-glazed ship tiles printed by John Sadler of Liverpool *c*1758–61.

Phillips & Co. of Sunderland *c*1820 (plate 13). The plate is transfer-printed with a merchant brig under sail with an ensign composed of a white cross on a red ground. The inscription below reads:

Success to the Coal Trade
Here's may Colliers Flourish, our Trade increase
And Victory bring us a lasting Peace.

The initials *AVDK* and *KVS* are handpainted beneath, presumably in reference to the giver and recipient of the gift. A frog mug and a teapot by Dixon & Co. of Sunderland with the same transfer are in the Sunderland Museum.

Similar ship designs appear on other pottery pieces of the late eighteenth and nineteenth centuries, particularly on jugs and mugs. Again it was quite usual to decorate a piece with a standard ship transfer and add a handwritten inscription below, naming the vessel. Such designs are frequently taken to be individual ship portraits, whereas this clearly cannot be so, as identical transfers appear with a variety of ship names. At Greenwich there is a Liverpool creamware jug of *c*1805 which is transfer-printed in black with a brig on one side and an engraving of the god Jupiter on the other. The combination of transfers was well chosen on this occasion, for the words below the brig are *Success to the Jupiter*, in reference to the ship's name. *Lloyd's Register* lists a brig *Jupiter*, registered at Barnstaple and owned after 1805 by Blake and Company. This ties in neatly with a handwritten inscription under the lip, *Miss Susan Blake, Barnstaple.* An identical transfer of the brig appears on another jug, however, previously on loan to the Museum, which carries the inscription *Success to the Claveland. Capt John Williams of Appledore.*

The square scrolled border of the design on these two jugs suggests that it was originally designed for use on a tile. Ships of various types appear on a series of decorative delftware tiles by John Sadler of Liverpool *c*1758–61. Some are shown broadside, and others from bow or stern view, and all are surrounded by a scrolled border (plate 14).

One Liverpool creamware mug is transfer-printed in black with a warship captioned *A first Rate Ship of War with Rigging etc at Anchor* (plate 15). The design of the flags indicates that the transfer must be earlier than 1801, when the St Patrick's saltire was added to the Union Flag to symbolise political union with Ireland. The ship flies a Royal Standard at the mainmast, an Admiralty flag at the fore and Union Flag at the mizzen, as well as a jack and ensign. This combination of flags was seen in the eighteenth century at the launch of a naval vessel or when the Sovereign was afloat, but in this case it is probably simply an attempt to symbolise the might of the Royal Navy.

Another unusual print is a sailing pilot boat which appears on a creamware jug at Greenwich (plate 16). The jug is printed with a dandy-rigged boat, with its typical small mizzen-sail, within a flowered cartouche with a little hand-colouring. Above the boat, in a scroll, is the legend *Safety depends on Conduct*, and the jug is exactly dated by a handpainted inscription, *JO 1802,* below the lip.

The pilot boat is identified as such by a large *2* on all the sails and a red and white no. 2 flag. Local regulations would have operated in the various ports, and it is interesting to compare the regulations in the 1807 Act for Bristol pilot craft:

Each pilot's skiff shall be marked with the number appointed for her by the haven master, in black

15 Liverpool creamware mug transfer-printed with a warship.

16 Liverpool creamware jug transfer-printed with a pilot boat.

paint on the three lower sails, such number to be at least 4 feet in length; the hull to be painted black, with a white streak under the gunwale; to be also numbered on the bow and the pilot's name on the stern, and to carry a flag constantly at the mast-head, with blue and white horizontal stripes, of the dimensions 4 feet by 5feet.[15]

There are also a large number of interesting handpainted mugs and jugs made in Liverpool and other factories, some of them bearing personal names. One pair of ceramic tankards, probably intended as a wedding gift, was made in Sunderland in about 1780. They are decorated in colour with wreaths of flowers and a painting in sepia of a coasting vessel. The two differ only in size, one being 5 inches and one 4 inches high, and both are inscribed: *Thos & Mary Marsh. Success to the Union*. Whether Thomas Marsh was master of the vessel *Union* or the toast simply refers to the marriage, or whether a pun was intended, we will never know for certain.

Of similar date is a creamware mug painted with a merchant brig outlined in black, flying red pennants and sailing on a green sea (plate 17). On the other side, within a wreath of coloured flowers and leaves, is a four-line verse:

May God above
Preserve the free
And hearty Tar
That plows the Sea.

The same subject of a merchant brig appears on a Liverpool pearlware jug of *c*1800 (plate 17). Both sides are decorated with wreaths of handpainted coloured flowers and leaves, and on the opposite side to the brig is a verse:

By untouch'd credit
& by honnest trade
the upright dealer
Eminent is made.

A later piece of Liverpool interest is a ceramic flagon or spirit bottle, probably made at the Herculaneum factory in Liverpool *c*1837 (plate 18). The flagon has a narrow neck, wide body and scroll handle, and has the same transfer engraving on each side showing a two-funnelled paddle steamer under sail, with the Liverpool waterfront in the background. The only inscription is a handpainted *AS*, but the vessel can be identified as the *Liverpool* from a lithographic print by J R Isaac. A similar flagon in Liverpool Museum has a transfer of a sailing boat flying a flag identifying her as *Phebe*. The *Phoebe*, probably built in 1813, was one of the two flats used by the Herculaneum factory for carrying coal, and was named after the wife of William Smith, factory owner 1810–21.[16]

Later in the nineteenth century many ship portraits appeared on jugs, mugs and wall plaques of Sunderland lustreware. The subjects chosen might be either naval or merchant vessels. A large jug of pink lustreware, probably by Moore of

17 Liverpool jug and mug handpainted with merchant brig and verse *c*1800.

18 Spirit bottle by the Herculaneum Factory at Liverpool, printed with the paddle steamer *Liverpool*, *c*1837.

Sunderland *c*1824, is printed with a view of the four-masted barque *Columbus* and is inscribed with a verse, dimensions of the vessel and the words *Columbus the largest ship ever built.* She was built at Quebec in 1824 and was designed to freight a large cargo of timber from Canada to Britain. Having reached London safely, the timber was unloaded and she was despatched to St Johns for another cargo, but foundered on the voyage in May 1825.

A typical oblong wall plaque by Dixons of Sunderland, in its distinctive pink-splashed frame with moulded copper lustre border, has a transfer of HMS *Northumberland*, 74 guns, with men on the yards furling sails. The same design also appears on lustre jugs. This was the ship that conveyed Napoleon to exile in St Helena in 1815. Another similar plaque, also with holes in the frame for hanging, has a hand-coloured transfer of a 1st Rate under sail, identified underneath as HMS *Duke of Wellington 131 Guns* (colour plate 19). She was a screw ship, built at Pembroke Dock in 1852 and only sold to the shipbreakers in 1904. Less warlike, even though it depicts a warship, is a plaque inscribed:

> *May Peace and Plenty*
> *On our Nation Smile*
> *And Trade with Commerce*
> *Bless the British Isle.*

Ship portraits appeared on porcelain as well as pottery. At the end of the eighteenth century the Derby factory sold pieces with finely painted shipping scenes of unnamed vessels by George Robertson and John and Robert Brewer. Derby also produced a number of pieces with naval actions painted after contemporary prints. A porcelain vase of *c*1785 sold in 1992 was painted *en grisaille*, probably by Zachariah Boreman, with a scene of the Siege of Gibraltar, 1782, after an aquatint by William Hamilton RA.[17] There is also a cream jug in a private collection, painted by George Robertson of Derby, with a large panel depicting the action between the frigate *Anson* and *La Loire* in October 1798, from an engraving of 1816 by T Sutherland after Thomas Whitcombe's painting. Other pieces from the same cabaret service show the action from different angles.[18]

One ship bowl in the collection at Greenwich is of particular interest as it represents a naval vessel instead of the usual merchant ships or privateers. The bowl is of handpainted porcelain by Pennington of Liverpool, and the warship is identified by its inscription *Success to the Perseus Capt Gibson 1790.* The exterior is decorated with floral sprays. HMS *Perseus* was a 6th Rate of 20 guns, first commissioned in 1776, and broken up at Sheerness in 1805.

In the mid-nineteenth century a series of porcelain bowls were handpainted in colour with named ships in an oval cartouche on one side, usually against a background of Kronborg Castle at Elsinore in Denmark. An example in the National Maritime Museum has a brig on one side, and on the other side another cartouche with an inscription in Gothic script. Gilt scrollwork covers the rest of the bowl. The gold inscriptions were not fired, so they are usually more worn than the pictures, but this example includes the toast *Success to the Catharine of London.* The firm of Major Wright & Co. of Elsinore had the bowls made as gifts for foreign ship captains who were customers. Major Wright was the son of Henry Wright of Hull, who had set up his ship clearance firm in Elsinore in 1778. The bowls depict brigs and topsail schooners, and although it is unlikely that they are exact portraits of particular named ships they probably show the correct rig with the appropriate flags. The bowls were made at an unknown porcelain factory, possibly German, and were probably painted in Elsinore by Chapman Norris, who worked there as an enamelier. Some bowls include a reference to Major Wright & Co. of Elsinore in the inscription. All of the bowls date from the middle of the nineteenth century.[19]

The so-called *captain's cups* are another mid-nineteenth century type. They are cups and saucers of heavy German porcelain, painted in full colour with ship portraits. An example in the Town Docks Museum at Hull depicts the three-masted paddle steamer SS *Lord Cardigan*, launched at Hull in 1857. The saucers are lettered with the captain's name and decorated in gold. The sets would be purchased by visiting captains to take home from their voyage. Many of the ships depicted are registered in Hamburg, and there is a collection of these cups in the Altonaer Museum in Hamburg. One example, showing the barque *Schön* of Hamburg, built 1857, is signed by J G Hauthal & Co., listed in a Hamburg register as *Dealer in shipping materials, porcelain and glassware, painter on porcelain.*[20] Another with the same maker's mark depicts the *Criterion*, a barque built in Sunderland in 1853.

20 Three rummers by an East Coast engraver, decorated with local vessels. Left to right: merchant brig dated 1866, cutter dated 1864, topsail schooner, 1854.

22 Two glasses engraved with paddle steamers. Left: *Phoenix*. Right: Unnamed vessel.

Ships were also frequently engraved on glass. In the eighteenth century there are some fine privateer glasses, usually elegant wine glasses with opaque twist stems, expertly engraved with a view of a ship and a legend such as *Success to the Eagle Privateer*. Another at Greenwich is engraved *Success to the Duke of Cornwall Privateer David Jenkins Commander*. These glasses date from between the 1760s and 1790s and are most likely to have been made in Bristol. Unfortunately the interest in these rare and valuable glasses has led to the production of many clever fakes which may be difficult to distinguish from the genuine pieces.

In the nineteenth century many engraved glasses with named ship portraits were produced. One type of the 1860s, by an East Coast engraver, illustrates small local sailing vessels of various rigs (plate 20), and these are distinctive because of their decoration of fruiting vines surrounding the inscription on the other side. Glasses of this type at Greenwich include a rummer engraved with a merchant brig inscribed *William & Susannah Jenkinson, Filey 1866*, a rummer with a gaff cutter inscribed *Welfare. Thomas & Jane Hatton, Ramsgate 1864*, and another with a topsail schooner inscribed *Julia of Wells Francis Southgate 1854*. Some of the glasses made in Sunderland have views of sailing ships, or sometimes steam vessels, passing under the bridge on the River Wear (colour plate 21). One Sunderland Bridge rummer at Greenwich, dating from *c*1830, is engraved with a brig sailing into harbour past a lighthouse on one side, and passing under the bridge on the other. It also has a George II florin in the hollow-knopped stem. These glasses are companions for the lustre pottery, also made in Sunderland, which is decorated with similar views. There are also some glasses in the collection which have finely-engraved views of paddle boats (plate 22). One of these, a rummer also engraved in about 1830, shows the paddle steamer *Phoenix* towing a merchant brig.

There are some unusual ship portraits in the form of framed paper sculptures which have survived from the 1760s. One, which is signed and dated *A.V.Omeringh 1764*, is a shipping scene with warships and a Dutch sailing boat off a Dutch port with figures on the quayside. Two other paper sculptures at Greenwich portraying individual vessels are signed by Augustine Walker of Rye and dated 1761 (plate 23) and 1765. He is known to have produced other sculptures in the same style, all depicting British warships under sail, the entire picture, including the sea and the ships' rigging, being worked in paper.

Professionally produced ship portraits embroidered in silk make an interesting comparison with the more homely sailors' woolwork pictures which feature in chapter 4. In the late nineteenth century some particularly distinctive silkwork ship pictures were produced by Thomas Willes of Brooklyn, USA. The detailed portraits of merchant ships and barques are worked on a silk background, the hull being of velvet with embroidered details, and the sails made of silk-covered card, curved to give a convincing three-dimensional effect. The vessels are shown under full sail to show off the manufacturer's art to best effect, and most of the pictures include other smaller vessels in the background.

One of these pictures by Willes, at Greenwich, shows the three-masted iron barque *Halton Castle* (colour plate 24), a Liverpool vessel of 159 feet length, built in 1862 by H M Lawrence & Co. and owned by John F Angel of Oakhampton. She is shown flying the signal flags *TWFP* of the Commercial Code. The picture, which dates from 1881, was ordered by the master, A E Haynes of Newport, who had it sent back to England by another ship. The *Halton Castle* sailed from New York bound for Queenstown with a cargo of grain on 17th April 1881, but was posted missing at Lloyd's on 17th August the same year.

Other similar relief pictures in the collection show the ship *Ravenshall* of London, of 1,663 tons, Master A Telfer, and the *Plymouth Rock*, Captain N Madsen. Both of these have velvet hulls and silk sails, but the *Plymouth Rock* picture has a sewn silk sea and coastal view, like the *Halton Castle*, whereas the *Ravenshall* is on a canvas background with a painted sea, sky and coast. *Ravenshall* was built at Glasgow in 1874 by J Elder & Co., registered in London, and appears in *Lloyd's Register* until 1891. *Plymouth Rock* was built at Boston in 1849 and sailed under the Norwegian flag, disappearing from *Lloyd's Register* in 1892. Another large and finely-worked silk ship portrait in the collection is by another hand. It shows the barque *Dunfion*, Master Thomas John Roberts of Fowey. The sails are worked in cream silk stitching and she sails on a lively green sea embroidered in silks.

It has long been a tradition when a famous ship reaches the end of its life to manufacture mementoes from parts of her timber. It is still possible for visitors to HMS *Victory* at Portsmouth and the SS *Great Britain* at Bristol to buy small souvenirs made from timber and metal removed during the continuing restoration of the vessels.

23 Paper ship by Augustine Walker of Rye, dated 1761.

When Francis Drake returned to Deptford in the *Golden Hind* in 1580 after his voyage round the world, Queen Elizabeth knighted him there and commanded that his ship be preserved in the dockyard. Here the vessel became an attraction for visitors for many years. Eventually the ship broke up, but the master shipwright, John Davis, had a chair made from some of the timber and presented it to the University of Oxford in 1662. The chair can still be seen in the Bodleian Library.

The chair inspired the poet Abraham Cowley to write his *Ode: Sitting and Drinking in the Chair made out of Reliques of Sir Francis Drake's Ship*. A verse in Latin is now attached to the chair. The translation ends:

> *Drake and his ship could not have wish'd from fate*
> *A more blest station or more blest estate;*
> *For, lo! a seat of endless rest is given*
> *To her in Oxford and to Him in Heaven.*[21]

26 Chair made from timber of the Dutch fleet captured at the Battle of Camperdown, 1797.

At Greenwich there are several examples of furniture made from the timber of ships captured in the late eighteenth century, and chapter 6 will consider other pieces made from the timber salvaged from ships accidentally lost at sea, such as the *Mary Rose* and the *Royal George*. The Spanish 1st Rate *San Josef* was captured by Nelson at the Battle of Cape St Vincent in 1797. She became a floating gunnery school, and was broken up in 1849. An octagonal table was made from the timber and presented by the Admiralty to the Nelson family, and a century later it came to the Museum.

The Board of Admiralty also ordered a sideboard to be made from part of the *San Josef* timber for presentation to Lady Berry, widow of Rear Admiral Sir Edward Berry, who had served as first lieutenant of the *Captain* in the battle. This elaborate piece of furniture (colour plate 25), designed and manufactured by Mr Frederick Morris of Bath, was exhibited in the Royal Naval Exhibition at Chelsea in 1891, and is now in the collection at Greenwich. The back panel is carved in high relief with a scene from the battle, after a painting by Nicholas Pocock, showing the boarding and capture of the Spanish ships, flanked by flags and guns.

On loan to the Museum is a set of chairs commemorating the Battle of Camperdown with an inscription carved on the back rest: *This wood was part of Adml De Winter's Fleet captured by Adml Duncan Oct 11 1797*. The arms are carved in the shape of cannon barrels, and there is a plaque on the back carved with a fouled anchor. The chairs vary in detail; one has a cane seat and another (plate 26) a silver plaque on the seat inscribed: *This chair was made for Admiral Edward O'Bryen who commanded his Majesty's Ship Monarch in the battle of Camperdown*. Of very similar style is an armchair made of oak and copper from Nelson's flagship, *Victory*. Again there is a central panel on the back carved with a fouled anchor, and the arms terminate in guns. *The Nautical Magazine* for 1843 illustrates a different type of armchair made from *Victory* oak which was presented to the Royal Naval School at Camberwell. The chair was said to be from timbers *selected from those nearest to the place where Nelson breathed his last*. The back of the chair is shield-shaped and carved with a large anchor, flags, crown and mitre, and a ribbon inscribed with the words of Nelson's Trafalgar signal. The chair was designed by Mr R Blake, master builder of Portsmouth Dockyard, made by Samuel Arnold, a dockyard shipwright, and carved by Robert Bray. *The Nautical Magazine* adds:

> *To render the whole in keeping, on the presentation of the chair, it was borne into the schoolroom, in which the examination of the pupils takes place, by the following four veteran seamen of Greenwich Hospital, all of whom had fought on board the Victory, at the memorable Battle of Trafalgar – James Bergam (lost a leg), William Welch, George French, and Peter Moses.*[22]

Another of Nelson's flagships which ended her days as souvenir material was HMS *Foudroyant*, 80 guns, launched in 1798. In June 1799 Lord Nelson shifted his flag to HMS *Foudroyant*, until July 1800 when Sir Edward Berry took over command. She was present at the capture of the *Guillaume Tell*, 80 guns, in March 1800, and took part in the capture of the *Belle Poule* and *Marengo* in March 1806. After service on the American Station she became a guardship at Devonport until 1892. During that year she was sold to a German shipbreaker, but Mr Wheatley Cobb bought her back, fitted her out and sailed her round the coast as an exhibition ship. However, on the night of 15th June 1897 she was wrecked off the coast at Blackpool. The Manchester firm of Goodall, Lamb and Heighway Ltd purchased the timber and copper from the wreck and produced furniture and small souvenirs for sale.

In 1899 the company published a catalogue which illustrated the wide variety of *Foudroyant* timber items which could be purchased. The smaller pieces, like bookcases, chairs, boxes and occasional tables, could be ordered from the illustrated catalogue. For instance, a birdcage and stand in oak and copper cost 11 guineas, a table easel was 14s 6d and a glazed wall cabinet designed like a ship's stern was £60. Several of the items on offer were copies of furniture with Nelson connections or other historic associations. Copies of Anson's chair from the *Centurion*, the leather-covered chair from Byng's cabin, and a chair once belonging to Nelson's father were available. Even the chairs made earlier from the wood of the Dutch prizes after Camperdown were reproduced again in *Foudroyant* oak. For those with grander ideas anything else could be made to order. To whet the appetite the catalogue suggests a hall staircase and a yacht interior. Evidently there were customers for some of these more elaborate projects, and we know of a boardroom, probably now demolished, which was panelled in the relic wood, complete with Nelson coats of arms and references to his battles. Another *Foudroyant* oak-panelled room in a private house in Preston survived until 1972, when it was demolished.

The catalogue includes a sample of the certificate which accompanied the goods, giving the bond of the company that £50 would be paid to the purchaser *in the event of any article furnished by us to be made from timbers salved from Nelson's Flagship Foudroyant containing any oak that was not so salved from the Foudroyant.*

Other well-known ships also became the source of souvenirs. The Museum has a small table with a parquetry top and bobbin-turned legs from the wood of HMS *Temeraire*, 98 guns, commanded by Sir Eliab Harvey at the Battle of Trafalgar. She was broken up at Rotherhithe in 1838, and two chairs from her timber are in St Mary's Church at Rotherhithe. A chair from the timber of HMS *Bellerophon*, the ship on which Napoleon surrendered to Captain Maitland in 1815, has front legs in the shape of gun barrels and a carved anchor as the back rest. In St Mary's Parish Church at Whitby is an elaborately carved chair from *Royal Charter* timber, with anchors and a compass on the back above a relief scene of the wreck of the ship off Anglesey in 1859.

Boxes were also popular, some made from the wood of more than one vessel. One circular box, made in 1824, is inlaid with rings of wood from the *Royal William*, the *Royal Escape*, Cook's *Discovery*, the *Royal George*, *Bellerophon* and *Victory*. Other boxes and trinkets were made from the wood of the *Chesapeake* and *Shannon*, the *Euryalus* and *Eurydice*, the *Northumberland*, *Terrible* and many other famous ships.

Nelson himself treasured mementoes made from the timber of the French flagship, *L'Orient*, which exploded at the Battle of the Nile. Captain Benjamin Hallowell of the *Swiftsure* gave him a strange gift of a coffin made from *L'Orient*'s mainmast, which Nelson not only kept for the rest of his life, but was actually placed in after his death. He kept *L'Orient*'s lightning conductor in his hall at Merton.

In 1880 two writing tables were made from the timber of HMS *Resolute*, abandoned in the Arctic in 1854 during the search for Sir John Franklin (1786–1847). She was recovered by an

American whaler, returned to England, and presented to Queen Victoria. When she was broken up in 1879 the two tables were made by Edward Praill from her oak and teak, and one was presented to the American President. Boxes, photograph frames and paper knives were also made.

The tradition of ship relic mementoes survived into this century. Many souvenirs made from ships associated with Nelson were produced to commemorate the Trafalgar Centenary of 1905. The British and Foreign Sailors' Society, a charity founded in 1833, bought up scrap copper and oak while *Victory* was undergoing major repairs, and sold and presented various items from *Victory* and *Foudroyant* timber and copper, including commemorative plaques, Nelson busts, walking sticks, medallions and smaller items for the benefit of the society.

At Greenwich there is a set of folding slatted deck chairs and tables made in 1935 by the Hughes Bolckow Shipbreaking Company of Blyth, Northumberland, of teak taken from the Admiralty Steam Yacht *Enchantress*, built by Harland and Wolff in 1903. At about the same period there were many small souvenirs, such as miniature wooden barrels made from the wood of well-known ships like *Mauretania* and HMS *Iron Duke* when they were broken up. Castles Shipbreaking Company at Millbank on Thameside produced wooden garden benches and other practical ship mementoes as a by-product of their trade. These usually had an identifying plaque, such as that on a teak footstool at Greenwich: *Timber ex HMS Arethusa. Launched 1849. Broken up 1933. Odessa. Sebastopol. The last ship to sail into action. Castles Shipbreaking Co Ltd.*

Some of the wood panelling in Liberty's famous Regent Street shop is taken from the timber of HMS *Impregnable* and HMS *Hindustan,* broken up in 1921. Even the main staircase of the National Maritime Museum is made from the teak of HMS *Ganges* (launched 1821), *Arethusa* (1849), *Defence* (1861) and *Defiance* (1861), all ships which were broken up between 1933 and 1935, at the time the building was being converted into a museum.

NOTES

1 Denis Diderot and Jean Le Rond d'Alembert: *Encyclopédie Méthodique: Marine* Vol IV (1783)

2 Illustrated in Jean Mudge: *Chinese Export Porcelain for the American Trade* (1981)

3 John E Barnard: 'John Barnard the Younger, Shipbuilder of Ipswich and Harwich 1705–1784' (*Mariner's Mirror* Vol 78 no. 2 1992) pp155–75

4 Bernard Rackham: *Catalogue of the Schreiber Collection* Vol II (1930) p83 no. 414

5 M K Stammers: *West Coast Shipping* (1976)

6 Illustrated in James Ayres: *British Folk Art* (1977) plates facing pp40 and 65

7 F H Garner and Michael Archer: *English Delftware* (1972) plate 91B

8 Robert Latham and William Matthews (eds): *Diary of Samuel Pepys* Vol V (1971) pp305–6

9 See Rosemary Weinstein: 'City Patronage and the Warship London' (*Antique Collector* no. 10 1984) pp64–7

10 E Alfred Jones: 'Some Builders of Ships for the Royal Navy and their Gifts of Plate from 1708 to 1736'. (*Burlington Magazine* XXXVII 1920) pp130–37; Public Record Office: Admiralty, A G, Miscellaneous, Various 161

11 National Maritime Museum: ADM/A/3099, Admiralty to Navy Board (10th August 1814)

12 Charles Dickens: 'Chatham Dockyard' (*The Uncommercial Traveller* 1969) pp259–60

13 Sylvia Rodgers: 'The Symbolism of Ship Launching in the Royal Navy' (unpublished DPhil thesis 1983, Linacre College, Oxford)

14 Jonathan Horne (Antiques) Ltd: Exhibition of Early English Pottery (March 1984)

15 See Peter Stuckey: *Sailing Pilots of the Bristol Channel* (1977)

16 *Herculaneum: the Last Liverpool Pottery* (catalogue of exhibition at Warrington Museum and Art Gallery, 1983) no. 100

17 Sotheby's (14th April 1992) Lot 336

18 D A Hoyte and G L Pendred: 'Shipping Decoration on 18th Century Derby' (*Antique Dealer & Collector's Guide* March 1967) and 'The Decoration of Derby Porcelain – Some Interesting Sources of Inspiration' (*Antique Dealer & Collector's Guide* February 1976)

19 *Arbog 1964* (Handels-og Sofartsmuseet, Kronborg, Elsinore) pp136–8

20 See Manfred Meinz: *Schausammlung des Altonaer Museums* (1968) pp48–9

21 *Nautical Magazine* Vol IV (1835) pp457–9

22 Ibid. Vol XII (1843) pp558–60

CHAPTER 2 Battles and Heroes

Naval victories have always seized the public imagination and demanded thanksgiving and celebration. Great paintings and other major works of art have resulted, but it is was not until the eighteenth century that popular souvenirs of such actions were produced for sale. The Spanish Armada of 1588, for instance, was commemorated in contemporary paintings, tapestries, silver medals and costly jewels. A set of Armada tapestries commissioned for Charles, Lord Howard of Effingham (1536–1624), which had hung in the House of Lords since the Commonwealth, perished in the 1834 fire. Our detailed knowledge of their appearance depends on John Pine's set of published engravings of 1739. The tapestries, designed by Hendrick Vroom for completion by the Delft workshops of Frans Spierings, show views of the rival fleets within a border of medallion portraits of the naval commanders.

No contemporary ceramics were produced to commemorate the events of 1588. Later periods attempted to put this right, and the Chamberlains Porcelain Factory in Worcester designed a costly Armada service for the Earl of Bandon of Castle Bernard in County Cork in 1801, costing £500. The service was decorated with badges representing the destruction of the Spanish Armada, and was known as *Queen Elizabeth's Pattern*.[1]

In 1974 a Chamberlains Worcester part dinner and dessert service with printed Armada medallions on a coral-red ground was sold in London, which may be the service referred to in the Worcester records.[2] The design is from the reverse of an Armada medal showing the Spanish fleet being driven against the rocks, with the date 1588 and Latin inscription *Tu deus magnus et magne facis ut solus deus* (Thou God art great and doest wondrous things; thou art God alone, Psalm LXXXVI.10).[3]

The year of the Armada was also commemorated on iron firebacks, which were cast with anchor motifs and the date 1588. Some of these firebacks have panels of fruiting vines on either side of the anchors. However, it is usually difficult to identify which ones are the contemporary versions since good copies have continued to be produced until the present day.

In the seventeenth century sailing ships were a common motif on Dutch tiles and stained glass panels, and were a favourite choice for the interior decoration of houses. Engraved silver was also to be found in the houses of the wealthier citizens. The earliest commemorative piece of silver in the collection of the National Maritime Museum is a seventeenth century Dutch octagonal dish commemorating the capture of the Spanish silver fleet by the famous Dutch admiral, Piet Hein (1577–1629). The centre of the dish (plate 27) is finely engraved with a scene of the fleet, and above it a portrait medallion of Piet Hein. On 8th September 1628 he captured the Spanish treasure fleet in Matanzas Bay, east of Havana, Cuba, and in the

27 Silver dish, Amsterdam 1629, engraved with Admiral Piet Hein's capture of the Spanish silver fleet.

Netherlands he is still famed for this success. The shaped border of the dish is engraved with other shipping scenes, interspersed with emblematical figures of the four seasons.

The dish was made in 1629, and may be by Andreas Kauxdorf of Amsterdam. It is the largest of a series of eight dishes dating between 1624 and 1635 which are now in Dutch collections. An inscription on the back can be translated:

> *The brave deed of Piet Hein's victory you see produced here to his everlasting memory, who risked his life for his fatherland. His name is eternal to the disgrace of the enemy. This is given by Philip Castel to Machtel Castel. Until he goes to his God give him a good and Christian life.*

The Anglo–Dutch Wars of the seventeenth century were commemorated with medals in precious metals and rare pieces of engraved silver. The Dutch are known to have produced engraved silver beakers with portraits of their admirals. One made in Enkhuizen in 1656, which has a frieze of Dutch warships, commemorates Admirals De Ruyter and De Witt, and also names the English admirals, Penn and Blake. There are other fine contemporary engraved medals associated with Penn and Blake. Vice Admiral William Penn (1621–1670) was presented with the Commonwealth Gold Naval Reward and chain in commemoration of naval victories over the Dutch in 1653. Four of the medals struck by Thomas Simon of London were awarded by Parliament to the senior flag officers, and Penn's, which is on loan to the National Maritime Museum, is the only one to survive complete with its heavy 8-yard length of chain, meant to be worn as a collar.

There is also an important tapestry at Greenwich which celebrates an incident in the Battle of Solebay, the first battle of the Third Dutch War. On 28th May 1672, 140 ships of the English and French fleets, under the command of James, Duke of York and Comte d'Estrées, met the Dutch fleet, under De Ruyter, with 91 ships, 54 fireships and 23 tenders. The wool and silk tapestry (colour plate 28) depicts the burning by Dutch fireships of the *Royal James*, flagship of the Earl of Sandwich. She can be seen on the extreme left of the tapestry, with the burnt Dutch fireships. The deep borders are woven with putti, sea monsters and tritons.

This is one of a set of six tapestries commemorating the battle which were woven at the famous Mortlake factory after drawings by Willem van de Velde the Elder, who was present at the battle. One of the original drawings is in the Boymans Museum in Rotterdam. The first three tapestries were made under the direction of Francis Poyntz for King Charles II and are now in the Royal Collection at Hampton Court Palace. The Greenwich tapestry is one of the second three, which were ordered to complete the set but apparently never delivered. They are signed by Thomas Poyntz, younger brother of Francis. These passed into the possession of the Walpole family, whose arms were added to the border in 1720, and were subsequently sold. The other two are now at Hampton Court.[4]

So far we have considered only the precious items made to celebrate naval events, but in the eighteenth century public interest in naval and military affairs created a demand for cheaper and more available decorative objects. The earliest large-scale production of maritime commemoratives came with Admiral Edward Vernon's (1723–1794) victory at Portobello in 1739. Speaking in Parliament for the Opposition on the subject of Spanish interference in British trade to the West Indies, Vernon had claimed that he could capture Portobello, the fortified Spanish base on the Isthmus of Darien, *with six ships only*. So he was sent with the six ships *Burford, Hampton Court, Worcester, Strafford, Princess Louisa* and *Norwich*, and indeed took the town on 20th November 1739, and the next March also captured the fort at Chagres, in Panama. In April 1741, reinforced by a squadron under Rear Admiral Sir Chaloner Ogle, Vernon's fleet captured the forts at Carthagena and destroyed the Spanish squadron in the harbour.

A marble bust honouring Admiral Vernon is in the Museum's collection. The bust was sculpted by J M Rysbrack *c*1743–4, and depicts Vernon wearing a curled wig and a decorated breastplate. It remained with descendants of the Vernon family until the 1930s. But the great popularity of Vernon's achievements in England was indicated by the immediate mass production of cheap souvenirs. In particular, bronze medallions were issued, many of them by Edward Pinchbeck of Fleet Street. Some 270 variations are known, most of them incorporating the admiral, the town and the ships. In some cases the designs appear in uniface form as buttons, and one example is enamelled, probably for use as a patch box lid. The victory was also the first opportunity for the developing pottery industry to meet a major demand for souvenirs from a patriotic public. Most of the commemorative pieces depict Portobello, although dishes showing Chagres are also known. As ceramic printing had yet to be developed, all the commemorative designs were either hand-painted or moulded in relief.

Among the productions were the delftware or tin-glazed earthenware plates made in London at Lambeth, and possibly in Liverpool too. One plate at Greenwich is freely painted in blue with a view of Portobello Harbour with its fort, and Vernon's warships approaching (plate 29). The border is decorated with a foliage pattern, and the painted sprigs beneath the rim suggest that it was probably made in Liverpool rather than London. Another important delftware plate at Greenwich, which was made at Lambeth, is also painted with a Portobello scene, but has a brown powdered manganese border decorated with four naval guns mounted on wooden carriages bearing the royal cipher *GR* and a crown (colour plate 30). Some features of the Portobello design may be derived from W H Toms's engraving of Samuel Scott's painting of the scene. The Victoria & Albert Museum has two delftware chargers commemorating the taking of Chagres, and a plate which may be a portrait of Vernon. In a private collection there is a very rare tin-glazed mug with a half-length profile portrait of Admiral Vernon, painted in blue.

A large Fulham stoneware tankard of 1741 commemorates the same action (colour plate 31). The tankard has a silver rim, and the body is decorated in relief with an oval cartouche depicting the taking of Portobello. Round the bottom of the tankard is a stag hunt, and other standard reliefs of cottages and trees fill up the remaining areas, as well as the inscriptions *Portobello* and *1741*. The other important Portobello group is of white Staffordshire saltglaze. Teapots and bowls of various designs were popular, and the National Maritime Museum has an example of both. The small bowl bears applied reliefs of the fort and ships, and a full-length representation of Vernon (colour plate 31). There is also a fine mug, similarly decorated, at the Victoria & Albert Museum, in the Schreiber Collection. Lady Charlotte Schreiber, a tireless collector of decorative art, described the acquisition of this piece in her journal for 26th September 1884: *While I was yet at dinner they brought me in a mug which Kerridge had left for my approval–salt glaze–with portrait–ships–cannon, etc., and inscription ... A wonderful acquisition.*[5] Another Staffordshire saltglaze Vernon mug appeared in 1991 in a London saleroom, this time moulded in relief with a large Royal coat of arms in addition to the figure of the admiral and view of Portobello.[6]

29 Tin-glazed earthenware plate *c*1739 painted with Portobello Harbour.

An amusing hexagonal teapot (colour plate 31) with a serpentine spout and handle has a view of the ships before the town on one side and a different full-length figure on the other, with the inscription *R Ad Vernon. Fort Chagre Portobello taken.* Birds on sprays decorate the smaller panels, and the cover is surmounted by a seated animal, probably a Chinese lion. Lady Schreiber bought one of these teapots in London a few weeks after she bought her mug, and records on 30th October: *Kerridge bringing a Salt Glaze Teapot with portrait (and inscription) of Admiral Vernon–very desirable, very ugly and very dear. He wants £5 for it, but of course I must have it.*[7]

Presumably there were a number of more ephemeral souvenirs of Admiral Vernon's victory, but these have only rarely survived. One such piece in the collection at Greenwich is an ivory and paper fan (plate 32), the paper leaf printed and hand-coloured with a depiction of Portobello and verses, and signed *F Chassereau April 22 1740*. One verse runs:

> *Hark the British cannon thunders,*
> *See my lads six ships appear;*
> *Every Briton acting wonders,*
> *Strikes the Southern World with fear.*
> *Porto Bello fam'd in story*
> *Now at last submits to fate;*
> *Vernon's Courage gains us glory,*
> *And his mercy proves us great.*

From a slightly later date come the London and Liverpool delftware punch bowls decorated with patriotic naval and military slogans which do not refer to any particular action, although some may date from the Seven Years War (1756–63). A Liverpool bowl is painted in a simple cursive script *Britons Still Will rule the Main*. Another bowl, painted inside with a floral pattern in *bianco sopra bianco*, has a blue inscription *Success to the British Arms*. This technique, in which a pure white pattern contrasts with the blue-white of the tin glaze, is normally associated with Bristol, but this example is now thought to be have been made in London, and to date from 1747–55.

The Seven Years War, in which Britain supported Prussia against attack from Austria, France, Sweden and Saxony, was fought in distant theatres, and was marked by ceramic productions which included the first printed commemorative porcelain pieces. Edward Boscawen (1711–1761), who had served under Vernon at Portobello, was made Admiral of the Blue in 1758, and appointed commander-in-chief of the expedition to the French-held island of Cape Breton, Nova Scotia.

There is a fine first-period Worcester porcelain mug, printed by Robert Hancock, commemorating Boscawen's part in the Siege of Louisbourg in 1758 (colour plate 33). The copperplate engraving is a three-quarter-length portrait of Boscawen holding a chart of Louisbourg, and on the other side two warships and the admiral's coat of arms. The pose and naval uniform are taken from John Faber's mezzotint of 1747 after Allan Ramsay's painting of Boscawen as Rear Admiral of the Blue, but the head and wig are different. In fact the print on the mug is a composite portrait incorporating the head from Robert Sayer's engraving of a painting of Admiral Boscawen by Joshua Reynolds. This is one of the many occasions when a print was re-used and adapted to suit the purpose of the moment, and, as we shall see in other later examples, the engravers tended not to worry too much if some of the details were a little outdated.

32 Fan by F Chassereau, 1740, painted with a scene of Portobello.

Another Worcester piece is a small porcelain bowl of *c*1760 with an indented rim, printed inside and out with views of naval victories during the Seven Years War (plate 34). The interior has a scene of warships outside the harbour at Senegal, and on the outside are ships engaged in action at Cape Breton and Guadeloupe. Fort Louis, on the Senegal River, surrendered to Captain Henry Marsh and Major Mason on 1st May 1758, and Cape Breton capitulated to the British, under Admiral Boscawen and General Amherst, after the surrender of Louisbourg on 26th July 1758. The island of Guadeloupe finally succumbed on 1st May 1759 after bombardment by Commodore Moore and the military forces led by General Hopson, who sickened and died before victory was achieved.

34 Worcester porcelain bowl *c*1760 printed with naval victories of the Seven Years War (1756–63)

Minorca, which had been held by the British at the beginning of the war, was lost in 1756. Admiral John Byng (1704–1757), with a poorly equipped squadron, failed to relieve the island and, being found guilty of neglect of duty, was condemned to death and shot. Only some engraved glasses and a flurry of medals commemorated the event publicly, although satirical engravings were produced. One such contemporary broadsheet holds quite a different interest for us, since it shows Byng holding a council on board his ship, and we can clearly see that the cabin is lined with shelves holding rows of porcelain vases and figures. A member of the council is just remarking:

Pray let's go back to Gib
And there invent a Fib.[8]

The National Maritime Museum has an interesting souvenir of the war in the form of a small circular silver box some 2¼ inches in diameter containing sixty engravings. The box, which has the appearance of a deep medallion, has a relief profile of George II on the lid and George III on the base. The circles of paper inside have illustrations on one side and text on the other, detailing: *A Short History in Miniature of the Origin and Progress of the late War from its commencement to the Exchange of the Ratification of Peace between Great Britain, France and Spain on the 10th of Feby 1763.*

Also dating from this period is a polychrome wax plaque of Captain Richard Gwyn RN (*d*1766). The plaque is unsigned, but is in the manner of Samuel Percy, the famous wax modeller. He is shown three-quarter-length, seated in profile, and rests a telescope on his right shoulder. The portrait is of particular interest because he is shown wearing captains' undress uniform of the 1749–67 pattern – one of the first official naval uniform patterns. The relief figure is realistically coloured and glazed in an oval mount. Captain Gwyn commanded the *Falcon* sloop in 1747, under Anson, and was promoted to captain of the *Ambuscade* frigate of 40 guns. With Duff of the *Rochester* he captured five large Dutch ships, and in 1759 was appointed to the *Rainbow*, 44 guns, and served on the Mediterranean Station until near the end of the war.

The Twelth [sic] *of August is a Very Good Toast* is the evocative inscription on a wine glass which commemorates the capture of Havannah on that day in 1762 (colour plate 35). The small glass stands on a shaped foot with a facet-cut stem, and is painted with a gilded scene on each side depicting a palm tree, standing figure and military trophies. In the distance is a coastline with a fortress, and by the figure is a shield of arms bearing three scallop shells, the arms of the Keppel family. George Keppel, 3rd Earl of Albemarle, was commander-in-chief of the expedition. His brothers – Commodore the Hon. Augustus Keppel, who had earlier voyaged round the world with Anson, and Major General the Hon. W Keppel – also took part in the capture of Havannah in August 1762. All three brothers were awarded considerable sums in prize money.

A few months after the reduction of Havannah, Augustus Keppel (1725–1786) was promoted to rear admiral. By 1778 he had become Admiral of the Blue and commander-in-chief of the Channel

36 Bristol tin-glazed earthenware punch bowl for Rodney *c*1768 and plate for Keppel *c*1780.

Fleet. An encounter with the French fleet off Ushant that year, in which the enemy escaped under cover of darkness, led to charges of misconduct and neglect of duty being brought against Keppel by his second-in-command, Sir Hugh Palliser. At the subsequent court martial he was acquitted with honour, and later received the thanks of Parliament; popular feeling was on his side, and public houses were named after him. From this period there survive a number of Lambeth delftware plates and punch bowls painted with a crude portrait of the admiral and the inscription *Admiral Keppel for Ever* (plate 36). These pieces may have been made to commemorate the war against the French, and indeed similar pieces celebrate other admirals of the period, or they may alternatively have been intended for electioneering purposes. Keppel sat in the House of Commons as the Member for Windsor in the Parliaments of 1761, 1768, and 1774, and for the County of Surrey in 1780. In 1782 he was appointed First Lord of the Admiralty, and raised to the peerage.

A number of other interesting pieces commemorating Augustus Keppel are known. At Greenwich there is a Leeds creamware teapot (colour plate 37) transfer-printed in black and hand-coloured with a half-length portrait of the admiral in uniform holding a telescope, and inscribed *The Honble Augtus Keppel.* Naval trophies surround him, small figures of Fame and Justice hover in the background, and a warship appears under sail on the other side. The teapot was made in *c*1780 and the engraving is by William Greatbatch. A privately- owned teapot of slightly different shape has the Keppel portrait on one side and another topical subject, *Captain Cook being directed by Britannia,* on the other.

Other Keppel commemoratives include a Pratt ware plaque moulded in relief and painted, in the distinctive bright colours of the ware, with a crude portrait and trophy of arms. There is also a small creamware bowl from the studio of David Rhodes of Leeds which is handpainted with the admiral wearing a uniform coat incorrectly coloured red, but identified beyond doubt by the inscription *Admiral Keppel* (colour plate 37). An Irish linen damask tablecloth is a more unusual souvenir of Keppel's period of greatest fame. Presumably intended for practical use by his supporters since it could not be displayed in any other way, the tablecloth has the inscription *Keppel and Victory 1779* woven into the white damask, together with a warship, all within a decorative border. A matching Irish linen napkin is woven with *Keppel and Honour.*

From the same date is a vitreous paste profile plaque of Augustus Keppel by Tassie, signed and dated 1779 (colour plate 38). He is shown in profile, with short hair and bare shoulders. The Scottish father and son, William and James Tassie, perfected the art of casting these detailed profiles of notables of the day from an opaque glass paste, and we shall later see other naval figures reproduced in the same medium. Wedgwood also produced portrait medallions of Keppel in 1779 and 1780, and the authors of a book on the subject have pointed out how the manuscript evidence sheds interesting light on the speed of their production. Other etched and wax portraits of the admiral were evidently already being advertised by the time Wedgwood complained, on 1st March 1779: *Oh Keppel Keppel–Why will you not send me a Keppel. I am perswaded if we had had our wits about us as we ought to have had 2 or 3 months since we might have sold 1000£ worth of this gentleman's head in various ways.* Twelve days later the portrait was in production.[9]

The Anglo–Dutch Battle of the Dogger Bank in 1781, claimed as a victory by both sides, has been seen depicted on a Japanese gold and black lacquered copper panel. At Greenwich there is also a paper fan commemorating the action, with a central painting of the rival fleets in line of battle, and a triton holding the Dutch flag. From a similar period is a silver verge watch of 1777 by J Brant of London, which has an enamelled dial painted with five warships and the inscription *Success to the British Navy.*

The next major production of souvenirs was associated with George Brydges Rodney (1719–1792), and particularly with his victory over the French at the Battle of the Saints in April 1782. A few pieces commemorate his earlier exploits. The earliest is a Bristol delftware punch bowl of *c*1768, with a naive portrait and the inscription *Admiral Rodney for ever* (plate 36), but this probably relates to his political campaign when he was elected Member of Parliament for Northampton. A transfer-printed creamware jug by J Aynsley of Lane End has a portrait of Rodney and naval trophies (plate 42). The transfer dates from about 1780 and the jug commemorates Rodney's relief of Gibraltar. There is a printed verse:

You Frenchmen and you Spaniards
Interrupt us if you dare.
We'll give you thundering broadsides
From our English Men of War.

Another earlier piece, a creamware mug, is hand-painted with floral sprays and an inscription *Rodney for ever 1781*. The sentiment is repeated on a Leeds pearlware mug, decorated in the studio of David Rhodes and Robinson, with a painting of a naval officer in uniform and the inscription *Rodney for ever*. Also from the earlier period is a small earthenware figure showing Admiral Rodney standing full-length, coloured in mottled green and blue glazes, and believed to be by Ralph Wood of Staffordshire. The figure wears naval uniform, and stands beside a gun about to draw his sword. The word *Rodney* is moulded vertically beside his right leg. Another version of this figure is known in the same pose, but without the hat.[10]

On 12th April 1782 Rodney won the greatest naval victory of the American Revolutionary War by defeating the French fleet under the command of the Comte de Grasse in the West Indies, off the islands known as Les Saintes. Britain may have lost the American Colonies, but this important victory over the French in the Caribbean was still cause for celebration back in Britain. The souvenir manufacturers had a field day, and the ceramic factories turned out commemorative items of all types: bowls, mugs, jugs, plates, teapots and figurines. These varied from fine porcelain to naive earthenware pieces, and might be printed, hand-painted or moulded. The top end of the scale is represented by a Chelsea-Derby porcelain jug with its lip modelled as the head of Admiral Rodney, and underneath it the inscription *April the 12th 1782*, the date of the Battle of the Saints (colour plate 40). The sides of the jug are painted with flower sprays, probably by Edward Withers of the Derby factory.

Similarly intended for the richer market was a series of Chinese export porcelain punch bowls decorated with a grisaille painting of the Battle of the Saints. The painting is after the oil painting by Robert Dodd which was engraved by F Chesham and J Peltro and published by Sayer and Bennett on 21st March 1783. The bowls must have been individually produced to order, for each example has a different design in a reserve on one side. Of the two Saints bowls in the National Maritime Museum one is painted with the coat of arms of Sir Charles Douglas Bt, (*d*1789) Rodney's captain of the fleet at the battle, and the other has a caricature of an Englishman and a Frenchman exchanging abusive remarks. *You be damm'd* says the Englishman to the Frenchman, who replies *Vous êtes une bête*. The source is a James Gillray etching, *Politeness*, originally published in 1779, depicting the confrontation between national stereotypes. It is most likely that the bowls were specially commissioned for presentation purposes rather than for sale to the public generally, as most of them have no inscription referring to the battle to tempt a casual buyer.

41 Staffordshire mask mugs *c*1782 modelled as Lord Rodney.

More attractive to the pocket of the general public were the colourful Rodney mugs and jugs which were being mass produced in cheaper materials (colour plate 39). The earthenware pieces are decorated with yellow, green, black or marbled glaze, and some have applied swags and a cartouche with a portrait of Admiral Rodney (1724–1816). Others have applied relief figures of both Rodney and Admiral Hood, and a medallion with de Grasse's flagship *Ville de Paris*. Dating from the same period are the amusing but well-modelled mask mugs, shaped as the head of Lord Rodney (plate 41). They were probably made in Staffordshire, and some are attributed to Ralph Wood Jr. The same idea was also used to commemorate Lord Nelson and other later heroes. The mugs are variously coloured in blue and white, or pastel shades, and the foot is modelled as the collar of a naval uniform. In the case of one large mug or jug the handle is modelled as the upturned *queue* (or pigtail). The rim is inscribed in relief lettering and is sometimes decorated with a signal flag. One example in the collection at Greenwich is a double-sided mask mug, with Rodney's face on both sides, large scroll handles, and the inscriptions *God save the King* and *Success to Lord Rodney*. But perhaps the most amusing piece is a double-headed pottery vessel, randomly daubed with colour, inscribed *Lord Rodney*, and pierced at the top as a flour sifter.

Other ceramic commemoratives of Rodney include a Liverpool creamware plate which is transfer-printed in black with his portrait and trophy of arms, and the inscription *Sr Geo. Bridges Rodney Bart.* (plate 42), and an earthenware mug with a painted portrait of the admiral wearing an incorrectly coloured red coat and purple waistcoat, with the toast *Success to Brave Rodney*.

Although the most numerous souvenirs of Rodney's victories appear to have been ceramic, other commemorative pieces do appear from time to time. One unusual item at Greenwich is a finely carved coconut flask depicting Rodney's ship, *Formidable,* breaking through the French line at the Battle of the Saints. The inscription below the scene provides a key to letters which mark the *Diadem* sinking and the dismasted *Glorieux*. The other side of the coconut is carved with a similar scene showing the landing of troops on St Kitts earlier in the year, on 28th January 1782.

Commemorative shoe buckles are also known in at least two different designs. One pair of large rectangular brass buckles has a cast inscription in the border: *Sr George Brydges Rodney Admiral of the White*. There is evidence that buckles of this pattern were also produced in silver and pewter. Another pair of buckles with silver rectangular frames are inscribed *Victory over the French. Admiral Rodney and Admiral Hood 1782 12th of April*. These words are on the underside of the frame, so they would be hidden in normal wear. The maker of the steel fastener of these buckles was Thomason, and it is interesting that this maker's name appears on a shoe buckle recovered from the wreck of the ill-fated HMS *Royal George,* lost at Spithead in the same year, 1782. An eighteenth century gold ring set with an oval amethyst glass intaglio by Tassie also commemorates the Saints. The bezel, cut as a seal, has a fouled anchor and inscription *12 Apl 1782 Rodney L'Espérance Réalisée*.

Another particularly rare and interesting celebration of the Battle of the Saints appears to have belonged to Lord Rodney himself. This is a dioramic model of the action by an unknown maker, taken from an engraving after the painting by Richard Paton of 1783 (colour plate 43). Model ships are mounted in a gilded wooden case, and dramatic effects of sky and sea behind the vessels are achieved by the use of painted glass sheets, false perspective and a hidden light source reflected into the case from a mirror. A central glass sheet with painted gun smoke bisects the finely-modelled ships and gives a realistic impression that a precise moment in the action has been captured. Rodney's flagship, *Formidable,* is on the

42 Creamware mug, jug and plate, and an enamel plaque of Rodney.

left, and on the right the French flagship, *Ville de Paris,* surrenders to Rear Admiral Hood in the *Barfleur.*

There are a few rare pieces made of precious metals which are associated with the Battle of the Saints. A gold Freedom box from the City of Cork and an engraved silver goblet were both awarded to Admiral Rodney himself, and appear in chapter 3 with the presentation pieces. Gold pendants were also produced to commemorate the battle, although the details of their original commissioning have now been lost. All the known examples are of oval form, and pierced with a design showing the French flagship, with variations in detail, but in each case an inscription along the lines of *Ville de Paris taken by S G B Rodney in the Glorious Action 12th April 1782.*

It is unusual to find items of furniture of this period designed specifically to commemorate a naval action. There is one long-case clock at Greenwich, however, which marks the victory at the Saints (plate 44). The clock is by John Chance of Chepstow, and the mahogany case is decorated with a scrolled pediment and fretwork design. The arch dial incorporates a rocking ship beneath the inscription *Success to Brave Rodney.* John Chance (1750–1800) was the best-known of Chepstow's eighteenth century clockmakers, and many of his long-case clocks have survived locally, but not, apparently, another Rodney example. However, there is another of his clocks of similar design which also has a moving ship below an inscription which reads *High Water at Brockware.*[11]

War broke out between Britain and France in February 1793. The first major naval action of the Revolutionary War was the Battle of the Glorious 1st of June 1794, when Admiral Lord Howe (1726–1799) defeated the Brest fleet of Admiral Villaret-Joyeuse, sent out to escort an essential grain convoy from the United States to France. The victory was commemorated by the production of a few ceramic souvenirs and other pieces. Among these is a Leeds creamware mug (plate 45), transfer-printed in black with a portrait of Admiral Howe, sword in hand, gesturing towards the stern of his flagship, *Queen Charlotte.* Below is an inscription *Right Honble Earl Howe Commander of His Majesty's Fleet in the Channel.* The print is from a mezzotint published by Laurie and Whittle on 11th June 1794, engraved by Corbutt after R Purcell. Another version of the print omits the

44 Detail of long-case clock by John Chance of Chepstow, inscribed *Success to Brave Rodney.*

45 Leeds creamware mug commemorating Howe and the Glorious 1st of June 1794.

name on the stern of the ship. Liverpool Museum also has a creamware jug with an oval view of the battle, inscribed *A representation of the glorious Defeat of the French Fleet of Brest by Earl Howe June 1st 1794.*

Other souvenirs of the battle included decorative enamel patch boxes made to hold the small cosmetic patches of the period, produced in Bilston, Staffordshire. One such box has a transfer-printed profile of Admiral Howe, and another has a view of ships in action and the inscription *The glorious Victory of Earl Howe On the 1st of June 1794.* Wedgwood produced one of the well-known oval portrait medallions of Admiral Howe a few years later, modelled by John de Vaere in 1798. This same portrait was often used as part of a set of Admirals comprising Howe, Duncan, St Vincent and Nelson, appearing either as a framed set, or as part of the relief decoration on a single jug. Coloured wax profiles, apparently after the Wedgwood medallion, are also known, some

46 Japanese lacquer writing box with a view of the Battle of Camperdown, 11th October 1797.

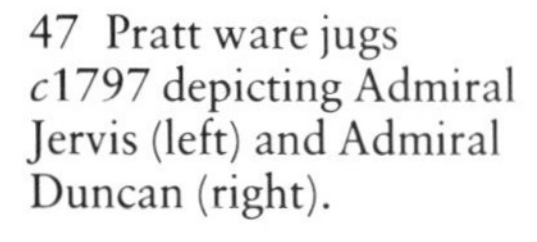

47 Pratt ware jugs *c*1797 depicting Admiral Jervis (left) and Admiral Duncan (right).

signed by Wyon. A similar portrait profile was produced at the same time by Tassie, and appears both as portrait plaques in white vitreous paste and as small gems to adorn pins and brooches, or for the collector's cabinet.

Gold badges were also made at this period to commemorate Earl Howe and the Glorious 1st of June, either in the shape of anchors or pierced with a design incorporating various naval motifs. Both types were made with a loop for suspension, but it is not known whether they were intended to be worn by officers who had served in the battle or were made as presentation pieces. The ladies in the Royal party in Henry Briggs's oil painting of King George III's visit to Howe's flagship on 26th June 1794 can certainly be seen wearing small gold anchors on chains around their necks.

The Battle of Camperdown, fought between the British fleet under the command of Admiral Adam Duncan (1731–1804) and the Dutch under Admiral De Winter (1750–1812) on 11th October 1797, resulted in a decisive British victory after a hotly-contested action. The victory was marked by the production of souvenirs in great variety: pottery, glass, jewellery, and even furniture. Among the more elegant productions was an oriental lacquer writing box inlaid with mother-of-pearl, with a view of the battle set into an oval in the lid (plate 46). The box is Japanese and dates from the first third of the nineteenth century. A Dutch inscription below the scene is translated: *Naval battle, between the Batavian and English fleets off Egmond on the eleventh of October 1797.*

Other fine pieces include engraved drinking glasses, evidently specially commissioned. One engraved tumbler at Greenwich has a warship under sail on one side, a family coat of arms with boar's-head crest, and an inscription *Adml. Duncan and the Glorious 11 Oct 1797.* Another tumbler, perhaps by William Absolon, is inscribed *Duncan's Victory. Loyalty from Yarmouth JFH 1798.* Also specially commissioned were the decorative chairs made from the timber of the captured Dutch fleet which have already been considered in chapter 1.

Among the most popular of the cheaper mass-produced souvenirs of Camperdown were the Pratt ware jugs decorated with a brightly coloured relief profile of Admiral Adam Duncan wearing a uniform hat (plate 47). On the other side are either two female figures of Peace and Plenty in classical dress, or Captain Henry Trollope of the *Russell.* The profiles are identified by the names *Admirel* [sic] *Duncan* and *Captain Trolop* which appear on the sashes of their orders, fortunately for us, since the two portraits are hardly distinguishable. An even cruder profile of Duncan is on a rare bowl and saucer decorated with transfer printing and hand-colouring – perhaps used by a child, as the name *Cathrine Chalmers* is handpainted in cursive script on both pieces. Far better likenesses of Duncan, this time without the hat, appear on the Tassie profile of 1797 and the Wedgwood portrait medallion modelled by John de Vaere in 1798 (plate 48). At the other end of the scale is an amusing earthenware jug with a reversible portrait which is identified as Admiral Duncan one way up, but when turned upside down appears as Admiral De Winter, although they are hardly recognisable.

An interesting creamware jug with a fine transfer-printed portrait was produced by Thomas

6 (far left) Liverpool delftware bowl painted with a launching scene, dated 1752.

7 (left) Launching plate presented to master shipwrights in the Royal Dockyards. Left: Tankard by Thomas Farren, for the launch of the *Captain* at Woolwich in 1743. Right: Candlesticks by John Bache, for the launch of the *Feversham* at Plymouth in 1712.

11 (left) Top row: Tin-glazed bowls from Bristol and Liverpool painted with vessels rigged as a cutter, a ship and a snow.
Bottom row: Liverpool creamware bowls painted with a brig and a ship.

12 (above) Liverpool delftware plate *c*1760 painted with a Baltic galeas wearing Danzig flags.

19 (right) Two lustreware wall plaques by Dixons of Sunderland.

21 (below) Three glasses engraved with shipping passing through the bridge over the River Wear at Sunderland.

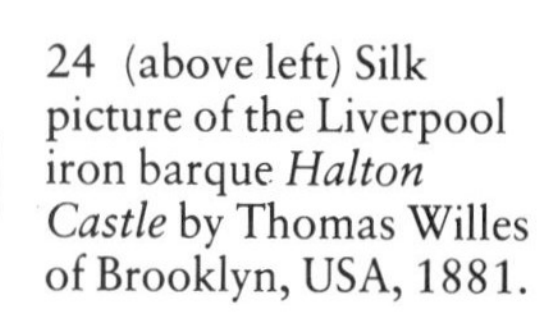

24 (above left) Silk picture of the Liverpool iron barque *Halton Castle* by Thomas Willes of Brooklyn, USA, 1881.

25 (above right) Sideboard made in 1849 from the timber of the Spanish 1st Rate *San Josef* captured at the Battle of Cape St Vincent, 1797.

28 Mortlake tapestry by Thomas Poyntz depicting an incident in the Battle of Solebay, 1672.

38 Vitreous paste profile plaque of Keppel by Tassie, 1779.

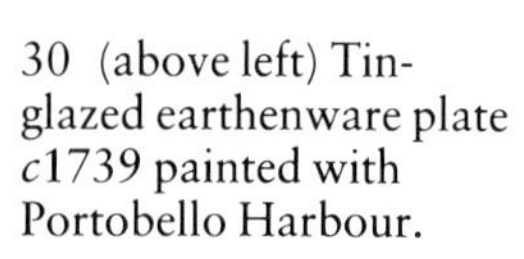

30 (above left) Tin-glazed earthenware plate *c*1739 painted with Portobello Harbour.

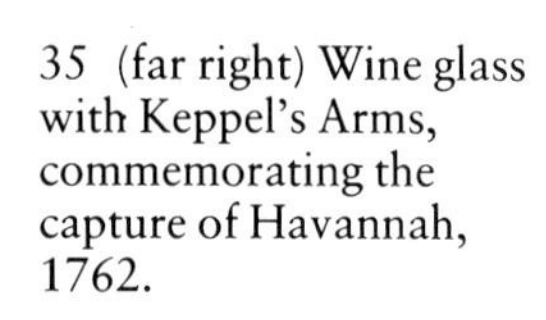

33 (right) Worcester porcelain mug by Robert Hancock *c*1758 printed with a portrait of Admiral Boscawen.

35 (far right) Wine glass with Keppel's Arms, commemorating the capture of Havannah, 1762.

37 (left) Leeds bowl and teapot *c*1780 with portraits of Keppel.

40 (below left) Chelsea-Derby porcelain jug with Rodney mask lip and the date of the Battle of the Saints.

39 (below) Earthenware mugs and jugs *c*1782 commemorating Rodney and the Battle of the Saints.

31 (bottom) Staffordshire saltglaze teapot and bowl and a Fulham stoneware tankard commemorating Vernon's capture of Portobello and Chagres.

43 (above) Model of the Battle of the Saints, 1782, owned by Lord Rodney.

49 (left) Creamware jug transfer-printed with portrait of John Jervis, Earl St Vincent, *c*1797.

51 (above) Earthenware mugs and jugs decorated with an earlier engraving of 1758, used here to represent both the Battle of the Nile in 1798 and Trafalgar in 1805.

52 (above left) Derby mug, and porcelain chocolate cup and cover, made to the order of Alexander Davison after the Battle of the Nile, 1798.

57 (above right) Copenhagen porcelain punch bowl presented to Danish naval officers after the Battle of Copenhagen, 1801.

62 Porcelain vases by Chamberlains of Worcester, painted with the Battle of the Nile (left) and Trafalgar (right)

63 (above) Nelson medallion box containing a set of coloured engravings published by Edward Orme.

64 (far right) Silver-rimmed horn beaker engraved with the ships which fought at Trafalgar.

65 (right) Staffordshire portrait figures of Admiral Sir Charles Napier and Sir James Dundas, *c*1854.

67 Minton china bowl painted by J E Dean, commemorating the surrender of the German High Seas Fleet in November 1918.

Baddeley of Hanley at about the same date, also to commemorate Duncan's victory at Camperdown. However, it appears that the engraver must have been using the wrong source for his portrait, for the distinctive profile which appears on one side has quite different features from the admiral's, and even the details of the uniform appear to be foreign. It is easy to forget that, in the days before television and illustrated newspapers, public figures were far less instantly recognisable to the man in the street, and such mistakes mattered little. The engraver's intention of portraying Duncan is in no doubt, for he is clearly identified by a caption on the oval frame, and a verse below:

Long as the Sea shall fence our envi'd land
Long as the Navy shall that sea command:
So long shall Admiral Lord Duncan's Name
Be grav'd by Memory on the Rock of Fame;
The page of History shall his deeds repeat
With Britan's triumph and the Dutch defeat.

This jug is actually a double commemorative, marking two quite different actions, for the other side has a portrait of Nelson and a matching verse which ends:

For the best Piece of news we have heard a long while,
Is what gallant Nelson has sent from the Nile.

Since the Battle of the Nile was fought in August 1798, some ten months after Camperdown, it is interesting that the pottery manufacturers should still have regarded Duncan's victory as hot news, and even stranger that they had not by that time obtained an authentic likeness of Duncan, whose engraved portrait by Ridley had been published in the *European Magazine* in February 1798.

Bilston enamel patch boxes were once again produced to mark the victory over the Dutch. One of the most attractive is painted with ten ships against a bright blue sea, and is inscribed *Admiral Duncan forming the line against the Dutch Fleet.* Another, with a transfer-printed fouled anchor and laurel sprays, has *Duncan and Victory*, and a third has the slogan *Glorious 11th Octr English Valour Triumphant and Dutch Perfidy Defeated.* Occasionally an enamel box commemorates more than one hero of the period. One in the collection at Greenwich with a transfer-printed picture of Duncan's flagship, *Venerable,* is inscribed:

Howe and Jervis Victory did command
and Duncan's Glory doth unrivall'd stand.

Another is painted with figures of Fame and Plenty, and inscribed on Fame's scroll of honour are the names *Duncan, Jervis, Abercromby, Nelson, Howe.*

The Jervis mentioned above was Admiral Sir John Jervis (1735–1823), who in February 1797 defeated a Spanish fleet off Cape St Vincent, from which he took his title Earl of St Vincent. This was also the first of the four great battles linked with Horatio Nelson's name. Nelson (1758–1805) served under Jervis as a young commodore, and his capture of the Spanish *San Nicholas* and *San Josef* by boarding after his own ship, *Captain,* was disabled took the public imagination as *Nelson's patent bridge for boarding first rates.* On being created a Knight of the Bath following the battle, Nelson adopted as his crest the stern of the *San Josef*, a device which appears in various forms on his personal table silver and china services.

Admiral Jervis was himself celebrated in popular pottery, both individually and linked with other heroes of the moment. A Pratt ware jug was produced with a three-quarter-length figure on both sides wearing a cloak, holding a speaking-trumpet and identified as *Lord Jarvis* or *Lord Garvis* (plate 47). A rare porcelain version of the same jug is also known. Transfer-printed pottery was also produced with a portrait inscribed *Earl St Vincent KB Admiral of the Blue* (colour plate 49), and on the other side either Nelson or Marquis Cornwallis. Below the St Vincent portrait is a verse:

You have heard of a Howard, a Hawkins, a Drake,
Of a Raleigh Hawke Russel Howe Rodney and Blake.
But here is a man off St Vincents you'll find him
Who leaves those brave tars at a distance behind him.

The nearest source of the engraving is a print by W Ridley from the *Monthly Mirror*, published 2nd April 1797. This half-length engraving is derived in turn from a mezzotint engraving by J R Smith, also published in 1797, which is after Gilbert Stuart's full-length oil painting of the admiral, showing him standing on a rocky shore with his left hand extended to indicate the fleet lying at anchor. This use of an engraving of a current hero as source material for popular magazines and pieces of commemorative pottery is typical of the way illustrations reappear in a variety of guises at this period. Sometimes what starts out as a fine engraving of a good oil painting can end up, after

48 Profile portrait plaques of Admiral Duncan *c*1798 by Tassie (top) and Wedgwood (bottom)

numerous adaptations, as a crude and unrecognisable version of the original. In this instance the portrait which appears on the jug is still close to the Smith engraving, although some changes have already begun to creep into the details of the uniform and both the Ridley engraving and the print on the jug have different lacing on the coat, and a shoulder strap instead of an epaulette. A cruder version of the same print is also known on other earthenware mugs.

Rear Admiral Sir Horatio Nelson came into major prominence in 1798 with his resounding victory over the French at the Nile. Napoleon's (1769–1821) expedition to Egypt gave Nelson the opportunity to lead a squadron sent by Earl St Vincent to destroy the French fleet. The Battle of the Nile was fought on 1st August 1798, and news reached London on 2nd October. Nelson was created Baron Nelson of the Nile, and the victory was immediately taken up by the ceramic manufacturers. Both cheap pottery and expensive high quality porcelain were produced. At the cheap end of the scale are the relief-moulded Pratt ware jugs (plate 50), with Nelson on one side and on the other, Captain Berry, the captain of Nelson's flagship, *Vanguard*.

One particularly interesting example, which gives an idea just how cheaply these pieces were produced, shows that the mould was evidently reused seven years later to commemorate the Battle of Trafalgar, when the relief lettering of *Captain Berry* was overpainted with the name *Adml. Collingwood*. Another Pratt ware piece of this period is modelled as a smoking-pipe with a long coiled stem terminating in a half-length uniformed figure wearing a tall hat which forms the pipe bowl. The hat is inscribed in relief *Nelson forever*.

Transfer-printed creamware pieces were also made as souvenirs of the Battle of the Nile, both with portraits of Nelson and, more usually, with views of the action. One such mug is especially intriguing on two counts. It is a frog mug, one of those longstanding imbibers' jokes where a hollow pottery frog on the inside of the mug comes into view and gurgles alarmingly as the drinker quaffs his ale. On the outside is a view of a naval action and a caption *Lord Nelson engaging the Toulon Fleet of the Mouth of the Nile*. In fact the source of the engraving dates from forty years earlier. The design actually depicts HMS *Buckingham*, 66 guns, Captain Tyrrell RN defeating *Florissant*, *Aigrette* and *Atalante* on 3rd November 1758, as engraved by Robert Sayer after Swaine. Even more amusing is the fact that a few years later the pottery manufacturers speeded up their response to the news of Trafalgar in 1805 by producing the same transfer yet again, changing the caption and rushing through new souvenir mugs and jugs as mementoes of the latest battle (colour plate 51).

The Nile version of that particular engraving appears on a number of interesting pieces, includ-

50 Pratt ware Nelson jugs moulded in relief *c*1798.

ing a marriage mug with a handpainted inscription, *Frances and Grace Wilkinson Lincoln 1800*. Another creamware jug, presumably made at Sunderland, has the Nile transfer with some additional colouring on one side, and on the other *A West view of the Iron Bridge at Sunderland Begun Sept 24th 1793 and Opend 9th Augt 1796*. Strangely, another Sunderland lustreware jug with a view of John Rennie's bridge over the Thames at Southwark, which was not built until 1814–19, still has the same Nile engraving on the other side – this time attractively decorated in colour, with additional handpainted leaves and flowers – although it had been long outdated by Trafalgar.

A creamware jug with a transfer signed Barker and Brown depicts *A View of Nelson's Glorious Action on the Nile Augt 1 1798*. Only the sea is coloured green, and the other side has the verse:

Still o'er the Deep shall Britons Reign
Brave Nelson doth the Trident bear
Proud France's Boasting all is vain,
When British Heroes do Appear.

A plate and bowl transfer-printed in red-brown with a fairly crude Nelson portrait make an interesting pair. The bowl is entitled *Sir Horatio Nelson*, a reference to the Knighthood of the Bath which he received in March 1797 after the Battle of Cape St Vincent, but the plate has updated the caption to *Lord Nelson,* followed by a verse:

Here's a health to Brave Nelson
Old England's boast
'The Hero of the Nile'
Let this be our toast.

The victor of the Nile also appears on two transfer-printed creamware jugs. On one a figure of Lord Nelson stands on the deck of his ship, sword in hand, with the caption *Baron Nelson of the Nile and of Burnham Thorpe in the County of Norfolk*. This title records the honour newly granted to Nelson after the battle. Another jug, printed with an oval medallion portrait of Nelson supported by cherubs, has on the other side a coat of arms rather loosely based on Nelson's new arms, but correctly reproduces his new motto: *Palmam qui meruit ferat* (Let him bear the palm who deserves it). Beneath the portrait is a fleet plan of the Battle of the Nile, and under the lip, with a crocodile, is the inscription *Admiral Lord Nelson and the Glorious First of August 1798*.

A portrait of Nelson also decorates a Liverpool Herculaneum creamware dinner service made *c*1798. The centre of each piece is printed with an oval stipple engraving showing Nelson in uniform. The portrait is from an engraving by W Evans after a drawing by Edridge.

Of the more elegant porcelain pieces perhaps the finest are the rare Derby mugs and chocolate cups made to the order of Alexander Davison, Lord Nelson's friend and prize agent (colour plate 52). After the Battle of the Nile Davison paid for medals to be struck by Matthew Boulton of the Soho Works, Birmingham, for presentation to every officer and man who had taken part. Nelson and his captains received their medals in gold, lieutenants and warrant officers in silver, petty officers in gilt metal, and seamen and marines in copper. It is this medal which is painted in a full-colour version on the porcelain pieces which Davison commissioned from the Derby factory. Five of these Derby pieces are now known, two of which are in the collection of the National Maritime Museum.

One is a large mug with both sides of the medal depicted in colour, the obverse with a figure of Peace supporting a medallion portrait of Nelson, and the reverse showing the rival fleets in Aboukir Bay. Handpainted in gilt cursive script around the top of the mug is an inscription: *Done from a Medal presented by Alexander Davison Esqr to Lord Nelson, his Officers and Men, in commemoration of the Glorious First of August 1798*. A matching mug with the mark of Duesbury and Kean of Derby was sold in a London saleroom in 1990, and another similar example, sold in 1978, has the Nile inscription underneath rather than round the outside.[12]

The other two known pieces from this set are chocolate cups, covers and saucers decorated with gilded scrollwork. The cup at Greenwich has the reverse of the Nile medal showing the French and British fleets, and the inscriptions *Almighty God has blessed his Majesty's arms* and *Victory of the Nile August 1 1798*. Inside the rim is an additional inscription, *A tribute of regard from Alexr Davison Esqr St James's Square*. The pair to this cup, which depicts the obverse of the medal, is in the Royal Naval Museum at Portsmouth. In 1876 John Haslem described a pair of Nile mugs which not only had both sides of the medal but also the Alexander Davison inscription, now known only on the chocolate cups.[13] These were said to have been ordered by Davison as a gift to Lord Nelson

53 Porcelain crocus pot *c*1798 painted with a scene of the Battle of the Nile.

himself, after whose death they came back into the possession of Davison's son. We do not yet have any evidence how many of these presentation pieces were ordered, however, or who the original recipients were.

The Battle of the Nile is also the subject of a handpainted panel on the front of a porcelain crocus pot with five flower holders set in the cover (plate 53). The two side panels have trophies of arms and flags, and the scene of the action is inscribed *Adm. Nelson's gloryous victory over the French Fleet on the Nile August 1 1798.* Many Nelson busts were also produced for sale, including one published and sold by Robert Shout of Holborn, which shows him in rear admiral's full dress uniform, wearing the Nile medal. This bust was already in production in the Wedgwood factory when news of the battle arrived.

Once again the victory was taken up with enthusiasm by the Bilston enamel manufacturers, who produced drawer handles with portraits of Nelson and of his ship, *Vanguard,* as well as the usual colourful patch boxes (plate 54). One box depicts a pyramid, lion, winged Victory and Nelson medallion, with the inscription *Nothing can oppose virtue and courage. Victory of the Nile Augt 1 1798.* Another shows the destruction of the French flagship, *L'Orient,* which blew up during the battle with such a deafening explosion that firing from both sides ceased for some minutes. There is also an example of a different type of commemorative patch box, this time a narrow ivory box with the word *Nile* inlaid on the lid in gold piqué work.

The popularity of the Nile victory and the charisma of Nelson also had their effects in fashionable society. Judging by some of the surviving items, the battle was not forgotten by the ladies even at balls, where fans, jewellery and dress trimmings might be seen marking the latest victory. One wood and paper fan *sold by the principal Haberdashers in London* is printed both with details of the British and French lines of battle at the Nile, and with instructions for eighteen new country dances for 1799. Among the topical names of the new dances are *North Sea Fleet, Lord Duncan's Reel* and *Sprigs of Laurel for Lord Nelson.* Another wood and paper fan is printed with a half-length portrait of Nelson with a patriotic verse on either side.

Commemorative Nile jewellery is also known, particularly gold anchors engraved with the name

54 Bilston enamel drawer handles and patch boxes and an ivory and gold piqué patch box made to commemorate the Battle of the Nile.

55 Painted ivory lockets made to mark Nelson's victory at the Nile in 1798.

and date of the battle. One such anchor – made of a flat sheet of gold and mounted on a gold chain – has an inscription which runs over both sides: *Admiral Nelson and the British Tars relieves the World at the Mouth of the Nile 1st of August 1798*. It is not so surprising that such items were hoarded even after the event had passed into history, but it is interesting that even ephemeral novelties, such as dress trimmings or ribbons worn as favours on the dress or hat, have survived. One length of silk ribbon in the collection – probably made in Coventry – is printed in red, green and black on a white ground with a pattern of fouled anchors and the word *Nelson*. Another white silk ribbon – still rolled on its original wooden core, as sold – is printed in red, green, yellow and black with a Baron's coronet, Order of the Bath, fouled anchor, laurel sprays and the words *Baron Nelson of the Nile. Tria Iuncta in Uno*.

The most elaborate commemorative decorations of this type to have come down to us, however, are two lengths of a dress flounce said to have been worn by Emma Hamilton herself at the fête at Palermo. The gauzy material is worked in green silks, gold thread and sequins with a repeating swag design of oak leaves, acorns, fouled anchors and coronets, linking oval frames embroidered *Nelson* and *Bronte*.

Painted lockets were also among the many popular commemoratives produced to mark the victory of the Nile (plate 55). One such locket has a full-length picture of a sailor gesturing towards his ship, with the words *Nelson for Ever*. Another has the female figure of winged Fame blowing her trumpet while a naval battle rages out at sea, with the inscription *Nelson's Victory*. There was also a great variety of commemorative plaques showing scenes from the Battle of the Nile. Some of these are small paintings on glass and ivory set in circular wood or soapstone frames under domed glass. In some cases parts of the scene are painted on the reverse of two or three layers of glass to give an effect of depth.

In 1801 Nelson was sent to the Baltic as second-in-command of an expedition under Sir Hyde Parker (1739–1807) to counter the armed coalition of Russia, Sweden and Denmark by an attack on the Danish fleet. Having overcome the Danish defences he negotiated an armistice, and subsequently became commander-in-chief when Parker was recalled. Nelson was created a viscount, but the battle fought off Copenhagen on 2nd April 1801 was far less popular than the Nile with the British people, and produced little in the way of souvenirs. Pieces which did appear tended to have been individually commissioned for a particular purpose, rather than mass produced for general sale. One piece which has survived in the Greenwich Hospital Collection is a silver-mounted papier mâché wine coaster in the shape of a boat (plate 56), representing one of the ship's boats of HMS *Elephant*, Nelson's flagship at Copenhagen. A silver strake along each side is inscribed with the names of the British ships, and a silver plaque on

56 Wine coaster in the form of HMS *Elephant*'s jolly boat, commemorating the Battle of Copenhagen, 1801.

the stern is inscribed *Elephant's jolly boat, A bumper to Ld Nelson who bravely went on shore to save Copenhagen 2nd April 1801.*

In 1968 a similar decanter stand appeared in a London saleroom, this time complete with a four-wheeled waggon.[14] This boat also had the ships' names inscribed on the sides, and a plaque on the stern identifying it as *The Edgar's Jolly Boat, Captn George Murray*. Another plaque inside the stern makes it clear that the boat was actually owned by Captain, later Admiral Sir George Murray, which suggests that a small number of the boats may have been made for presentation after the battle. This type of decanter stand was already popular in earlier years. In 1799 John Emes of London is known to have made a silver clinker-built boat engraved *The Jolly Boat* on the stern, and Lloyd's has another by Emes which was presented by Nelson to Thomas Atkinson in 1801.

The most elaborate commemorative pieces following the Battle of Copenhagen were produced by the Royal Danish Porcelain Manufactory, Copenhagen, as a tribute to the Danish leaders of the defence against Nelson's attack. A limited edition of porcelain punch bowls was commissioned by Governor Roepstorff for presentation to Danish officers in the battle. Twenty-one of the bowls were painted in full colour with a continuous scene of the battle, after a watercolour by C A Lorentzen, and another twenty-three were painted in monochrome for the less high-ranking officers. One variation is complete with a stand and lid. All but eight of the forty-four pieces can be accounted for today. Most remain in Denmark, some in public collections and some in private possession, but there are at least four in the United Kingdom, including the National Maritime Museum's full-colour version (colour plate 57).

It is interesting that after the battle Nelson took the opportunity to buy porcelain at the Copenhagen factory to send to Lady Hamilton. In a letter dated 15th April 1801, a fortnight after the battle, he wrote to her from his ship HMS *St George*:

> *My Dearest Friend, I can get nothing here worth your acceptance, but as I know you have a valuable collection of china, I send you some of the Copenhagen manufacture. It will bring to your recollection that here your attached friend Nelson fought and conquered. Captain Bligh has promised to take charge of it, and I hope it will reach you safe.*[15]

The brief peace of 1802 inspired the souvenir manufacturers to produce only a few commemorative pieces. There was an earthenware mug from the Bristol Pottery with transfer-printed decoration and an inscription *Peace signed at Amiens between England France Spain and Holland March 27 1802*. Patch boxes appeared with

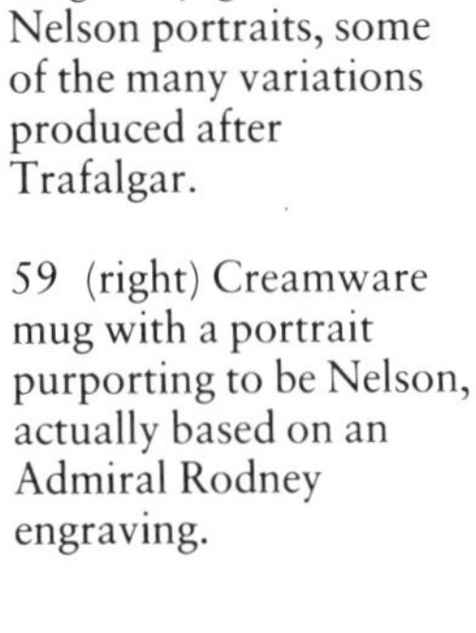

58 (left) Earthenware mug and jug with Nelson portraits, some of the many variations produced after Trafalgar.

59 (right) Creamware mug with a portrait purporting to be Nelson, actually based on an Admiral Rodney engraving.

inscriptions like *In Peace rejoice And War no more* and *Peace Rewarding Britannia* instead of the more usual warlike sentiments.

From 1803, with the resumption of the war, the danger of a French invasion became increasingly serious as Napoleon massed his troops across the Channel and prepared his Boulogne flotilla to attack the south coast of England. An unusual French watch has an enamel dial painted with a fleet of French sailing vessels off the coast, filled with troops preparing to land, below an inscription *Descente en Angleterre*. A semicircular aperture in the dial reveals a sinking ship.

In 1804 Spain declared war on Britain, and by 1805 the combined fleets of France and Spain were at Cadiz, but the British victory at the Battle of Trafalgar on 21st October 1805 effectively ended the threat of a French invasion. As Nelson's final victory, the battle produced more variations of commemorative ceramics, glass, ornaments, trinkets and ephemera than all his other naval achievements put together. Combining as it did a resounding victory with the tragic death of the greatest naval hero of the day in his hour of glory, the battle offered a heaven-sent opportunity to the manufacturers to exploit the popular mood. The report of the battle appeared in the London newspapers on 6th November, and Nelson's funeral procession and interment in St Paul's Cathedral took place on 9th January 1806. The souvenir sellers were prepared, already vying with each other in a joint celebration of victory and mourning for the lost leader. Some of the pieces which relate directly to the funeral will be discussed in chapter 6, but many of the commemoratives stressed the victory in battle.

Countless variations of cheap pottery mugs and jugs were produced with every possible attempt to depict the hero (plates 58 and 59). Some potters used good source engravings to achieve an acceptable likeness, while others were content to recopy a portrait with little regard to how far it had strayed from the original. Sometimes a transfer design intended to be used on a particular size and shape of pot was adapted to a new use to save time. This often happened with the popular blue and brown-printed jugs decorated with a portrait of Nelson, trophies of arms, flags, anchors, and ships. The verses and inscriptions referring to Copenhagen, the Nile and Trafalgar were sometimes spoiled when the transfers were cut through at random and lost their meaning, but it does not seem to have affected sales.

60 Staffordshire earthenware mug and jug produced after Trafalgar, transfer-printed with portraits of Collingwood on one side and Nelson on the other.

61 Transfer-printed Nelson mugs and jugs commemorating Trafalgar.

Some of the transfer-printed mugs have portraits of both Nelson and Vice Admiral Cuthbert Collingwood (1750–1810) his second-in-command at Trafalgar, but the two are almost indistinguishable, and all the interest was clearly with Nelson. These large blue-printed mugs (colour plate 60) are further decorated with an anchor and laurel border, and a seashell frieze inside, and between the two portraits is a laurel wreath containing the rose, thistle and shamrock with a Union Flag, gun and anchor. More primitive narrow-shouldered portraits of Nelson and Collingwood appear on blue- and brown-printed jugs with a view of HMS *Victory*, inscribed *Off Trafalgar Octr 21 1805*. The transfer has been cut so that the names of the admirals are partly obscured.

Many of the transfer-printed jugs combine a portrait of Nelson with a plan of the battle and lists of the British ships which fought at Trafalgar (plate 61). Various errors appear in some versions of the jugs, as a testimony both to the speedy production of the pieces and the difficulty of obtaining accurate information. One particular variation gives the size of the British fleet as 33 instead of 27, the Franco-Spanish fleet as 43 instead of 33, and Nelson's age as 48 rather than the correct 47. Later souvenirs, produced in rather less haste, corrected the errors.

At the other end of the market were the fine porcelain pieces. Chamberlains of Worcester produced a large pair of hexagonal vases (colour plate 62) which were said to have been presented to William, 1st Earl Nelson after Trafalgar. One is painted with the Battle of the Nile and the other with Trafalgar, after the aquatint by T Hellyer published in 1807. The National Maritime Museum also has a single Spode bone china cup and saucer, probably produced in 1806 as part of an elegant teaset. The cup is bat-printed with a portrait of Nelson after the famous painting by Lemuel Abbott, and the saucer is printed overall with a Trafalgar battle plan showing the opening positions of the battle.

Drinking glasses were also popular, especially the large heavy rummers which were frequently extensively decorated on the bowl. The majority were produced to mark the funeral, but one at Greenwich has an engraved view of the battle and the name *M Corser 1806*, as well as a memorial inscription to Nelson. Silver vinaigrettes were also made in quantity by the Birmingham workshops. These were tiny hinged cases which originally held a sponge soaked in aromatic vinegar behind a pierced grille, and were used to ward off bad smells or anticipate a swooning fit. The outer cases were frequently decorated with a well-engraved oval portrait of Nelson, while the inner pierced section covering the sponge had a view of Nelson's flagship, *Victory*.

Boxes in every size and shape evidently had a ready sale. The Bilston enamel patch box makers produced dozens of new designs to mark the latest victory, and toothpick cases, as well as snuff, tobacco and trinket boxes flooded the market. Circular brass boxes with a relief portrait of Nelson on the lid and a list of his battle honours on the base have survived in some quantity. They are based on a medal design, and similar boxes were also produced bearing likenesses of Sir Sidney Smith, George III, and the politicians Pitt and Fox. Even closer to the form of medals were the flat circular brass boxes – again with a Nelson portrait on the lid – which open to reveal a set of circular coloured engravings of recent *Naval Exploits*, published by Edward Orme (colour plate 63). A very similar souvenir was later made to commemorate Wellington (1769–1852) and the Battle of Waterloo (1815).

Textile souvenirs of the battle were also for sale. At Greenwich there are two attractive printed linen squares with different designs. Both quote the famous Trafalgar signal which Nelson ordered to be hoisted immediately before the battle, but both get the wording wrong. The squares are printed: *England Expects Every Man To Do His Duty*, the version probably encountered more often than the correct signal – *England Expects That Every Man Will Do His Duty* – which was hoisted in the flags of Popham's Telegraphic Signal Code. One of the linen squares is printed in red with a view of the line of battle below a Nelson portrait, and the other is brown-printed with a confused battle scene entitled *Victory or Westminster Abbey* and *The Memorable Naval Engagement*.

Tablecloths and table napkins were also made to commemorate the battle, with designs woven into the white damask. At Greenwich there are some large linen tablecloths over 4 yards long depicting a central battle plan of Trafalgar with named ships within a flowered cartouche. At each corner, within a border of oak leaves and acorns, is a phoenix, a fouled anchor, guns and flags, and at the sides are crossed tridents with entwined dolphins.

The matching linen napkins have a fouled anchor surmounted by a naval crown within a border of oak leaves, and the words *Nelson, Trafalgar 21st Oct 1805 Palmam qui meruit ferat*. Other napkins are woven with a crown, anchor and garter star in the centre, an overall pattern of flaming cannonballs, and Nelson's Orders of the Bath and the Crescent at the corners. These napkins are marked with the manufacturer's name, I W W Coulson, a firm in Lisburn, Ireland, which was established in 1750 and is still in existence.

Some interesting light has recently been shed on this type of Irish commemorative table linen by some earlier correspondence relating to damask items woven to commemorate the Battle of Copenhagen of 2nd April 1801. Rear Admiral Thomas Graves (1746–1814) was second-in-command to Nelson at Copenhagen, and ten years after the battle his daughter Mary Graves wrote to her Aunt Catherine – on 4th June 1811 – to explain her mother's idea of ordering commemorative cloths. One cloth – complete with matching napkins and the original bill from the manufacturer, Coulson of Lisburn – is still in the possession of the family. The letter is sufficiently interesting to justify quoting at some length:

Her Ladyship has a great wish to have the Battle of Copenhagen wove in a Table Cloth of the manufacture of my father's native Country [Ireland] *and he assured her that you would readily assist in the accomplishment of her wishes. Would you therefore have the goodness to inquire in your Neighbourhood, what kind of design would be required for the purpose. We could send you a print of the Battle of Copenhagen or an enlarged drawing of it, as also a drawing of the Crest to put round the border.*

Lady Graves also requests you to enquire what will be the expence of one Table Cloth three yards and a half long and a proper width which the makers will know, representing the battle of Copenhagen in the center and the family Crest round the border, and a dozen Napkins to suit made of the modern size which is not very large, and two Table cloths three yards long of the same pattern exactly with a dozen similar napkins to each Table Cloth.[16]

The bill from the Coulson's Damask Manufactory was dated December 1816, and itemised tablecloths to dine eighteen with matching napkins at £39 4s and smaller tablecloths at £33 8s. The total bill came to £160 7s 6d. The tablecloth has a central scene of the battle, with named ships and the words *Copenhagen April 2 1801*, together with the Graves crest and the name *Defiance*, his ship at Copenhagen. The border of naval trophies is the same as the Trafalgar tablecloths.

Even furniture was produced to commemorate Trafalgar. A mahogany long-case clock by William Northern of Hull has a dial by R Hipkiss of Birmingham, which is painted with a scene of Fame with an olive branch and Cupid holding a ribbon inscribed *Nile, Copenhagen and Trafalgar*. The arch is painted with a boating scene on a lake near a country house.

On loan to the National Maritime Museum is a round tortoiseshell box with a crystal intaglio of Nelson mounted in the lid. The gold-mounted clear crystal is cut with a profile portrait of Nelson with his hair worn loose, similar to the Simon de Koster portrait. The box was owned by Emma Hamilton, and given by her to Abraham Goldsmid, the financier. Another unique piece is a silver-rimmed horn beaker (colour plate 64) which is engraved with the ships which fought in the battle, with HMS *Victory* and the Spanish *Santissima Trinidada* named.

After Trafalgar there was never again such an outpouring of popular souvenirs to mark a naval victory, although from time to time some action took the public imagination. Occasionally this event was a single-ship action rather than a major battle, and indeed there had been some earlier instances of minor engagements being commemorated by the potters. Two Coalport porcelain plates from a set painted by Thomas Baxter in 1801 show just such scenes. One in the collection at Greenwich, signed and dated *T Baxter London Nov 1801*, is finely painted in the centre, and inscribed *The Arethusa taking La Pomone St George's Day 1794*. The gilt ground of the plate is further decorated with a black wave design, and a rim painted with mermen, sea beasts, dolphins, anchors and other nautical motifs. A matching plate in the collection of the Nelson-Atkins Museum of Art in Kansas City, also signed by Baxter, depicts the *Capture of La Virginie by Sr E Pelew in the Indefatigable the Concord coming up*. The plates were presumably commissioned specially for the 2nd Earl Spencer, First Lord of the Admiralty from 1794 to 1801, whose crest appears on the decorative border.

The nineteenth century appears to have produced far fewer naval commemoratives. A china cup and saucer – probably made in Herculaneum, Liverpool, for the American market *c*1815 – has bat-printed views commemorating an American naval victory. The pieces are decorated with pink lustre borders and the United States stars and eagle. Both the cup and saucer depict a ship wearing an American pennant at the mainmast, and show American colours flying above the British white ensign at the foremast. A teapot from the same set is also known. The set may commemorate either Captain James Lawrence's (1781–1813) victory in the *Hornet* over the British *Peacock* on 24th February 1813 or the American victory at Lake Champlain on 11th September 1814. On the other side of the cup is another interesting print, of an American paddle steamer with ladies and gentlemen on board.

Even the Crimean War (1854–6) failed to excite popular interest to the extent of previous wars. Pink lustre jugs were produced in Sunderland with a combination of hand-coloured transfer engravings depicting the bridge over the Wear, a sailor's farewell scene and a cartouche commemorating the Allies inscribed *May they Ever be United. Crimea. Vive l'Emperor. God save the Queen.* The sentiment *May they ever be United* also appears on a glass rummer engraved with a British and French seaman carrying flags and shaking hands on the deck of a warship. The same design is known on Sunderland lustre wall plaques. Staffordshire earthenware portrait figures were also very popular at this period, and in addition to the well-known sailor figures waving flags and supporting the wounded, some of the admirals of the period were represented as single standing figures. Among these perhaps the most commonly encountered is Sir Charles Napier (1786–1860), but figures of Sir James Deans Dundas (1785–1862) and Sir Edmund Lyons (1790–1858) also appear (colour plate 65), although in some cases the differently-titled figures are clearly taken from the same mould.

In the twentieth century, although individual naval commanders aroused considerable public interest, and their images were well-recognised and reproduced in newspapers and magazines, it was relatively rare to find them commemorated in popular souvenirs. There was evidently still a good market for decorative patriotic mugs and other ceramics, as the mass of Royal commemoratives indicates. From Victorian times to the present day pieces have been produced in a wide variety of quality to mark coronations, Royal marriages, jubilees and deaths, but there seems to have been no comparable level of production to mark naval events of this period. British gratitude to the war leaders came mainly in the form of valuable personal presentations of specially-commissioned items rather than cheap mass-produced souvenirs.

Admiral David Beatty (1871–1936) – recipient of a multitude of personal honours, Freedoms and expensive gifts to mark his services in World War I – appears on just one jug in the Museum's collection, compared with the scores of variations of Nelson pieces. The Beatty jug (plate 66) was produced after the war by Royal Doulton in moulded earthenware, in the factory's typical blue, green and brown colours. A medallion portrait of the admiral wearing a uniform cap appears on one side with the inscription: *Admiral Beatty. Peace with Victory. 1914 1919.*

66 Royal Doulton jug *c*1919 with a portrait of Admiral Beatty moulded in relief.

A series of eleven jugs modelled as the Allied war leaders in the form of seated Toby jugs was produced during World War I by Arthur J Wilkinson Ltd, Royal Staffordshire Pottery, Burslem. They were designed by Sir Francis Carruthers Gould, the political cartoonist and journalist, and sold in strictly limited editions. The National Maritime Museum has an example of the King George V jug, issued in 1919 in an edition of 1,000. He is shown seated on the throne, holding a globe with the British Empire coloured in red. Jugs moulded as Admirals Jellicoe and Beatty were also produced, in 1915 and 1917 respectively, in editions of 350. The Jellicoe figure holds a jug inscribed *Hell fire Jack,* and originally cost 2 guineas, while Beatty supports between his knees a shell labelled *Dreadnought,* and was paired with a Field Marshal Haig jug for 5 guineas. The other jugs in the series portrayed Sir John French, General Botha, Marshal Joffre, Lloyd George,

Lord Kitchener, President Wilson and Marshal Foch. The *Connoisseur* wrote in November 1917:

> *These jugs are to be welcomed as a revival of a thoroughly English type of pottery, brought up to a high standard of accomplishment by the Wood family and other celebrated makers, whose work today is deservedly highly prized. The modern jugs rival the old in the high quality of their workmanship and the originality and quaintness of their design, and are among the most artistic works of their kind which the war has so far called forth.*

A more exclusively-produced piece is the fine Minton china bowl (colour plate 67) painted by J E Dean to commemorate the surrender of the German High Seas Fleet to Vice Admiral David Beatty in the Firth of Forth in November 1918. The bowl is painted on the outside in full colour with a view of the fleet and an airship, and within a rope-bordered cartouche are the words of Beatty's signal: *The German Flag is to be hauled down at sunset to-day and is not to be hoisted again without permission. 21st November 1918.*

Other World War I admirals have appeared in the form of relief plaques or busts. Wedgwood produced a relief portrait plaque of Beatty, not represented at Greenwich, although the collection does include relief plaques of Admiral Sir John Jellicoe (1859–1935). There is one plaque of Jellicoe in iron, and another portrait in brass produced by the Arthur Cox Illustrating Company of Birmingham. The plaque, signed by Rex Osborne, is inscribed *Admiral Sir John Jellicoe Commander of the Home Fleets, Permanent souvenir of the Great European War 1914–Qui vivra verra.*

The ships were also sometimes commemorated. A silver model of HMS *Iron Duke* displayed at Greenwich was made by the Goldsmiths' and Silversmiths' Company Ltd. The model was presented to Admiral Sir John Jellicoe after the Battle of Jutland by his second-in-command at the battle, Admiral Sir Cecil Burney.

Another presentation piece at Greenwich is a silver cigarette case with a finely-enamelled lid painted in colour with a view of HMS *Warrior* at sea. The case is by George Unite of Birmingham and is hallmarked 1915–16. It was presented to Lieutenant Commander R W Bromley RN of HMS *Warrior* by his uncle, Captain Gerald Bromley RN, in June 1916. The inscription on the base is: *In remembrance of HMS Warrior, Cruiser 13,550 Tons Sunk in the North Sea off Jutland, against the German High Sea Fleet. May 31st 1916 and June 1st 1916. With a loss of 65 killed and 27 wounded.*

At Greenwich there are also one or two rather more personal wartime souvenirs, either made by the ladies at home or purchased by sailors serving overseas. One such piece is a velvet tablecloth, embroidered in white silk (presumably in Malta) with eight destroyers round the sides, and in the centre HMS *Stuart*, Leader of the 6th Flotilla, 1st and 2nd Division Mediterranean Fleet, Malta. The other ships are named as HMS *Tumult, Sportive, Tomahawk, Spear, Sparrowhawk, Seraph, Speedy* and *Sikh*. The corners are embroidered with flowers in coloured silks.

Another foreign souvenir, probably brought back from the East, is a professionally-embroidered silk square of a type often found, with a raised lifebuoy motif in the centre framing a family photograph. Around the lifebuoy are the flags of the Allied countries, and the words *Victory for the Allies. In memory of the War 1914–1918.* Another piece of handiwork, this time completed by a lady to mark the end of World War I, is a tablecloth with a crocheted border worked with motifs of warships, crossed French and British flags, fouled anchors and the words *Welcome Home.*

Although commemorative pieces were not produced in such quantity in the twentieth century as they had been in earlier periods, the war leaders continued to provide subject matter for major artists of the period. The National Maritime Museum has a bronze-painted plaster version of Jacob Epstein's powerful bust of Admiral of the Fleet Lord Fisher of Kilverstone (1841–1920). Epstein wrote about the work in an article in the *Weekly Dispatch* of 24th December 1916, and described his very rapid progress on the bust during the week of 5th June 1916. He was particularly anxious to portray Fisher, whom he described as: *one of the greatest men of this age, one of the greatest figures of this war, and the head and features are a wonderful expression of this tremendous personality.* His aim had been to: *put life into the inanimate metal and breathe into the graven image the dynastic personality that for so long was the soul of the British Navy.*[17]

World War II is represented by a silver-gilt cup and cover commemorating the evacuation of Dunkirk in 1940. The beaker-shaped cup was designed by Cyril Shiner and made by Wakely and

Wheeler of London. One side is engraved with the arms of the Worshipful Company of Goldsmiths, and on the other is an inscription which begins: *This cup commemorates the action of the Royal Navy and the Merchant Navy in the withdrawal of the British Expeditionary Force from Dunkirk from 28th May to 4th June 1940.* The cup was designed for the Goldsmiths' Company for sale in aid of the Red Cross, on condition that it should be presented to the Admiralty for ultimate retention in the National Maritime Museum. The idea of selling works of art to aid the Red Cross was started by Sir Eric Maclagan, then Director of the Victoria & Albert Museum. A competition was held and the winning design for the King's Gold Vase intended for Royal Ascot was selected. The Ascot Races were not held because of the war, and the cup – which was finished in the same month as the Dunkirk evacuation – was auctioned at Christie's in London. It was purchased at the sale in July 1940 by Lord Queenborough, a patriot who started the Society of St George, who subsequently gave it to the Admiralty.

A silver copy of the cup, engraved with the full story, was sent to America in December 1940 and sold in aid of the American Red Cross. It is now in the museum at Cleveland, Ohio. For many years the original Dunkirk Cup remained with the Goldsmiths' Company, being exhibited in a number of international exhibitions, and in 1980 it finally came to the National Maritime Museum, where it is displayed today.

NOTES

1 R W Binns: *A Century of Potting in the City of Worcester* (1865) p149

2 Christie's (1st October 1974) Lot 206

3 See Geoffrey A Godden: *Chamberlain-Worcester Porcelain 1788–1852* (1979). He dates a tureen from this service as c1815–20.

4 See 'Lord Iveagh's Solebay Tapestries' (*Country Life* 16th March 1929) p351

5 Montague J Guest (ed.): *Lady Charlotte Schreiber's Journals* Vol II (1911) p443

6 Christie's (11th February 1991) Lot 10

7 Montague Guest: op. cit. p452

8 Illustrated in Bevis Hillier: *Pottery & Porcelain 1700–1914* (1968) plate VIII

9 Robin Reilly and George Savage: *Wedgwood the Portrait Medallions* (1973); Etruria Manuscript Collection: E-18880-26 for 1st March 1779 and Oven Book for 13th March 1779

10 Illustrated in Frank Falkner: *The Wood Family of Burslem* (1912) plate XVI no. 71

11 Ivor Waters: *Chepstow Clock and Watch Makers* (1980)

12 Christie's (20th June 1990) Lot 190; Christie's (5th June 1978) Lot 27

13 John Haslem: *The Old Derby China Factory* (1876) pp194–5.

14 Sotheby's (1st February 1968) Lot 63

15 Thomas Pettigrew: *Memoirs of the Life of Vice-Admiral Lord Viscount Nelson* Vol II (1849) p33

16 I am grateful to the family for their permission to quote from this correspondence and for making the tablecloth and original bill available for examination.

17 Evelyn Silber and Terry Freeman: *Jacob Epstein: Sculpture and Drawings* (catalogue of exhibition at Leeds City Art Gallery and Whitechapel Art Gallery, London, 1987)

CHAPTER 3 Tokens of Esteem

Prestigious and valuable pieces commissioned from leading goldsmiths and other master craftsmen have long been regarded as fitting presentations to reward the heroes of battle and mark outstanding acts of courage and skill. Sea and land battles from the seventeenth century to the present day have been followed by the granting of honours and titles to naval and military leaders, and these Royal and State rewards for service were usually accompanied by a shower of gifts and privileges conferred by civic authorities and other interested parties.

The Freedom of major cities was a particularly distinguished reward, reserved for the most worthy victors, and was usually accompanied by a valuable gift in the form of a gold box or jewelled presentation sword. Such pieces were often unique designs specially commissioned from the most skilful workers in precious metals, and typically incorporated armorial and other devices personal to the recipient, or a reference to the event or deed performed.

In time of war, committees were often set up to administer special funds accumulated for the specific purpose of rewarding such deeds of valour. There were always groups of merchants, insurance underwriters, shipowners and dealers who were concerned to protect their vital interests in seaborne trade and who would reward exploits which went beyond the normal limits of duty. On a more personal level, too, individuals with either a vested interest, patriotic fervour, or simply admiration for the deed performed, frequently put up the money to provide a gift of intrinsic value. The individuals might be friends or relations of those serving in a particular action, members of ships' companies honouring their commanders, or foreign rulers grateful for support to their nation or people.

The National Maritime Museum is fortunate to have in its collections some fine examples of such presentation plate, including four eighteenth century City of London gold Freedom boxes. The earliest of these is a gold box (plate 68) presented to Admiral Edward Vernon upon his admission to the Freedom of the City of London in 1740: *as a testimony of the greatest sense this city hath of his eminent services to the Nation by taking Portobello and demolishing the fortifications thereof.* The box was made by Jasper Cunst, one of the finest London gold box-makers of the eighteenth century, although his main production is likely to have been gold watchcases. The lid of the box is finely engraved with the arms of the City of London within a scrollwork border, with figures of Hercules and Victory on each side. An illuminated Freedom scroll was included in the presentation.

Two of the Freedom boxes are by the same celebrated London goldsmith, James Morisset. Both are executed in gold and enamel, one being for Admiral Sir John Jervis and the other for

68 Gold City of London Freedom Box presented to Admiral Edward Vernon. By Jasper Cunst, 1740.

Captain Edward Berry (1768–1831). The Jervis box (colour plate 69), of 100 guineas' value, was made in 1794 and is of rectangular form, chased overall with trophies of arms, laurel wreaths, oak borders and cornucopiae. On the lid a large oval enamel panel depicts the Jervis Arms in full colour, and around the sides smaller enamel plaques show the City of London coat of arms and monogram *JJ* surmounted by a naval crown. An inscription inside the lid refers to the reason for the presentation:

> *that the Freedom of this City be presented to Sir John Jervis KB in testimony of the high esteem of the Citizens of London for his gallant conduct and essential service, whereby glorious and important advantages have been obtained by his Majesty's Naval forces under his command in the West Indies.*

A few years later James Morisset was responsible for the gold and enamelled hilt of a 200-guinea City of London presentation sword (colour plate 70) made by Robert Makepeace to mark John Jervis's part in the Battle of Cape St Vincent on 14th February 1797, the battle from which he took the name of his earldom. This small-sword, set with diamonds, was the first sword presented by the City of London. The box and the sword passed down in the Jervis family until they were acquired by the National Maritime Museum in 1977, having already been on loan to the collection for a number of years. Writing of the box and sword, Claude Blair has pointed out that the box represents one of only seventeen fully-hallmarked items by Morisset out of twenty-four surviving pieces by him.[1]

A very similar Morisset box, now in a private collection, was presented to Admiral Earl Howe after the Glorious 1st of June 1794, and bears his arms and monogram on the lid in place of those of John Jervis. Another gold box (now owned privately) was presented to Earl Howe with the Freedom of the Worshipful Company of Skinners.[2] The box, by Sebastian Guerint of London, has a lid finely chased with a quarter view of his flagship, and the words *Queen Charlotte Glorious 1 June 1794*. The sides are engraved with the coats of arms of Earl Howe and the Skinners' Company, between trophies of naval arms.

The other Morisset gold and enamel Freedom box now at Greenwich was presented to Captain Edward Berry in gratitude for his gallant command of HMS *Vanguard* at the Battle of the Nile on 1st August 1798 (colour plate 71). The box is oval with a chased oak leaf border surmounted by a naval crown, which encloses a large coloured enamel plaque finely painted with a view of the battle at the moment when the French flagship, *L'Orient*, exploded. The base of the box is finely engraved with a broadside view of the British flagship *Vanguard*, under sail, and around the sides are four enamel panels. Two of these plaques are painted with military trophies surrounding the arms of the City of London and of Captain Berry, another has the monogram *EB*, and the fourth a pyramid, crocodile and lion symbolising the Battle of the Nile.

The box, which bears the London hallmark for 1798–9, was originally *of One Hundred Guineas value*, and still contains the original City of London Freedom document. A similar box by Morisset, presented to Sir Robert Calder (1745–1818), First Captain of the Fleet at the Battle of Cape St Vincent, is now in the collection of the Royal Naval Museum, Portsmouth. Another for the same battle, presented to Vice Admiral William Waldegrave (1753–1825), was sold in London in 1991.[3]

The collection at Greenwich also includes a gold box – made by Samuel Godbehere and Edward Wigan of London in 1795 – which was presented to Admiral Alexander Hood, Lord Bridport (1726–1814) with the Freedom of the City of London after his victory over a French fleet off the île de Groix on 23rd June 1795. The rectangular box with canted corners is decorated on the lid with a relief portrait of the 100-gun *Royal George*, flagship of the Channel Fleet, and an inscription: *Royal George. Glorious 23 of June 1795*. The sides of the box are engraved with his coat of arms as Baron Bridport on the front, that of the City of London on the back, a *B* below a baron's coronet at each end, and the Hood crest (a Cornish chough) on the corners.

Nelson's Morisset City of London Freedom box of 1797 was stolen from the Painted Hall of Greenwich Hospital in December 1900, and only his Freedom of Thetford remains at Greenwich. He received the Thetford Freedom on 30th October 1798, in a small silver-mounted oak box by Thomas Phipps and Edward Robinson of London, hallmarked 1798. On the lid in silver is a trophy of guns, flags, anchors and other naval emblems, and inside the box the silver lid is inscribed: *The Gift of the Corporation of Thetford in Norfolk to their gallant Countryman Rear Admiral Sir Horatio Nelson KB (now Lord Nelson of the Nile) for his brilliant services to his Country on the Glorious 1st of August 1798.*

Other cities similarly rewarded victory in battle by conferring the honour of a Freedom upon an individual. After the Battle of the Saints of 12th April 1782 the City of Cork granted a gold box with the Freedom of the city to Admiral Sir George Brydges Rodney. The oval box, by William Reynolds, was engraved on the lid with the City of Cork Arms: a ship sailing between two towers surmounted by a naval crown. Another gold box in the Museum, by John Innocent of London, was made two years later to mark the same battle, and was presented to Sir Edmund Affleck with the Freedom of the Borough of Colchester. Affleck commanded the *Bedford*, 74 guns, in the battle, and the oval lid of the box is engraved with a view of the ship under sail and an inscription: *Bedford 12 Apr. 1782. Arma Virumque Cano.* There is a presentation inscription inside the lid, and the base of the box is engraved with the arms of Colchester.

After the victory of the Saints, Rodney also received an engraved silver goblet from the people of Martinique, made by John Schofield of London in 1783 (plate 72). The goblet is engraved with a scene of the French Admiral de Grasse handing the French colours to Britannia, with his flagship, the *Ville de Paris,* in the background and Neptune standing with his trident. The cup is engraved with the date of the action, 12th April 1782, and the crest of Captain, later Vice Admiral, John Symonds, captain of Rodney's flagship, *Formidable*, at the Saints.

In 1798 the County of Forfar presented to Admiral Adam Duncan a silver-gilt soup tureen to mark his victory at the Battle of Camperdown in the previous year, *and in testimony of their satisfaction that so great a service was achieved by a native of their county.* The magnificent tureen, cover and stand with matching ladle were made by John Schofield of London, and are decorated with maritime motifs. The tureen rests on a stand composed of four dolphins with entwined tails, the handles are mermen with twisted tails, and the cover is surmounted by a finial in the form of Neptune holding a trident and seated on a dolphin. On each side of the body is a trophy of arms, enclosing Duncan's coat of arms on one side and the presentation inscription on the other. A tureen

72 Silver goblet presented to Admiral Rodney by the people of Martinique after the Battle of the Saints, 1782. By John Schofield, 1783.

of similar design – also by John Schofield – which is now in the Lloyd's Collection, was posthumously awarded to Captain John Harvey of HMS *Brunswick*, 74 guns, after the Battle of the Glorious 1st of June 1794.

The Magistrates and Town Council of Dundee presented Duncan with a silver tea urn after the Battle of Camperdown. Coats of arms of both Dundee and Duncan are engraved on the urn, which was made by Henry Chawner of London in 1795. Since the urn must have been a stock piece purchased and engraved for the occasion, rather than being specially commissioned like the previous piece, the design and decoration includes no specific nautical references. A silver tray with a waved and pierced gallery was part of the same presentation by Dundee. It bears the same inscription and the two coats of arms, and appears to have been used as a stand for the tea urn, although it was made by a different silversmith John Emes of London, and has the date letter for 1797.

The tradition of conferring the Freedom of a city on an individual in the form of a scroll contained in a precious box continued into the nineteenth and twentieth centuries, although the containers have tended to become casket-shaped rather than of snuff box form. The City of London Freedom box presented to Admiral Sir Robert Stopford in 1841 for his part in the Syrian campaign is unusual in being designed as a triangular fortress flying a star and crescent flag. It represents the Egyptian occupied fortress of Acre, which was attacked by a squadron of British, Austrian and Turkish ships under Stopford's command on 3rd November 1840. The vellum Freedom document is contained within the oak and silver-gilt box, and the inside of the lid has a presentation inscription.

The honour of the Freedom of a city was not reserved only as a reward for warlike activities. In 1875 Sir George Biddell Airy, Astronomer Royal, was presented with a gold and enamel casket containing the Freedom of the City of London: *As a recognition of his indefatigable labours in Astronomy and of his eminent services in the advancement of practical science, whereby he has so materially benefited the cause of commerce and civilization.* The casket, which is on loan to the National Maritime Museum, was made by Ernesto Rinzi of London. The body of the box is covered with enamel panels representing the universe, with a presentation inscription at the back, globes at each end, telescopes at the angles, and the arms of the City of London form a finial to the lid.

After World War I Admiral of the Fleet Sir David Beatty was showered with honours and awards, including a number of civic Freedoms. The caskets containing the scrolls were still individually commissioned and designed with symbolic and heraldic references to the recipient and the conferring authority, but they lack the elegance of eighteenth century examples. Among Beatty's caskets, however, is a good twentieth century example by the well-known London maker, Omar Ramsden, made to contain the Freedom of Oxford (plate 73). The casket is of ebony mounted with silver bearing the hallmark for 1919, and stands

73 Presentations marking Admiral Sir David Beatty's achievements in World War I: City of Oxford Freedom box by Omar Ramsden, 1919, City of London presentation sword, and silver lion ornament from the ship's company of HMS *Lion*.

on silver claw feet with winged lion masks at the corners. On the lid is Beatty's coat of arms in silver, incorporating the heraldic punning bees and beehive. On the front in silver are the arms of the City of Oxford.

Several of Beatty's other Freedom caskets, including those from Bristol, Hull, Manchester, Dunfermline and Grimsby, are at Greenwich, as well as a silver lion rampant almost a foot high, standing on a rolling wave, with a plinth inscribed: *Presented to Lady Beatty by the Ship's Company of HMS Lion as a token of esteem 1915.*

Another Freedom box at Greenwich was presented to Vice Admiral Sir Roger Brownlow Keyes by the Borough of Dover in recognition of his services in command of the Dover Patrol and at the famous raid on Zeebrugge on 23rd April 1918. For that service he was also presented with the Freedom of Chatham and Folkestone. The Chatham presentation was in the form of a large cigar box, but the Dover silver casket – by Carrington & Company – is of an unusually nautical design (colour plate 74). There are dolphins set at each corner and on the front and back are panels depicting the two principal ships – HMS *Vindictive* and HMS *Warwick* – and a scene of Dover Harbour. The lid has a figure of St Martin, patron saint of Dover, on horseback, giving his cloak to a beggar, the act for which he is famed. The Mayor of Dover presented the casket at a reception on 12th December 1918 with the words:

> *Your name will always be associated with the town of Dover. It is right and fitting that the Freedom of this Town should be given to one who has done so much in bringing freedom to the world. I have to ask your acceptance of it in this casket from the citizens of the town, and trust that it will remind you for many years to come of their gratitude to you and your officers and men for the protection you have afforded us.*[4]

Foreign rulers have often conferred honours and awards upon leaders in battle, in gratitude for services towards their countries. After the Battle of the Nile Nelson received many such rewards for services rendered. The Sultan of Turkey, Selim III, granted him the Turkish Order of the Crescent as well as a *chelengk*, the diamond plume of honour – the first time it had been given to a Western leader. This elaborate jewel, made up of a spray of thirteen diamond rays issuing from a central rosette, could be worn as an ornament in the hat, and

75 Silver-gilt *kovsh* presented to Rear Admiral R F Phillimore by the Imperial Russian Navy in 1916. By Carl Fabergé of St Petersburg.

this is how it is depicted in some of the Nelson portraits, including that by Lemuel Abbott. Nelson adopted the *chelengk* as one of the crests for his revised coat of arms granted after the battle. Unfortunately, the original jewel, which survived until this century, was stolen in 1951 and never recovered. George Elphinstone, Admiral Lord Keith (1746–1823), later received the Order of the Crescent from the Sultan, and also a *chelengk* which is now at Bowood House. Sir William Sidney Smith (1764–1840) was also awarded this honour by the Sultan for his defence of Acre in 1799, which halted the advance of the French Army.

Ferdinand IV, King of Naples, honoured Nelson with the Order of St Ferdinand, and also presented Nelson's flag captain, Sir Thomas Masterman Hardy (1769–1839), with a gold snuff box. The oval four-colour gold French box is set with a glazed miniature of the King surrounded by a plaited hair frame, which by tradition is said to have replaced an original diamond surround. Ferdinand IV also presented a gold snuff box to Sir Thomas Louis (1759–1807), who had commanded the *Minotaur* at the Battle of the Nile. The box is rectangular with canted corners, and bears the monogram *TL* on the lid.

Some interesting foreign awards made in the twentieth century are also to be found at Greenwich. One such exotic item on loan to the Museum is a Russian silver-gilt *kovsh* made by Carl Fabergé of St Petersburg in 1916 (plate 75). The form of this traditional Russian boat-shaped

76 (right) Cup and cover presented to Captain John Allen by the East India Company. By William Cripps of London, 1761.

77 (far right) Cup and cover presented to Captain Francis Geary RN for the capture of French prizes, 1745. By R Gurney and T Cook, 1745.

bowl, which terminates at one side in a flat handle, was derived from a drinking vessel, but the *kovsh* later became a decorative symbol of honour awarded for outstanding service to the State: either a military achievement or a successful diplomatic mission.

The Fabergé example was presented to Rear Admiral R F Phillimore by the Imperial Russian Navy in 1916 to mark eighteen months' service, as British Naval Representative on the Czar's staff. He left Russia a few months before the Revolution, and the *kovsh* is thought to be one of the last pieces to come out of Imperial Russia. The silver-gilt bowl is chased in the centre with the double-headed Russian eagle, which also surmounts one end. On the opposite end, the flat handle is engraved with the dates of Rear Admiral Phillimore's service. The outside of the bowl has presentation inscriptions in English and Russian.

Another interesting piece of twentieth century silver marking foreign service is an inscribed salver by a Birmingham maker, which was presented to Lieutenant R Pote-Hunt on the occasion of his retirement after thirty-seven years as admiralty pilot on the Yangtse River. This was a token of appreciation from the commanders-in-chief, rear admirals, Yangtse captains and officers of the China Fleet whom he had piloted up and down the river between 1900 and 1937. The large salver is inscribed with the names of 146 ships arranged alphabetically.

During the wars of the eighteenth century, funds were established for the reward of valour and victory and as encouragement to the protectors of the country's merchant shipping. One of the earliest of these awards in the Museum is an ornate cup and cover given by the East India Company to Captain John Allen (plate 76). The cup, by William Cripps of London, is hallmarked 1761 and is decorated with fruiting vines and scroll handles, with a finial shaped as a toper holding a wine bottle and goblet. A cartouche on one side is engraved with the coat of arms of the New East India Company, and the inscription on the other side reads: *The Gift of the Honourable United East India Company to Captn John Allen of the Duke of Dorset, for his Gallant behaviour against the Dutch in Bengal River in the Year 1759.* On 24th November 1759 Captain Wilson of the *Calcutta* had led several British East Indiamen in a successful attack on seven Dutch East Indiamen which had attempted to seize Chinsura, on the Ganges. When Bernard Forrester, captain of the *Duke of Dorset,* was disabled in the knee by grapeshot during the engagement, the first mate, John Allen, took over command. The next March, Captain Forrester died of his wounds following an amputation of his leg, and John Allen's promotion to command of the *Duke of Dorset* was confirmed. The East India Company was particularly generous in rewarding their officers and men, and the crews of the *Calcutta, Hardwick* and *Duke of Dorset* received the sum of £2,000 for each ship for their part in the action.

An even earlier cup and cover at Greenwich, by Richard Gurney and Thomas Cook, went to Captain Francis Geary RN for taking three French prizes during the Siege of Louisbourg in 1745 (plate 77). Details of the presentation are not known, but portraits of his ship – the *Chester*, 50 guns – and the French prizes – *Heron*, *Elephant* and *Notre Dame de Deliverance* – are engraved in cartouches on the lower part of the cup.

One of the best-known of the committees giving rewards for distinguished service belonged to the Corporation of Lloyd's. After the battle of the Glorious 1st of June 1794 a subscription was raised for the relief of the wounded. Following the Battle of the Nile in 1798, £38,436 was subscribed for the wounded and dependants of men killed, and Nelson himself was voted £500 for the purchase of plate by the Subscription Committee. A second gift of £500 was announced on 30th July 1801 after the Battle of Copenhagen, and the choice of articles was left entirely to Nelson, the Copenhagen grant allowing additional items to be added to the original service.[5]

Several pieces from this service are displayed at Greenwich. The Greenwich Hospital Collection includes a pair of silver wine coolers by William Hall of London, hallmarked 1801. Another pair is now at Lloyd's. The wine coolers have lion mask and ring handles and are engraved with Nelson's coat of arms. A long inscription on the other side records the reason for the presentation:

> *Presented by the Committee appointed to manage the Subscription raised for the benefit of the Wounded and Relatives of those who were killed in the glorious victory obtained off Copenhagen on the 2 of April 1801, to the Vice Admiral Lord Nelson KB Duke of Bronte etc etc in testimony of the high sense entertained of his meritorious and unprecedented exertions in defence of his Country, which at the peril and danger of his life, he so nobly sustained previous to the Engagement, and as a token of his brilliant and gallant Conduct during the whole of that ever memorable Action. Lloyds Coffee House. John Julius Angerstein, Chairman.*

The same inscription appears on the boat-shaped sauce tureens by Daniel Pontifex of London, also hallmarked 1801. The Nelson Arms are on the other side, and the lids have the *chelengk* crest on one side and the *San Josef* crest on the other. There are also silver plates with gadrooned rims by Timothy Renou of London, marked 1801. All the plates at Greenwich are plain with a small Nelson coat of arms on the rim, but Lloyd's has six matching soup plates engraved with the Copenhagen presentation inscription. Three have the inscription on the front, the other three have it on the reverse. The boat-shaped salt cellars which match the service are by Robert and David Hennell of London, hallmarked 1800, and are engraved only with the Nelson crests.

Some of the earlier Nile pieces have also survived. Both Lloyd's and the Monmouth Museum have circular vegetable dishes by Paul Storr, London, 1800, with *chelengk* handles inscribed:

> *Lloyd's 1800. Presented by the Committee for managing a subscription made for the Wounded and Relatives of the killed at the Battle of the Nile to Vice Admiral Lord Nelson Duke of Bronti* [sic] *KB etc who was there wounded.*

The Patriotic Fund was founded at a meeting at Lloyd's Coffee House at the Royal Exchange on 20th July 1803. The fund, which also gave awards of money to wounded seamen, made many gifts of presentation swords and silver during the early years of the nineteenth century, and examples of both types of award are at Greenwich. There are four of the well-known Patriotic Fund vases, of which sixty-six went to naval and military officers in recognition of distinguished services between 1804 and 1809. The series of vases was designed by John Flaxman, and supplied by Rundell and Bridge, the Court goldsmiths. The marks of various makers appear on the individual vases, which varied in detail and value although they were basically of the same design. Most of the vases were originally of £100 value, but seventeen were of values from £150 to £500. The committee often offered a choice of a vase or sword or the equivalent value in money.[6]

The vases are of amphora form, with a flat cover surmounted by a lion. On one side is a figure of Britannia holding Winged Victory in her hand, and on the other Hercules slaying the Hydra. The vases have high handles and decorative borders made up of scrolls, rosettes, oak leaves, palms and laurel leaves. The presentation inscription usually appears on the shoulder.

Fifteen of the vases were presented to captains after the Battle of Trafalgar in October 1805, and Greenwich has three of this type. One presented to James Nicoll Morris, captain of HMS *Colossus*, bears the 1806 hallmark of Digby Scott and Benjamin Smith of London (plate 78). Captain Morris also received a £100 sword from the fund. Another similar vase, made by Benjamin and James Smith in 1808, was given to Mrs Louisa Cooke, the widow of John Cooke, Captain of HMS *Bellerophon*, who was killed during the battle. The inscription on this £200 vase, which is part of the Greenwich Hospital Collection, includes the verse:

Sacred to Cooke let this fair Vase proclaim
To thine Trafalgar, join'd his Honor'd Name;
Pledge of his Country's Gratitude to tell
How England Conquered when he Nobly fell.

The third Trafalgar vase at Greenwich was similarly presented to a relative after a distinguished officer had perished in battle. In this case the man honoured was Lord Nelson himself, and the recipient was his brother, William, who was granted the title of Earl Nelson after Trafalgar. This vase, made by Benjamin Smith of London in 1807, was of an original value of £500 and is significantly different in appearance. It is far heavier and larger than most of the other vases, is silver-gilt rather than silver, and stands on an additional silver-gilt plinth. Instead of the more usual Britannia and Hercules figures on the body of the vase, there is a large version of Lord Nelson's coat of arms in relief on one side and a Latin inscription on the reverse. The plinth, which is also inscribed in Latin on the sides, in turn rests on a platform with mermen blowing on conch shells on the four corners. The other £500 Trafalgar vases are both in the possession of the Queen, one being presented to Frances, Viscountess Nelson, and the other to Vice Admiral Lord Collingwood.

78 Lloyd's Patriotic Fund vases by Digby Scott and Benjamin Smith, 1806. Left: To Captain James Nicoll Morris at Trafalgar. Right: To Captain J F Timins commanding the Honourable East India Company Ship *Royal George*, 1804.

A fourth Patriotic Fund vase at Greenwich is very similar to the Trafalgar presentations, although it went to an officer of the Honourable East India Company as a reward for distinguished service in 1804 (plate 78). J F Timins, the recipient, also received a Lloyd's sword to the value of £50. The vase, by Digby Scott and Benjamin Smith, bears the date letter for 1806, and is similar to the Morris vase except for an additional inscription – *Britannia Triumphant* – above Britannia, and *Britons Strike Home* above Hercules. The presentation inscription on the shoulder of the vase reads:

From the Patriotic Fund of Lloyds to J F Timins Esq commanding the H.E.I.Cos Ship ROYAL GEORGE, in which he gallantly led the action and fought the MARENGO of 84 guns under command of Adm. Linois on the 5th Feby 1804 when a fleet of merchantmen defeated and pursued a squadron of French men of war as recorded in the Gazette of the 11th Augt 1804.

In 1811 Captain Thomas Greenwood of Lancaster was presented with a two-handled silver cup and cover by the Underwriters of Lloyd's for having completed many successful voyages to the West Indies in the Lancaster ships *Comet*, *Molly*, *Chatsworth*, *Aurora*, *Mars*, *Harriet Pasey Hall* and *William Ashton*. The *Lancaster Records* mention:

On the same day Feb 28th 1811 Captain Greenwood of this town was presented by the Underwriters at Lloyds with a piece of plate value 100 guineas for having made 32 successful voyages to the West Indies and for having in the William Ashton of this port mounting 16 nine pounders and 25 men beaten off a French corvette of 18 eighteen pounders and 125 men.[7]

The cup (plate 79), which is now on loan to the National Maritime Museum, has Thomas Greenwood's monogram on one side wreathed in laurel and surrounded by naval trophies and the presentation inscription on the other side. The lid has a decoration of fruiting vines, and the finial is a sprig of oak leaves and acorns. The handles are formed as double rope twists, and there is a scrolling border around the top which is reminiscent of the Lloyd's Patriotic Fund vases. This is not surprising as the makers were Benjamin and James Smith, who had also made many of those cups.

The presentation of swords by the Patriotic Fund at Lloyd's has already been mentioned. The committee which met on 20th July 1803 decided on a scale of value for the presentations dependent on the rank of the recipient. Swords of £30 value for mates and midshipmen, £50 for lieutenants and £100 for captains and flag officers were proposed. Since, in practice, lower-ranking officers had comparatively little opportunity to earn such a reward, very few of the £30 swords were ever presented, so they are consequently far more rare and valuable today than the £100 swords. After the Battle of Trafalgar the commanding officer of every ship present received a variant of the £100 sword. The design of the four different Lloyd's swords was based on that of a light cavalry sabre with a curved blade. They all have identical gilt hilts and similar blued and gilt blades, but the varying ornamentation of the scabbards reflects the difference in value. An inscription on the blade records the name of the recipient, his ship and the reason for the award. The swords were presented in fitted mahogany boxes, and examples have survived which still have pasted into the lid the original label explaining the symbolism of the ornate hilt.[8]

There are some discrepancies in the various lists of recipients. A few officers opted to take money or silverware rather than swords. For instance, Thomas Fremantle (1764–1819), Captain of HMS *Neptune* at Trafalgar, wrote to his wife on 17th May 1806:

> *I shall write to my brother William to endeavour to get for me from Lloyds, or the patriotic fund, an Eperne* [sic] *for the middle of the Table, of 100 pounds value, in lieu of the Sword which they have voted, the one will be both more useful, and ornamental than the other.*[9]

For various reasons some officers did not receive swords they were entitled to, but as far as can be deduced, some 177 swords of all values were awarded by the fund between 1803 and 1810, made up of 39 of the £100 swords, 28 Trafalgar swords (including 2 awarded to lieutenants in recognition of particular duties), 95 £50 swords and only 15 £30 swords.

Many of the swords were made by the sword-cutler Richard Teed of London. The collection at the National Maritime Museum includes a rare £30 sword presented to Midshipman Lamb for gallant conduct in the capture of the Spanish brig, *Raposa*, in the Bay of Campeachy on 7th January 1806, and a £50 sword awarded to Lieutenant Samuel Mallock of the Royal Marines for gallantry at the storming of Fort Muros in Spain on 4th June 1805.

Among the six £100 Trafalgar swords at Greenwich is one complete with its original gold wire-embroidered sword belt awarded to Captain

79 Cup and cover presented to Captain Thomas Greenwood by the Underwriters of Lloyd's for successful voyages to the West Indies. By Benjamin and James Smith, 1811.

80 Silver tea urn presented to Captain Nicholas Tomlinson by the Royal Exchange Assurance. By Robert Salmon, 1796.

Charles J Moore Mansfield for meritorious service in command of HMS *Minotaur*, and another presented to Lieutenant John Richards Lapenotière, who brought back the Trafalgar dispatches in the schooner *Pickle*. Another interesting £100 sword awarded after a later action bears the inscription:

> *From the Patriotic Fund at Lloyds to Lieut W.J.Hughes for his gallant and successful defence of H.M.Fire Brig Phosphorus on her being attacked by a French lugger privateer of much superior force, off the Isle of Wight on the 14th Augt 1806, as recorded in the London Gazette on the 16th of the same month.*

To mark the successful defence of a merchant ship against a heavily-armed privateer, awards were also made, and a committee was formed to encourage this form of self-defence. The earliest example at Greenwich is a silver cup and cover presented to Captain Lawrence Irvine by the Underwriters in recognition of his bravery in beating off a large French privateer which boarded his ship, the *Lyon*, in Auracabessa Harbour, Jamaica, on 12th April 1758. The presentation was evidently made some time after the event, as the cup is hallmarked with the date letter for 1766.

In 1781 another silver cup and cover was presented by the merchants and Underwriters of Bristol to Luke Crosby, commander of the *Three Sisters*, for: *his Gallant Defence of that Ship, with six 6 Pounders only, against a French Privateer of eighteen 6 Pounders off the Island of Scilly, on the 17 of March 1781*. This cup, which is on loan to the Museum, was made by Charles Wright of London in the same year. It is of urn shape with two loop handles and a tall lid with a finial which echoes the urn design. On one side the presentation inscription appears beneath a border chased with anchors, telescopes and speaking-trumpets, and the other side has an engraving of a ship under sail. It is interesting that we have some further evidence to fill out the brief details given on the cup itself, thanks to an entry in a Bristol newspaper of Saturday 24th March 1781:

> *Capt. Crosby, of the Three Sisters, in the Russia trade, who sail'd from hence the beginning of last week, off Scilly fell in with a French privateer of 18 six pounders, full of men, which he engaged for a considerable time and beat off and 'tis supposed killed a great number of their people.*
>
> *Capt. Crosby had only 8 six-pounders, and about ten men and boys, but by his bravery and great judgment he escaped being taken tho' much mauld. 'Tis suppos'd a more gallant defence has not been made this war, considering the inequality, and there is not a doubt but he will receive the thanks of the lords of the admiralty for his bravery – The Frenchman was so roughly handled, that she was oblig'd to lie to to refit.*[10]

In 1796 Captain Nicholas Tomlinson, commander of HM sloop *La Suffisante*, was presented with a piece of silver by the Corporation of the Royal Exchange Assurance: *as a testimony of the sense they entertain of his activity, and ability, in the capture of the Morgan French Privateer, and the recapture of six merchant ships on the 27th of June 1796*. The item was of rather more domestic use than the usual cup and cover: a large tea urn, which we can assume was Tomlinson's own choice of award (plate 80). The tea urn, which is of octagonal vase shape with a high lid and loop handles not unlike a cup and cover, stands on a four-footed base, and is fitted with a silver and ivory spigot. On one side is engraved the coat of arms of Tomlinson impaling Ward, and on the other is the presentation inscription surrounded by a trophy of flags and arms. It was made by Robert Salmon of London in 1796. A smaller matching tea urn by the same maker bears the same coat of arms and a less ornate inscription. As the silver is hallmarked 1792 it is clear that it was not specially commissioned but was a stock item with the added inscription: *Presented by the Committee for encouraging the Capture of French Privateers etc etc. To Captn. Tomlinson July 8th 1796.* Also at Greenwich is the matching teapot, sugar basin and cream jug, clearly intended to be part of the same service, although the teapot and jug are by Robert Salmon, and the sugar basin is by Charles Chesterman and bears the date letter for 1790. The Tomlinson coat of arms appears on all three of these pieces, but only the teapot has a presentation inscription which is identical to that on the smaller urn.

Another piece of silver in the collection at Greenwich was awarded by the same committee in 1796. This is also a domestic piece, being a large soup tureen, cover and stand, made by Robert Makepeace of London (plate 81). The lid is surmounted by a reclining figure of Neptune with his trident and a dolphin, a motif which is echoed on the stand with its border of dolphins, tails entwined, all within a rope cable rim. Both sides of the tureen have an elaborate oval cartouche made up of flags, arms and naval equipment, surrounding on one side a coat of arms, and on the other the inscription:

> *Presented by the Committee for encouraging the Capture of French Privateers, Armed Vessels etc To Lord Amelius Beauclerk of his Majesty's Ship Dryad in acknowledgment of his very gallant behaviour in the capture of La Proserpine French Frigate, in the Action on the 13th inst. and in testimony of the high sense this Committee entertain of the Protection he has thereby afforded to the Commerce of Great Britain. London 23rd June 1796.*

There are other silver presentation pieces in the Merseyside Maritime Museum which are gifts from the Underwriters to the captains of Liverpool ships who had defended their vessels against privateer attack.

After the Battle of the Nile Nelson received a valuable silver presentation from the Governor and Company of the Merchants trading into the Levant, which Nelson referred to as his Turkey Cup (plate 82). The cup and cover, which are now at Greenwich, were made by Paul Storr in 1799, the year after the battle, and the design includes a number of devices referring to the Nile. The handles are winged Egyptian female figures, and the cover is decorated with crocodiles. The prizes taken in the battle are listed in laurel wreaths around the top, and the finial is in the form of a seated Neptune holding a trident. Nelson's coat of arms – augmented by a palm tree and ruined battery which appears in chief, and his new motto and *chelengk* crest – is engraved on one side, and on the other, in a matching draped cartouche, is the inscription referring to the recent victory of the Nile:

> *on which ever memorable day by the defeat and capture of a French squadron, superior to his own he restored to his Majesty's Arms, the dominion of the Mediterranean, and to the British merchants, the Free enjoyment of their ancient and valuable trade to Turkey.*

Nelson mentioned this cup in a letter sent to his wife from the *San Josef* in Torbay on 3rd February 1801. He complains of the bad condition in which his personal property had arrived on board:

81 Soup tureen presented to Lord Amelius Beauclerk for his capture of a French privateer. By Robert Makepeace of London, 1796.

82 Turkey Cup presented to Nelson after the Battle of the Nile by the Company of Merchants trading into the Levant. By Paul Storr, 1799.

Not one thing that Mr Dods sent but is ruined, large nails drove through the mahogany table and drawers to fasten the packing cases . . . Mr D has sent only three keys, of the small table and chest of drawers not of the wardrobe, trunk, case of the Turkey cup etc etc By the by the trident of Neptune is bent double from ill package.[11]

Admiral Sir John Duckworth received an unusual presentation piece in the form of a circular silver tea kettle by John Emes of London (colour plate 83). The kettle has an ebony handle and is set above a spirit burner on a hinged stand with four lions'-paw feet. One side is engraved with his coat of arms and the other is inscribed:

Presented in the year 1804 by the merchants of Kingston, Jamaica, to Vice Admiral Sir John Thomas Duckworth KB as a token of their high Respect and Regard for the eminent services rendered by him to the Trade of the Island, during his command on that Station.

In February 1806 the Liverpool privateer *Shipley* was attacked by a French three-masted schooner privateer while bound for the West Indies. During the action four of her men were killed, Captain John Wilson was shot through the shoulder and hand, and the first mate had his thigh broken. The *Shipley* was eventually obliged to surrender, and had her cargo plundered by the French. Later in the year the captain received a small silver cup as a reward, made by Thomas Wallis of London, and inscribed:

To Captn John Wilson, for his Gallant defence of the Ship, Shipley; During an action of One Hour & three quarters with the Hebe French privateer in which he received two severe Wounds. Presented by the Owners Shipley Williams & Co. Liverpool 25th July 1806.

Many of the presentations of valuable items made to commanding officers after battle were not official tributes of governments or institutions, but were gifts from officers who had served under them in action, or even from grateful families. In 1782 a silver punch bowl was presented to Adam Duncan by an officer of the *Blenheim*, the ship which Duncan commanded in the action against the French and Spanish fleets off Cape Spartel on 20th October of that year. *Blenheim* was one of a squadron of thirty-four warships under the command of Admiral Lord Howe which, after leaving Gibraltar, defeated forty-six French and Spanish ships commanded by Don Cordova and M la Mothe Piquet. The bowl, by Thomas Daniel of London, is engraved on one side with broadside views of three ships – *Princess Royal, Victory* and *Blenheim* – and on the other an inscription ending: *This bowl, in testimony of Friendship and esteem is inscribed by George Richardson (on this expedition) seventh lieutenant of the Blenheim.*

Another interesting presentation piece at Greenwich is a silver salver given in 1798 to Captain Thomas Boulden Thompson RN (1766?–1828). Like Nelson, Thompson had been wounded at Santa Cruz, and he subsequently served at the Battle of the Nile in 1798, in HMS *Leander*, 50 guns. After the battle he had the honour of carrying back to England Captain Edward Berry with Nelson's dispatches announcing the victory. Several days later, on 18th August, after a heroic defence, the *Leander* was captured by the French frigate *Généreux*, 80 guns. The *Leander* had 35 crew killed and 57 wounded, including Captain Thompson. The much larger crew of the *Généreux* lost 100 men and 188 were wounded. Thompson was honourably acquitted of blame for the loss of the ship, was knighted for his valour and went on to serve at the Battle of Copenhagen in 1801, where he lost a leg while in command of HMS *Bellona*.

The salver, by William Bennett of London, is a plain silver oval with a central inscription surrounded by oak and laurel branches and surmounted by the Thompson Arms. This is set into a separate Sheffield plate stand on lions'-paw feet. The salver is unique in being not only a presentation piece to honour Captain Thompson's gallantry but also a memorial to the death of a midshipman serving under him in the *Leander*, as detailed in the inscription:

> *To Thomas Thompson Esq., Captain in the British Navy, who so bravely defended the Leander to the very last extremity on the 18th of August 1798, this Memorial is presented by the surviving Brother and Sisters of Peter Downes, late Midshipman under his command who, led by his Example and encouraged by his Friendship to aspire after Glory, fell gallantly fighting in the hard Contest of that fatal Day in the Sixth year of his Service and the twentieth year of his Age.*

The most massive piece of plate in the collection of the National Maritime Museum was commissioned for presentation to Admiral Edward Pellew, Lord Exmouth (1757–1833), after the bombardment of Algiers of 27th August 1816. This silver-gilt centrepiece (plate 84), made by Paul Storr of London in 1817, was modelled as the lighthouse fort at Algiers, complete with guns and surmounted by a lantern. At each corner are pairs of figures, two representing seamen freeing a Christian slave, and the others showing a seaman overcoming an Algerian corsair. The base of the yard-high centrepiece has a relief view of the bombardment, as well as Lord Exmouth's coat of arms, and a presentation inscription, which ends:

> *This tribute of Admiration and Esteem is most respectfully presented by the Rear Admiral the Captains and Commanders who had the honour to serve under him at the memorable Victory gained at Algiers on the 7th of August 1816. Where by the judgement valour and decision of their distinguished Chief, aided by his brilliant example, the great cause of Christian freedom was Bravely fought and nobly accomplished.*

Lord Exmouth's new coat of arms, which appears on the centrepiece, incorporated references to Algiers, including a freed Christian slave as one of the supporters. The centrepiece was exhibited at the Royal Naval Exhibition held at Chelsea in 1891, and remained in the possession of Pellew's descendants until 1975, when it came to the Museum.

A more modest presentation piece commemorating the same event was given to Captain Charles Ekins (1768–1855), who was wounded during the bombardment while in command of the *Superb*. This is a gold snuff box by Alexander Strachan of London, and it is also at Greenwich. The lid of the simple box is engraved with a star and crescent and the word *Algiers* surrounded by a laurel garland, and inside is the presentation inscription: *This box was presented to Captn. Charles Ekins, by the Junior Officers of H.M.Ship*

84 Silver-gilt centrepiece presented to Admiral Edward Pellew, Lord Exmouth, after the bombardment of Algiers, 1816. By Paul Storr of London, 1817.

Superb as a mark of their Esteem and Admiration of his Conduct on the Glorious 27 of August 1816.

In 1818 a massive silver salver was presented to Rear Admiral Sir Charles V Penrose KCB (1759–1830) by the captains serving under his command in the Mediterranean Station between 1816 and 1818. The salver was made by Smith, Tate, Nathan and Holt of Sheffield in 1818, and the presentation inscription in the centre is surrounded by an elaborate decoration of engraved baskets of flowers and vines, all within a waved gadrooned border.

Another rather unusual piece in the Greenwich Hospital Collection is a circular salver with the arms of the Hospital in the centre made up by order of the Lords Commissioners of the Admiralty in 1875 from 125 unclaimed war medals of deceased In-Pensioners of Greenwich Hospital.

Most of the presentations for gallant service have been made to officers, and it is unusual to find presentation pieces for men of the lower deck. On 7th May 1900, however, the Corporation of Lloyd's held a reception at the Royal Exchange for the Naval Brigade of HMS *Powerful*. A souvenir programme and menu was provided, and each man was presented with a circular tobacco box of Birmingham silver engraved with the shield of the Lloyd's Corporation coat of arms and inscribed: *Lloyd's 7th May 1900. Silver Tobacco Box Presented by Lloyd's to the Men of HMS Powerful who took part in the gallant defence of Ladysmith.*

NOTES

1 Claude Blair: *Three Presentation Swords* (Victoria & Albert Museum Brochure no. 1, 1972) p9

2 Sold Christie's (28th June 1972) Lot 23

3 Christie's (21st October 1991) Lot 109

4 *Dover Express* (13th December 1918)

5 Warren R Dawson: *The Nelson Collection at Lloyd's* (1932); John May: 'The Nelson Silver' (*Antique Collecting* October 1985)

6 Leslie Southwick: 'The Silver Vases awarded by the Patriotic Fund' (*The Silver Society Journal* no. 1, 1990) p27–49. Includes a list of all recipients 1803–9.

7 *Lancaster Records 1801–50* (1869)

8 Derek Spalding: 'Trafalgar Swords of Honour' (*Arms & Armor Annual* 1973); Peter Dale: 'Swords of Honour & Glory' (*American Society of Arms Collectors Bulletin* Vol. I no. 40 Spring 1979); Leslie Southwick: 'Patriotic Fund Swords' (*Journal of the Arms & Armour Society* Vol XII no. 4 September 1987 and Vol XII no. 5 March 1988)

9 Anne Fremantle (ed.): *The Wynne Diaries 1789–1820* Vol 3 (1940) p270

10 *Sarah Farley's Bristol Journal* (24th March 1781)

11 George P B Naish (ed.): *Nelson's Letters to his Wife 1785–1831* (1958) p619

CHAPTER 4 Jack Tar

While individual admirals and captains were celebrated in pottery and porcelain, and their deeds in battle rewarded with Freedoms and valuable presentations, it is very unusual to find sailors – who came to be known as 'the lower deck' – similarly honoured. With the rare exception of the occasional hero of battle who had caught the public eye, seamen were seldom commemorated by name, although the *Jack Tar*, so often the saviour of his country's trade and honour by sea, was a deservedly popular figure and constantly makes his appearance in decorative form.

We are fortunate that throughout history the sailor's costume has been so easily recognised. An official uniform for naval officers was introduced as early as 1748, making it possible to identify the rank of an individual officer and to date his uniform within a fairly narrow period by its pattern. Although equivalent uniform regulations for ratings were not laid down until 1857, the need for a practical working dress at sea meant that, long before that date, a costume had evolved which became the distinctive mark of the sailor, both afloat and ashore at leisure. Through the ship's purser, seamen could purchase suitable ready-made *slop* clothing, provided by contractors, and this inevitably led to a certain degree of uniformity in appearance.

Jack Tar took his nickname from the seventeenth century *tarpaulin* (meaning a thorough seaman and referring to the waterproof clothing made of tarred sailcloth worn in rough weather). His costume underwent changes throughout the years and, most obviously, the wide petticoat breeches (or slops) of the seventeenth and early eighteenth centuries gradually gave way to loose-fitting trousers later in the century, but change was slow. In the absence of surviving examples of sailors' costume from this period we must depend on illustrations for our information. The variations of costume are well represented in the popular prints of the eighteenth century, but only occasionally occur as an incidental feature of an oil painting.

Early three-dimensional representations of sailors are even rarer. None are known before the middle of the eighteenth century, but later there are some excellent porcelain and pottery figures, which complement the prints and give a good impression of a seaman's typical dress of the period. They are particularly valuable in depicting the back view of garments seldom shown in pictures. In *c*1752 the Bow factory produced what was perhaps the first of these (plate 85), a standing porcelain figure of a sailor, with left hand on hip, wearing wide trousers, a long jacket with back slits, mariner's cuffs which could be turned back out of the wet, and a distinctive hat of the type described in the *London Chronicle* on 18th March 1762: *Sailors wear the sides of their hats uniformly tacked down to the crown, and look as if they carried a triangular apple pasty upon their heads.*[1] The National Maritime Museum and the Victoria & Albert Museum both have white versions of this figure, but a coloured version is also known, complete with a matching lass. This sailor wears striped trousers, a floral waistcoat and a spotted neckerchief.[2]

85 Bow white porcelain sailor *c*1752.

The same factory produced both white and coloured versions of a dancing sailor figure in *c*1753–8. In this example (colour plate 86) he stands in a theatrical pose, wearing a long pink jacket, blue fancy waistcoat and neckerchief, with yellow striped petticoat breeches, and the *apple pasty* hat. While the style is in keeping with the mid-eighteenth century sailors' costume shown in contemporary prints, it has obviously been somewhat fancifully coloured by the Bow decorator to attract the porcelain buyer.[3] A variety of colours was still being worn by seamen at this time, however, and striped breeches and waistcoats and check shirts were common. Grey and red were originally the most usual colours for slop clothing, but by the 1760s blue and white had begun to predominate.

The Derby factory also made an attractive pair of sailor and lass porcelain figures in *c*1760. The sailor stands against a flowery background on a scroll base, wearing a brightly-coloured waistcoat under his jacket, and he carries a stick. He displays gold coins in the palm of his left hand, while the lady beckons.

The popularity of these porcelain sailor figures led to less expensive but equally attractive figures being produced in earthenware to appeal to a wider market (colour plate 88). In *c*1775 Ralph Wood of Staffordshire was producing a standing sailor figure with a matching lass. The figure appears in white with a little blue, in black basalt, and also fully coloured. In one coloured version the decorator has painted the sailor's tunic a most unlikely bright green with red facings – presumably to match his lass's costume – and has completed the outfit with a yellow waistcoat.

87 Silver sailor taperstick by William Cafe, 1761.

The sailor image was equally attractive to the richer classes. A very rare cast silver taperstick of 1761 (plate 87), by William Cafe of London, is modelled as a sailor of the period in loose trousers, a long jacket with back flaps, frilled shirt, buckled shoes, tricorn hat and, of course, a flowing neckerchief. Sadly he lacks his lass, who would almost certainly have made up the original pair, and it is an enticing thought that she exists somewhere, unrecognised, waiting to be matched up. Two families of silversmiths, the Cafes and the Goulds, virtually monopolised the manufacture of silver candlesticks in the mid-nineteenth century. However, a very similar pair of sailor and lass candlesticks by Samuel Siervent is known, dated 1762. The sailor wears long slop hose rather than trousers, and his lass, who might well resemble the missing Cafe figure, wears a dress with a waisted tunic and a wide-brimmed hat.

From the same period is an interesting Worcester porcelain bowl made for the Marine Society in *c*1760 (plate 89). This bowl, by Robert Hancock, is transfer-printed in black with a design showing Britannia and Charity overseeing the Marine Society's reclothing of ragged boys as seamen. One boy is shown pulling on the distinctive loose canvas protective trousers over his breeches. The print was designed by Samuel Wale RA and engraved by T Major (plate 90), and first appeared in Jonas Hanway's letters on the subject of the Marine Society published in 1757 and 1758.[4] On the other side of the bowl is a sea battle, and inside is a printed bust portrait of George II after Thomas Worlidge's painting of 1753, which presumably dates the production before 1760. Worcester porcelain mugs and jugs with this same portrait of the King are well known, and are of interest as the series represents the first ever printed Royal commemoratives.

The Marine Society still exists as a seafarers' charity today. The records of the society (which are deposited in the National Maritime Museum) make no mention of these bowls, although several are known. The minutes, however, do refer to presentation silver anchors and medals being ordered as tokens of the society's esteem for Jonas Hanway and other benefactors, and it is likely that the bowls were also intended for presentation purposes. The Museum has in its collection the silver-gilt medal presented to Hanway in 1769, which is inscribed:

> *The Marine Society instituted in London July 1756, during the War with France and Spain, by voluntary Subscriptions clothed and fitted out 5,452 Landsmen as Seamen, and 4,787 Boys to be bred Seamen for the Service of the Royal Navy and also provided for all the Boys who apply'd to them at the close of the War in 1762.*

Reclothing ragged recruits and destroying their dirty clothes was a sensible precaution to prevent the spread of infection at sea, but it sometimes resulted in the newly kitted-out volunteers deserting before they had even joined their ship.

Apart from inspiring a few prints, the activities of the press gang were seldom a subject for popular commemoration. A rare creamware mug of *c*1800 has a transfer-printed scene of impressment on Tower Hill, based on a coloured etching *Manning the Navy*, by Barlow after a drawing by Collings of 1790. A sailor is seen seizing a vagrant while officers stand by. Impressment was a perfectly legal method of manning naval vessels in time of war.

Once at sea the sailor's life was hard and hazardous. The safety of all depended on the skill and efficiency of every individual in the ship's company, and one would expect to meet with items commemorating everyday life on board and scenes of the sailor about his typical sea duties. Perhaps such subjects were thought too mundane to ornament the mantelpiece, but whatever the reason there is no doubt that scenes depicting the sailor at work or employing his seamanship skills are very rare compared with illustrations of Jack at play. The odd example does occur, however. A Liverpool creamware mug in the Museum's collection has a sailor preparing to heave the leadline on one side, and taking a navigational sighting on the other, with the inscription: *We have had a good observation today And I hope we shall make the Land Tomorrow.*

A Nelson creamware jug of *c*1798, commemorating the Battle of the Nile, has a small vignette below the lip showing three sailors in a small boat, one taking soundings. Another Liverpool tobacco jar of *c*1805 in the Merseyside Maritime Museum, has the same engraving with the inscription:

From rocks and sands And every ill
May God preserve the sailors still.

As we saw in chapter 2, naval battles are well represented by pictures of the ships involved and their commanding officers, but the sailors' major part in these battles seems to have gone almost unrecorded on commemorative wares. Just occasionally a named sailor's heroism would become part of the mythology of battle, and he would be celebrated in verses, medallions and popular prints. Even so it could take many years before such recognition was forthcoming. During the Battle of Camperdown in 1797:

The foe thought we had struck,
But Jack cried out 'Avast'
And the Colours of Old England
He nailed to the mast.

This sailor was Jack Crawford, who served in Duncan's flagship, the *Venerable*, at Camperdown. In April 1890, nearly a century after his exploits, a statue was unveiled in his honour in his home town of Sunderland, and pottery souvenirs were produced to mark the event. The local factory at Sunderland, which specialised in lustre-decorated ware, sold mugs and teapots transfer-printed with a design of Crawford nailing a red ensign to the mast after the admiral's blue flag had been shot away by the Dutch. This mug is inscribed: *Jack Crawford the Hero of Camperdown Octr 11th 1797.* The original source of this rather crude print was an engraving by Daniel Orme published in November 1797, soon after the battle, but it has been reversed and the flag changed.

89 Worcester porcelain bowl by Robert Hancock *c*1760 for the Marine Society.

90 Marine Society engraving from Jonas Hanway's published letters (1757) showing poor boys being clothed as seamen.

A bronze medallion was also produced at the time, with Admiral Duncan as the main subject, and on the reverse an unnamed sailor nailing a Royal Standard to the mast, with the legend: *Heroic courage protects the British flag.* Sunderland Museum has another mug which is considerably closer to the original print.

Pottery figures of sailors continued to be produced throughout the nineteenth century, and the gradual changes in costume can be followed in the development of the cheap Staffordshire figures produced for the cottage mantelpiece. Striped trousers began to predominate as the mark of a seaman, and by the end of the eighteenth century the hat with brim pinned back in three places had been replaced by a low crown and narrow brim, which eventually developed into a tall hat. Sennit hats made from straw plait were also being worn from early in the nineteenth century, and did not go out of use until 1921. Some of these sailor figures are fashioned as Toby jugs, such as the early nineteenth century coloured earthenware figure of a sailor in striped trousers seated on a chest of dollars, with his clay pipe in one hand and a foaming tankard in the other, inscribed *Success to Our Wooden Walls* (plate 91).

The Royal Navy brig *Daring*, 12 guns, launched in 1844 at Portsmouth, carried a figurehead (plate 92) in the form of a sailor wearing sidewhiskers and the typical seaman's rig of the period prior to the 1857 Regulations. He wears a sennit hat with the name of his ship on the cap ribbon and also on the front of his jumper. HMS *Daring* was broken up by Messrs Castles of Charlton in 1864.

The Crimean War (1854–6), not surprisingly, produced the next wave of patriotic pottery figures, and standing figures of sailors waving ensigns, raising their sennit hats or leaning against guns were all popular. One such sailor figure is standing with one foot on a gun and the other on a chained and muzzled bear, symbolising victory over Russia in the Crimean War. Another figure group entitled *The Wounded Soldier* is modelled as a sailor with frock tucked loosely into his trousers, a sennit hat and red neckerchief, holding his bundle of possessions in one hand and supporting a wounded soldier on his other side. Like many of these Staffordshire figures it is based on a popular engraving of the time, in this case an illustration in *Cassell's Illustrated Family Paper* in April 1855.[5] Other Crimean War-period sailors are to be found as transfers on Sunderland lustre pottery and engravings on glass goblets.

In 1857 the uniform regulations for the first time set out details of dress for naval ratings, but what they introduced was little different from the costume which had become the accepted norm. Individual captains had already introduced considerable uniformity, and the crew of the Royal Yacht, in particular, had its own uniform some years before the regulations. In 1846 the five-year-old Prince Albert Edward, later King Edward VII, was painted by Franz Xaver Winterhalter wearing a sailor's rig of a white frock with blue cuffs and blue jean collar edged with three white lines, tucked into bell-bottomed trousers, and a black silk neckerchief. This costume was based on the uniform worn by the crew of the Royal Yacht *Victoria and Albert*. Queen Victoria wrote in her journal on 2nd September 1846:

> *After passing the Alderney Race it became quite smooth; and then Bertie put on his sailor's dress, which was beautifully made by the man on board who makes for our sailors. When he appeared, the officers & sailors, who were all assembled on deck to see him, cheered, and seemed delighted with him.*[6]

91 (right) 19th century sailor figure seated on a chest of dollars.

92 (far right) Sailor figurehead of HMS *Daring*, 12 guns, launched 1844.

The oil painting was reproduced in engravings and as bronze and earthenware figurines (plate 93). The popularity of these ornaments is indicated by their variety in quality and size, ranging from a small, barely recognisable earthenware copy to a Minton Parian ware figure modelled by permission of the Prince Consort, of which the *Illustrated London News* said: *The likeness is very striking, and the characteristic accessories of the nautical costume very nicely executed. This is certainly one of the most interesting presentments of the youthful Royal Family yet published.*[7] The child's sailor suit, made popular by such publicity, became for many years the fashionable dress for children, and has enjoyed periodic revivals up to the present time. The costume worn by the Prince in the Winterhalter painting has survived and is in the collection of the National Maritime Museum.

93 (left) Staffordshire earthenware figure of Prince Albert Edward, later King Edward VII, in sailor dress *c*1850.

95 (below) *Handyman* stoneware jug by Doulton & Co. of Lambeth *c*1899.

Later in the nineteenth century the sailor in his working dress was still seen as a decorative image. A bronze figure of a British seaman of the Naval Brigade, dating from *c*1882, made by a foundry in Brussels, is now at Greenwich (colour plate 94). The bearded seaman is depicted in his landing rig, with a Martini-Henry rifle, complete with cutlass bayonet, sennit hat, bedding roll, gaiters, ammunition pouch and water bottle. It is an excellent representation of the equipment used by bluejackets of the Naval Brigades when they were sent ashore after the bombardment of Alexandria. The figure is very close to the engraving which appeared on the front page of the *Illustrated London News* on Trafalgar Day 1882.[8] A later advertisement in the same magazine in 1895 offers for sale by Elkington & Co. two figurines of seamen with different uniform and accoutrements, dressed for a landing party.[9] One is rather like the bronze figure described above. The other wears a cap and ammunition belts reminiscent of a silver figure in a private collection which was retailed by Emanuel & Sons of Portsmouth in 1897. That figure, however, wears the name *HMS Blanche* on his cap band, and is hinged above the cartridge belt to reveal an inkwell.

During the Boer War (1899–1902) Doulton & Co. of Lambeth produced a stoneware jug to commemorate the landing of the Naval Brigades in South Africa and the defence of Ladysmith. In 1899 Captain Percy Scott, in command of HMS *Terrible,* devised mountings to enable the heavy guns from his ship to be transported to Ladysmith on board HMS *Powerful*, sister ship to the *Terrible*, under the command of Captain the Hon. Hedworth Lambton. The portraits of both captains appear on the Doulton jug, but pride of place is given to a full-length figure of an unnamed armed bluejacket (colour plate 95). Below the sailor figure is an inscription, *The Handyman*, a title frequently applied to naval ratings at this period in recognition of their multifarious skills.

In 1889 William Witney, a Royal Naval seaman born in 1857, embroidered a woolwork picture on canvas. Such pictures will be examined more fully later in this chapter, but this example is unusual because, instead of choosing to portray his ship, the seaman has used his coloured wools to depict two sailors in uniform. One figure is dressed in the blue uniform of the period with a naval cap, and the other in white uniform with a sennit hat. They are shown against a background of white and blue ensigns and an anchor, and the work is signed *WW1889* in wool, at the bottom. William Witney served in HMS *Superb* in 1883, and later in HMS *Black Prince* and HMS *Mistletoe*. Many of the representations of sailors show them wearing the wide-brimmed straw sennit hats.

The sennit hat also appears as a brooch with an enamelled ribbon inscribed *HMS Bellerophon*. A similar gold brooch by Emanuel of Portsea, dated *c*1900, bears the name of the Royal Yacht, *Victoria & Albert,* on the enamel cap ribbon.

Also dating from the end of the nineteenth century are two anonymous bluejackets' portraits on the sailors' printed neckerchiefs which were issued to new entries as late as 1899. The blue-bordered kerchiefs are also printed with useful nautical information, which is packed into every square inch. Around the central compass rose are details of uniform badges, cutlass exercise, semaphore, bugle calls, weapons, clothing and accoutrements, salutes and first aid.

The design can be dated quite closely by the presence of the Lee-Metford Rifle Mark II, which was only introduced in 1892, and by the fact that the ending of cutlass drill in 1901 rendered the instructions obsolete. This design was patented in 1894. Two similar military handkerchiefs, printed with the equivalent handy information for soldiers, were also produced, but had red borders. These were printed with information on either the Martini-Henry Rifle, patented in 1885, or the Lee-Metford Rifle of 1892, as appears on the naval version. Patents for all three designs were taken out in the name of Lieutenant Colonel K Fulton of the Durham Light Infantry.[10]

98 Swansea ship bowl transfer-printed in blue, late 18th century.

If an army marches on its stomach, it goes without saying that the maxim applies equally to a ship's crew, dependent as they are for their sustenance on what their vessel can carry and maintain in good condition on a long voyage. Food, as anyone who has put in any sea time can testify, soon becomes a major priority in a sailor's day. Having looked at the meagre commemoration given to the seaman's working life in decorative art form, it would seem reasonable to look for better three-dimensional evidence of his eating arrangements.

Most of the pottery described so far was made for use ashore, and although seamen might well have had a particular interest in buying items decorated with nautical subjects, they would not have used such pieces on board. Until the second half of the nineteenth century the drinking vessels and tableware used in naval messes were fairly basic and not of a specifically nautical design, but later, specially designed tableware and decorative items began to appear. Plates and bowls with patterns appropriate for seafarers were produced which were widely used in naval messes, although they were not official issue.

Most pieces were of unmarked pottery, but much of the ware was produced by the Bovey Tracey Pottery Company in Devon. It is thought that victualling contractors supplied sets of these plates and bowls free of charge with victualling orders. The most usual design from the 1880s to 1901 was a blue-printed earthenware plate with a border made up of alternate panels of sailors with flags and Queen Victoria's profile (colour plate 96). After the accession of Edward VII the King's head replaced the Queen's. The mess number was printed in the centre of the plate below a Royal crown, and in the case of the matching mess bowls the number was placed on the outside, upside down, so that it would be correct when the bowls were stacked base uppermost. Variations of the standard design also appear, and there are some with anchors, flags, ships and decorative borders. One bowl of *c*1870 is known which is decorated with views of Plymouth, one showing the Saltash Bridge and the other a view of the old pier.

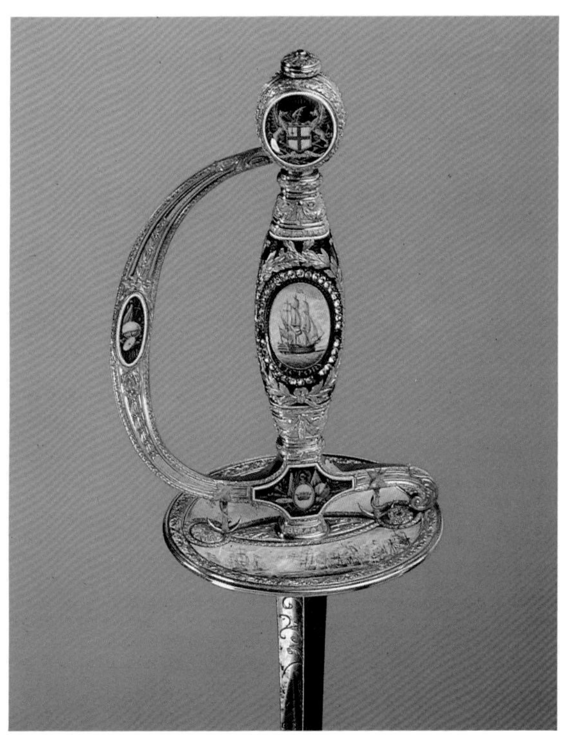

69 (far left) Gold City of London Freedom box presented to Admiral Sir John Jervis, whose coat of arms appears on the enamel plaque on the lid. By James Morisset, 1794.

70 (left) City of London presentation sword awarded to Admiral Sir John Jervis after the Battle of Cape St Vincent, 1797. By Robert Makepeace.

71 Gold City of London Freedom box presented to Captain Edward Berry after the Battle of the Nile. The enamel plaque on the lid is painted with a view of the battle, with the French flagship, *L'Orient,* exploding. By James Morisset, 1798.

74 Silver Freedom box presented to Vice Admiral Roger Brownlow Keyes by the Borough of Dover after the Zeebrugge Raid of 1918.

83 Tea kettle presented to Admiral Sir John Duckworth by the merchants of Kingston, Jamaica. By John Emes, London, 1805.

88 Earthenware sailor figures.

86 (far left) Bow porcelain sailor *c*1753–8.

94 (left) Bronze statuette of a British seaman of the Naval Brigade, *c*1882, made in Brussels.

96 Mess plates and mess bowl, the most common design with the heads of Queen Victoria and Edward VII.

97 Variations of the plates in use in seamen's messes in the late 19th century.

99 Tumbler engraved with sailors and the East Indiaman *Berrington,* launched 1783.

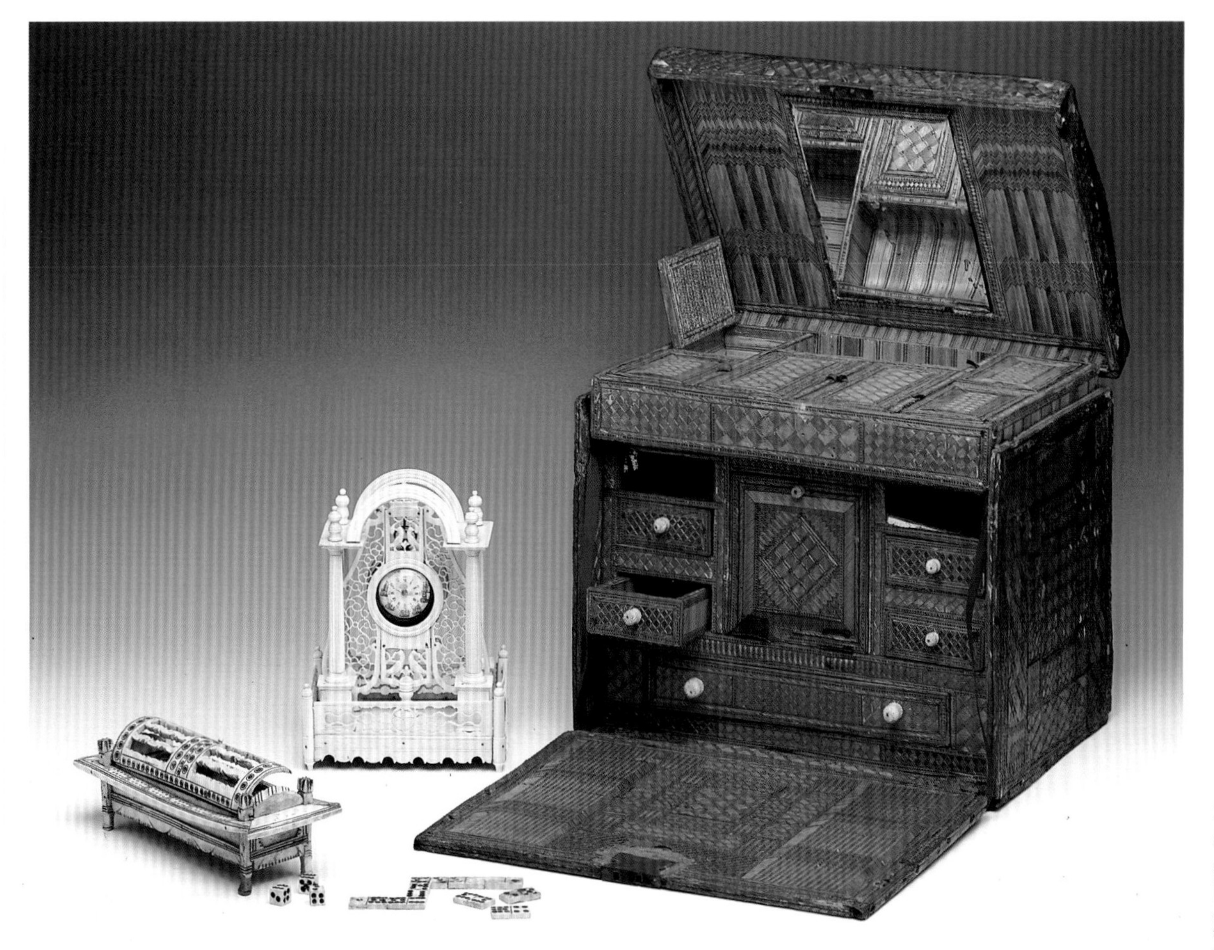

105 A straw-work casket, bone watch-stand and bone domino box, made by French prisoners during the Napoleonic Wars.

107 Sailor-made woolwork picture of HMS *Warrior* c1860.

111 (top left) Staffordshire earthenware figure of Captain Cook, *c*1840.

114 (bottom left) Leeds creamware teapot *c*1776 painted with a whaleship, *Polar Star*.

116 Scrimshawed sperm whale tooth decorated with a sailor boy engraving, and on the other side a theatrical portrait.

118 Staffordshire earthenware figures of Sir John and Lady Franklin *c*1848.

122 Two nautilus shells and a green turban shell engraved with Brunel's ships, by C H Wood.

A plate design dating from about 1890 has a fouled anchor within a garter in the centre, and a double rope border enclosing panels of rose, thistle and shamrock (colour plate 97). There is a mess bowl to match, which also has a compass rose and sailing ship. A rare variation of this plate design, so far seen only in private collections, illustrates an identifiable warship: HMS *Hercules*. Another slightly earlier plate by the Bovey Tracey Pottery Company has a border with panels of ships, naval trophies and flowers. The border of one of the most unusual plates represents country scenes of the four seasons, with a maypole, raking the fields, harvesting and ice-skating.

Far more common than representations of life at sea are scenes of Jack at leisure and ashore. Drinking was always one of his great pleasures, and it is not surprising that this subject should so often have appeared on ale mugs and jugs, punch bowls and drinking glasses. Many such pieces are inscribed with a suitable toast. A typical sailor's toast is seen in the late eighteenth century blue transfer-printed Swansea bowl depicting a warship under sail and the inscription *Success to the British Tars* (plate 98).

On a Dutch-engraved English glass of *c*1783 a more specific toast to a named ship, the *Berrington*, is illustrated not only by a picture of the vessel, but by a charming engraving of two sailors with a large punch bowl, dancing, smoking and drinking (colour plate 99). The *Berrington* was an East Indiaman launched in 1783, and the glass may have been made to celebrate a successful first voyage.

Similar drinking scenes frequently appear as prints on pottery of the 1760s. The earliest printed tiles by John Sadler of Liverpool included a number of scenes of sailors ashore. One of them – a view of a sailor sitting with a girl outside an inn while his friend kisses another over the garden fence – appears also as a transfer-printed creamware marriage plate with a feather moulded rim and a handpainted inscription: *Iohn & Sarah Artis, Yarmouth 1769* (plate 100). The scene is taken from an engraving entitled *Tom Clueline's Call; or the Sailor's Farewell.* In the engraving the inn is the *Duke of Clarence*, but in the ceramic version it has become the *King of Prussia*. The design is one of a pair depicting the *Sailor's Farewell and Return*, and an earlier woodblock-printed tile of the return is known which has a country scene instead of the sea background, and a *Lion of Scotland* inn sign. A Liverpool jug of the 1790s, with a print of *Poor Jack* on one side, has a group of merry Jacks on the other, toasting and drinking from a punch bowl set on an alfresco table, sometimes entitled *The Carousal*.

Most of the drinking scenes also show a sailor smoking one of the long clay pipes of the time, although at sea he would be more likely to chew his tobacco. He often carried a brass or copper tobacco box, which he might decorate with appropriate nautical motifs, or inscribe with his name and personal details. One such copper box in the collection at Greenwich is inscribed on the base with a ship under sail identified as *Perseus*, 1782. The owner's name, Lewis Carr, also appears on the lid, together with the words:

It is no repining can losses repay
Take a pipe with me & smoke sorrow away.

This is the same *Perseus* which appears on the Liverpool porcelain ship bowl of 1790 mentioned on p13. An engraving of 1790, entitled *The Tobacco box, or Jack taking a quid of comfort in a*

100 Liverpool creamware plate dated 1769, the design after a *Sailor's Farewell* print for tiles.

101 Pair of tiles printed by John Sadler of Liverpool c1760 with the sailor's farewell and return (top). Print of the sailor's return published 1744 (bottom).

Storm, shows a sailor in his canvas apron holding a tobacco box during a gale, with a verse from Charles Dibdin's song, *The Token*:

> *He shar'd the Grog, their Hearts to cheer,*
> *Took from his 'bacco box a Quid,*
> *And spell'd for comfort on the Lid,*
> *If you loves I, as I loves you, No pair so happy as we two.*

But perhaps Jack's chief pleasure ashore was attracting the ladies, and it is this subject which inspired the greatest number of popular sailor prints, both on paper and on ceramic mugs and jugs. One large Liverpool creamware jug of the late eighteenth century is transfer-printed with a sailor dressed in striped trousers walking with a girl on his arm, and inscribed with a verse entitled *Jack Spritsail coming on Shore.* The background of the scene is a cottage with a path leading from the seashore, where a boat has just put the sailor ashore from his ship. The source of the print is an engraving, *Jack Spritsail and his Nancy on a Cruise*, published in 1789 by J Roach, and in another variation the lady appears less modestly clad, the background becomes a shady alley outside an inn, and the title is *Jack Spritsail's Frolic.*

On the other side of this particular jug is another similar print of a sailor who has found his girl, accompanied by the verse:

> *A sailor's life's a pleasant life,*
> *He freely roams from shore to shore;*
> *In every port he finds a wife*
> *What can a sailor wish for more.*

The title of the print is *A Man-of-War towing a Frigate into Harbour*, and this is one of a series of popular engravings published by Carington Bowles of London in 1781 which are enlivened by humorous nautical titles. Another of these prints is entitled *An English Man-of-War taking a French Privateer.* In a third, *A Rich Privateer brought safe into Port by two First-rates*, a somewhat merry sailor is being importuned by two women who have their eyes on his hat full of gold coins, while a large bowl of punch is brought in to speed up the operation.

Similar humour inspired the punning captions of some of the prints published during the same period by Robert Sayer and J Bennett. *Jack Oakham throwing out a Signal for an Engagement* (1781) has the sailor holding out his stocking purse full of money to interest the lady, who glances coyly around her fan. Another, published by Sayer and Bennett in 1780, shows the same lady holding a closed parasol and being followed by an admiring Jack. The original print, which is set in an elegant garden with a temple and stone monument, is entitled *Jack on a cruise: Avast there – Back your Mainsail* (or in land parlance, 'Stop!'). Translated into pottery, the print appears, sometimes in reverse, on creamware mugs and jugs of *c*1798, but the background has become a rural scene of cottages, church and trees, and the characters appear rather less elegant. The same distinctive figures also appear on coloured oval relief plaques, either together or as single figures, and in this form are sometimes known as *Patricia and Her Lover.*

Jack's pleasure was all too shortlived, however, and soon he would be subjected once more to the rigours of naval discipline. When the time came to set sail the final heartrending scenes of parting provided an ever-popular subject for the pottery manufacturers. One transfer-printed creamware jug of *c*1798, inscribed *The Sailor's Adieu,* accompanies the sad scene with the patriotic sentiment: *What should tear me from the arms of my Dearest Polly but the undeniable calls of my country in whose cause I have engag'd my Honour and my Life.* A finer version of the engraving, on a jug in Hanley Museum, Stoke on Trent, is entitled *Tom Truelove going to sea.*

It was usual for representations of Jack's tearful departure to be accompanied by a matching scene of his joyous return from a successful voyage, often holding a heavy purse of prize money. The earliest such scenes on pottery are the delftware tiles printed by John Sadler of Liverpool. There is a very fine pair printed in red-brown in *c*1760 with sailor's farewell and return scenes (plate 101). The first scene shows the sad parting in sight of the sailor's ship, while his shipmates wait. The second scene is the reunion after the voyage. By now the sailor is elegantly dressed and able to shower his love with riches.

In fact the scene is considerably earlier than the date of the tile, and is taken from L P Boitard's paintings of the return of sailors from Commodore George Anson's circumnavigation of 1740–44, published as engravings by T Booth in December 1744. The return depicts in the background the wagons filled with the treasure captured by Anson's *Centurion* from the Acapulco galleon *Nuestra Senora de Covadonga* on their way to the

Tower of London. At Shugborough Hall, the Anson seat in Staffordshire, there are still some fine silver bowls and other pieces commemorating the circumnavigation. The same prints appear in less finely-engraved versions on other Liverpool pottery. They are among the Liverpool transfers on the outside of a creamware ship bowl of *c*1780, decorated with a brig and the name *John Dawson*.

But when the moment of departure came it was difficult to imagine a happy outcome, bearing in mind the sailor's hazardous life battling against the enemy and the elements. Another popular print of the late eighteenth century which reflected such fears was *Poor Jack*, which took its title from Charles Dibdin's sea song of 1788. The third verse runs:

I said to our Poll, for, d'ye see, she would cry,
When last we weigh'd anchor for sea,
What argufies sniv'ling and piping your eye?
Why, what a damn'd fool you must be!
Can't you see the world's wide, and there's room for us all,
Both for seamen and lubbers ashore?
And if to old Davy I should go, friend Poll,
You never will hear of me more:
What then? all's a hazard: come don't be so soft;
Perhaps I may laughing come back,
For d'ye see, there's a cherub sits smiling aloft,
To keep watch for the life of poor Jack![11]

The print shows Jack on the shore, hand in hand with the weeping Poll, while his ship prepares for departure, cherub duly perched aloft. Jack wears the typical wide petticoat breeches with striped waistcoat, tunic, spotted kerchief, buckle shoes and a jaunty hat with a ribbon rosette. This print appears on a Liverpool creamware jug of *c*1790 (plate 102) together with the Dibdin verse quoted above, and is also known on a Liverpool soup plate and a beaker. The pottery proved so popular that later the print had to be adapted to take account of sailors' changing fashions of costume. Another plate at Greenwich, made at the Herculaneum factory at Liverpool in *c*1805 has a very similar print – still called *Poor Jack* – in which he wears striped trousers instead of the earlier slop hose, and his lass, not to be outdone, has also changed her costume.

Another farewell print shows the lady left behind on the seashore waving to the departing fleet. A creamware jug of 1802, which has a print of a sailing pilot boat on one side, has a transfer on

102 (left) Liverpool creamware jug *c*1790 with engraving and verse from Dibdin's *Poor Jack*.

the other, with the title *Susan's Farewell: Adieu, she cry'd, and wav'd her lily hand*. The reference is to John Gay's song, *Sweet William's Farewell to Black-eyed Susan*, in which Susan, having found her *sweet William* on board a ship moored in the Downs, is obliged to lose him again when the fleet sails, although he swears his constancy:

Change, as ye list, ye winds, my heart shall be
The faithful compass that still points to thee!

After a final promise that he would return safely from battle, protected by her love:

The boatswain gave the dreadful word,
The sails their swelling bosom spread,
No longer must she stay aboard:
They kiss'd, she sigh'd, he hung his head.
Her less'ning boat unwilling rows to land;
Adieu! she cries, and waved her lilly hand.[12]

The ballad later became the inspiration for a nautical drama – *Black-Ey'd Susan, or All in the Downs*, by Douglas Jerrold – which was first performed in 1829, with the famous ex-seaman actor, T P Cooke, taking the role of William. The same print has been seen with the title *Mary's Farewell*.

Farewell and return scenes also feature on Chinese export porcelain and paintings on glass.

103 Liverpool creamware mug *c*1800 with a *Sailor's Return* print by J Johnson.

Nearer to home we find them also in three-dimensional Staffordshire pottery groups. Examples dating from *c*1800 comprise a pair of figure groups, one showing the sailor with his small bundle of possessions taking leave of his lass, while in the other he greets her on his return with a purse of money and a chest of dollars. Another happy ending appears on a Liverpool creamware mug which is transfer-printed with a sailor standing in the bow of a small boat as it sails up onto the beach (plate 103). He is ready to leap ashore, his arms held out to embrace his sweetheart, who stands on the breezy beach risking her fine dress and elegant coiffure. The engraving is signed *J Johnson Liverpool*, and dates from *c*1800.

Sadly, not all the tales had such a happy ending. The well-known pair of illustrations *Jemmy's Farewell* and *Jemmy's Return* appear both as prints on paper by Sayer and Bennett (published 1784–6) and on Liverpool pottery of the 1790s. The farewell print shows Jemmy comforting the weeping lady before he sets off to sea, and the return depicts him in a similar pose with the lady turned away, still weeping into her handkerchief. When the print appears on a large Liverpool punch bowl, the scene of the return seems even more pathetic, for now the lady needs her apron to wipe away her tears. The explanation is that the prints illustrate the popular ballad *Auld Robin Gray*, written by Lady Anne Lindsay in 1771, and the reunion is too late, for the lady has just married another.

I had na been a Wife, but weeks only four,
When sitting so mournfully at my own door,
I saw my Jemmy's wrath, for I could na think it he,
Till he said I'm come back, for to marry thee.[13]

The homecoming sailor, as we have seen, would often return richer than he had gone – although once ashore the bag of prize money would soon be spent. Sailors must always have brought back souvenirs of their travels, but the majority of existing mementoes of this type date from the nineteenth and twentieth centuries. The souvenirs might be reminders of exotic ports or examples of foreign craftsmanship not obtainable at home, or love tokens for a wife or sweetheart, purchased abroad, or made by the sailor during quiet moments on the voyage.

One typical foreign gift was a sailor's valentine. These were shellwork pictures, generally made in matching pairs of octagonal glazed wooden frames, hinged at one side to form a protective case. The small and delicate shells are set out in intricate patterns, and usually include heart motifs and a loving message picked out in shells of a contrasting colour. Favourite legends were *Forget me Not*, *Home Sweet Home, With Love*, *For My Sister*, and *When This You See Remember Me.* The shells used were all native to the West Indies, and most shell valentines are now known to have been made in Barbados, since examples exist which still bear makers' labels on the back, although for many years they were mistakenly thought to be sailors' work. They were being produced from the early nineteenth century until *c*1880, and must have been popular with whalers and merchant vessels calling at Barbados. The souvenirs would have had an obvious appeal to those left at home in Victorian England, where shellwork crafts were so fashionable.

Another favourite foreign souvenir was an Oriental silkwork picture embroidered to order by a professional Eastern craftsman. These ranged from the extremely detailed silk embroidered ship portraits already described in chapter 1 to standard designs of flags grouped around a blank space which could be filled to the sailor's choice.

He might want to use it to display a favourite photograph, or he could buy an embroidery or painting on silk depicting his ship to fill the space. Details of the voyage would then be recorded on the background before the finished work was rolled in a protective paper backing to be carried back home, where it could be framed for display. A picture of HMS *Narcissus* at Greenwich is typical of such souvenirs, with its surround of naval flags, Royal coat of arms, portrait of the cruiser *Narcissus*, launched 1886, and inscription *In remembrance of my cruise in China and Japan 1896–1898*. Another example of slightly later date has the inscription *Stoker J C Bartlett HMS Hawkins 1923–1926*, and on the original paper backing has the maker's name, Murahashi of Yokohama.

Less exotic souvenirs would be brought home to wives and families from British and European ports of call. Pottery decorated with nautical motifs was bound to be popular with sailors, and even if they could not afford the finer productions, the cheap and cheerful wares of the types seen in previous chapters were readily available in Liverpool and other towns. In the nineteenth century the brightly-coloured lustreware of Sunderland was particularly popular. The mugs, jugs, bowls and wall plaques were splashed with pink or copper lustre and transfer-printed or occasionally handpainted. Views of the bridge over the River Wear at Sunderland sold especially well, judging by the number of variations of the print which appeared. A print of London Bridge is also known, but more popular were the simple ship designs with a homely verse beneath, or sometimes a view of a famous battle such as Trafalgar.

Ships fashioned from fragile glass threads, and other glass novelties, could be bought at fairs, especially in the Nailsea area of Bristol, but it is doubtful whether they often survived the journey home! More substantial glass items, such as decorated rolling pins from Sunderland, Bristol and elsewhere, were popular with sailors in the middle years of the nineteenth century, and often sported a painted ship and personal inscription, or transfer-printed decoration with a nautical flavour. Much folklore surrounds these objects, and they have been variously identified as containers for rum or salt, or to have been used by smugglers, but it seems unlikely that they were intended as anything more than ornaments which could be used as rolling pins if required. Although they were usually made of blown glass the size of a typical rolling pin, plenty of larger ones are also known, up to 30 inches long.

Life aboard a sailing ship often meant long periods when the sailor was obliged to make his own amusements to pass the time off watch. As a result many men became skilled in practical crafts. The sailor was never without a good knife, and many a useful item was carved during leisure hours. The slow pace of life during long passages encouraged the elaboration of such items by additional decoration. Boxes and other trinkets were often decorated with nautical motifs. One such box – hollowed out from a single piece of wood – has a flying fish on the base, inspired presumably by a recent sighting in the tropics. The sliding lid of the top is carved with a heart and arrow and the initials *IB* and *EL*. At Hull there are knitting sheaths carved as flying fish, made by the whalers. At Greenwich a marquetry box, complete with inner lidded compartments, made by the ship's carpenter of the clipper *Corinth* in the late nineteenth century, is inlaid with an intricate geometrical design composed of Australian and New Zealand woods (plate 104).

Voyages to the farthest corners of the globe gave seamen the opportunity to experiment with unfamiliar woods, shells and other natural materials, and some of the more specialised trades produced entirely new areas of decorative art which have become highly prized today. The men of the whaleships, for instance, had a never-ending

104 Marquetry box made by the ship's carpenter of the clipper *Corinth*, late 19th century.

supply of whalebone, baleen and whales' teeth to polish, carve and engrave with *scrimshaw* designs, and examples of these will be considered more fully in chapter 5.

Less well-known are the carvings on coconut shells. A fine example of such work, depicting the Battle of the Saints, has already been mentioned on p26, but less professional examples made by the sailors themselves are also known. An example at Greenwich is a flask made from a wild coconut carved over the whole of one side with a warship under sail. The vessel has a lion figurehead, and an ensign at the stern. On the other side are two shields with the initials *W S* and *E S* and the date *1760*. The remainder of the surface is inscribed with an intricate design of hearts and lovers' knots.

It was not unusual for a sailor to make a model of his ship, which might be either a conventional rigged model, or a flat framed picture with wooden sails fixed to a painted scenic background. Rather different in origin are the distinctive ship models produced during the French Revolutionary and Napoleonic Wars (1793–1815) by French prisoners of war incarcerated in British prison hulks at Portsmouth, Chatham and elsewhere, as well as ashore in prisons such as Dartmoor, and Norman Cross near Peterborough. Some prisoners with specialised skills could make detailed ship models, not only from bone – the type usually associated with French prisoner work – but also from wood, often with decorative straw-work stands or cases. Such models frequently incorporated ingenious devices to enable guns to be run out of the ports.

Working models of guillotines and spinning-jennies were also particularly popular, and several amusing examples can be seen in the museum at Peterborough, which has an extensive collection of French prisoner work. In addition to a fine collection of bone, wood and miniature woodchip ship models which are outside the scope of this book, the National Maritime Museum has a pierced watch stand made at Norman Cross in 1811, and a straw-work casket with a fall-front and many small drawers and compartments, as well as a mirror inside the lid (colour plate 105). There are also two French prisoner domino boxes constructed from bone panels, with pierced domed covers and a cribbage board in the outer frame. The sliding bone lids under the covers are painted with commemorative designs somewhat incongruously lamenting Nelson's death. The reason is that the prisoners were allowed to work with whatever materials were available to them in the prisons to raise a little money to improve their living conditions, and the toys, models and other trinkets they made were sold at the local markets. Evidently pieces commemorating Nelson sold well even if made by the enemy, and often the ship models bore the flags and names of well-known British ships.

In the nineteenth century, when mass-produced clear glass bottles became widely available, some ingenious seaman first had the idea of mounting a fully-rigged ship model inside a bottle to mystify the uninitiated. Andrew Crawford's journal of his voyage to Australia in the iron sailing ship *Patriarch* in 1885 mentions that among the entertainments and pastimes on board: *One of the sailors has made a model of a ship in a glass bottle, which has been put up to raffle. Mr Burridge drew the prize and handed it over to the youth Herbert who is very proud of it.*[14] The collection at Greenwich includes some elaborate versions with as many as three different square-rigged vessels under sail in the same bottle (plate 106), and one demonstration model in which a dowel is pegged – apparently impossibly – through the inner end of the plug in the neck of the bottle. Frequently there is additional ornament in the form of a harbour scene with lighthouse or quayside buildings. Although several books have been published which reveal the trick of erecting the prefabricated masts by means of cotton threads running through the neck of the bottle, ships in bottles have never lost their popularity, and are still being made today, although not necessarily by seamen.

The sewing and repairing of sails and canvas-work, and other less heavyweight items of personal clothing, gave many sailors surprising skill with the needle, which some used to great effect in decorative work. One of the most characteristic crafts associated with British seamen in the second half of the nineteenth century is the embroidery of woolwork pictures. These were worked in coloured wools on a canvas ground in a variety of basic stitches, and the subject of the picture was very often a broadside view of the sailor's own ship. His knowledge of the vessels and their rigging meant that the finished image was usually fairly accurate even if the overall effect might be deceptively naive. There are several such sailors'

106 19th century ships in a bottle.

pictures in the collection at Greenwich, in some good private collections, and in museums in many of the seaport towns.

The pictures vary considerably in size, and one of the intriguing questions is how the larger examples were worked in the cramped conditions provided by a ship at sea. To work them evenly and tension the rigging correctly it would have been helpful to mount the picture on a stretcher, which would have been difficult to accommodate in a confined space. Of course it is possible that only the smaller ones were made at sea, and that some of the surviving examples were made by retired sailors, or during spells ashore. We have very little evidence about the conditions in which they were worked, but one interesting reference is Elizabeth Linklater's description of a voyage round the Horn as a child in 1890, in the *Orpheus*:

> *One might think that in such a small community nothing could happen to amuse us, yet there was always some joke to be told, something new to be shown in the way of models of ships, or ships in bottles, or pictures sewn in wool. The steward, for instance, presented mother with one of the most remarkable pieces of work I have ever seen: a representation of the* Orpheus, *sewn in thick wool on a piece of white duck. The woollen sea was a bright green and the sky an equally bright blue.*[15]

This reference to the *Orpheus* is also of interest because not many examples depict merchant vessels. Woolwork pictures do not appear before the 1850s, but thereafter there are many good examples of sailing warships, later steam and sail vessels, and even ironclads. Surprisingly, the tradition of working wool pictures continued into the present century, and evidently boys were still being encouraged to learn the craft in 1901 when the Rev. G Goodenough RN wrote of the Royal Hospital School at Greenwich:

> *Going into these reading-rooms one finds some boys reading stories, some studying their seamanship or signal books, others doing woolwork, which consists in working designs (chiefly combinations of flags or pictures of ships) in bright-coloured wools on canvas stretched on a frame, and is a very favourite pastime.*[16]

Public interest in sailors' woolwork was already evident in the early years of this century, when at least three exhibitions featured good collections of the work. In 1927 Flemings, antique dealers of Southsea, lent fifty such pictures for display in London in aid of disabled sailors and soldiers.

A number of makers' names are known, and they developed distinct and recognisable styles, especially different treatments of the sky and sea. At Greenwich there is a series of four wool pictures by Charles Weeden, whose background is unknown. All show two-decked warships dressed overall, with a small two-funnelled paddle steamer in the foreground, and a sky worked in unusually bold zigzags. Another, by an unknown maker, depicts HMS *Warrior*, the first iron warship, built at Blackwall in 1860 (colour plate 107). She is wearing the red ensign, which dates the picture before 1864. At this date the squadronal system was abandoned and, instead of wearing red, white or blue ensigns according to their squadron, all Royal Navy ships adopted the white ensign. The ship portrait is framed within a surround of flags and flowers, and has the Order of the Bath motto, *Tria Iuncta in Uno,* below.

Another well-embroidered picture shows a 28-gun frigate of *c*1850 surrounded by national flags. It was made by William Brookman RN, who joined the Navy in 1871, and is believed to have worked the picture as a trainee on board HMS *Implacable.* Like many of the pictures, this one is still in its original maple frame.

There are some interesting pictures which incorporate a photograph of the sailor or his family into the design, and others which include an actual cap tally. In 1893, while serving as a rating aboard HMS *Warspite* in the Pacific, Alfred Allen worked a wool picture incorporating flags of all nations, anchors, a crown, a photograph frame enclosing a photograph of a young seaman at the ship's wheel, and the legends *Forget me not* and *Remember me.* He also worked another, of his ship, HMS *Warspite.* The flag design as a decorative border to a photograph or woolwork ship was typical of sailors' work at this period, and these seem to owe something to the design of the professional silkwork pictures purchased as souvenirs in the East.

Sometimes it is possible to identify a historical event, and some of the most decorative examples include a number of ships dressed overall at a Fleet Review. One picture in a private collection shows fourteen vessels of various sizes at the Spithead Review of 1856 after the Crimean War, with a row of small gunboats along the bottom edge. Pictures of merchant ships are unusual, but there is even the occasional fishing vessel. At Greenwich there is a rare wool picture of the *Great Eastern*, Brunel's great paddle steamer, worked in 1858 by James Collins, who served in the ship as an engineer. Another, by Henry Robert Fisher, shows a Lowestoft sailing trawler, the *Forget me Not*, easily identifiable by her name pennant and the number *LT30* on her mainsail. This fishing vessel last appears in Olsen's *Fisherman's Almanac* in 1909. Rarest of all is the scene of home, and perhaps a sailor taking his leave or returning to his sweetheart. In the main, sailors' woolwork pictures seem to be worked from the imagination, rather than being copied from other illustrative sources. Their direct and personal feeling and their colourful, attractive design give such pictures as much appeal today as they had for the people for whom they were made.

Ropework, which started as a necessary everyday skill employed by the sailor, also became an ornamental craft. Utilitarian objects like bell ropes were elaborated into items of beauty to display the skill of the maker, and simple objects, like the rope sea chest handles called *beckets*, were fashioned from ornamental ropework, and often painted or varnished to make them more attractive. Other fancy work like macramé (which in recent years has enjoyed a revival among handicraft enthusiasts) was used by seamen to decorate items like hanging wall pockets to hold personal possessions. Elizabeth Linklater again recalled from her early years in the 1890s:

> *I was very proud when I was asked to make a macramé mast-coat to go round the part of the mast nearest to the deck. The old mast-coat was made of canvas partly teased out to make a fringe, and this was the usual finish used on all ships. But I wonder if any other ship but the Orpheus ever attained the glory of being decorated with macramé lace?*[17]

Sailors in the merchant service also frequently decorated their sea chests with paintings. The recent interest in folk art has resulted in fake painted chests, purporting to be by seamen, coming onto the market, but these are generally painted on the exterior to increase their decorative effect. Such paintings would never have survived the wear and tear of a sea voyage, and the genuine chests are usually painted only on the inside of the lid, where the work would be protected from damp and damage. They usually date from the last third of the nineteenth century, and the subject is often a broadside view of the seaman's own ship. Sometimes this is elaborated with signal flags, a shipping company house flag, or references to home. One example has a painting of a sailor and a girl on either side of a ship under sail, and the inscriptions *Homeward Bound* and *Welcome Home.*

At the end of his sea career a sailor might well become an In-Pensioner of Greenwich Hospital, the naval equivalent of Chelsea Royal Hospital.[18] The first Pensioners entered the Hospital in 1705, and the last left in 1869. The colourful lives previously led by these seamen, and their obvious battle scars, made them a popular subject for books, prints and pottery. Amputations were not

108 Greenwich Pensioners. Left: Staffordshire earthenware figure. Centre: creamware jug with Greenwich Pensioners and a Dibdin verse. Right: creamware mug with view of Greenwich Hospital from the Isle of Dogs.

unusual, and artists of the eighteenth and nineteenth centuries were not in the least squeamish about depicting the Pensioners with wooden legs, hand hooks and eye patches. A drawing in an early nineteenth century General Register of Greenwich Hospital shows a Pensioner with two wooden legs and an eye patch, contentedly smoking his pipe.[19] A transfer-printed creamware jug has a scene of two Greenwich Pensioners drinking and smoking outside an inn in sight of Greenwich Hospital (plate 108). One has a wooden leg and the other a hook for a hand, and the four verses of Charles Dibdin's song *The Greenwich Pensioner* are printed beneath. The third verse runs:

Next in a frigate sailing,
Upon a squally night,
Thunder and lightning hailing
The horrors of the fight,
My precious limb was lopp'd off;–
I, when they'd eas'd my pain,
Thank'd God I was not popp'd off,
But went to sea again.[20]

The transfer is taken from a coloured mezzotint (plate 109), and the original grey monochrome watercolour painted by Isaac Cruikshank, father of George Cruikshank, is in the local history collection at Woodlands Art Gallery, Blackheath.

There are also examples of a circular wooden snuff box decorated on the lid with a relief design of two wounded Pensioners talking animatedly over their ale and clay pipes. The illustration is taken from Robert Dighton's print, *Descriptions of Battles by Sea and Land*, published in March 1801. Popular interest in the subject persisted well into the nineteenth century, when Staffordshire earthenware groups of Greenwich Pensioners were still being produced (plate 108).

The buildings of the Royal Hospital for Seamen at Greenwich (founded in 1694 and built to the design of Sir Christopher Wren) feature on a number of printed mugs and jugs. A creamware mug of the 1790s (plate 108) is printed in black with a view of the Hospital from the Isle of Dogs on the opposite bank of the Thames, and the inscription:

Greenwich Hospital
Where seamen prattle o'er their former wars
And proudly shew their wooden legs and scars.

The view is adapted from an engraving by W & J Walker after a drawing by F Nicholson, published in 1792. The length of the engraving has been reduced to fit it into an oval surround on the mug, and another version on a jug in the Willett Collection in Brighton has a ship in place of the tree on

109 Mezzotint after a watercolour of Greenwich Pensioners by Isaac Cruikshank.

the left. The same view of Greenwich Hospital appears later on a brown transfer-printed jug of *c*1825 with the whole body decorated with a design which retains all the features of the Walker engraving.

Another jug, transfer-printed in blue and with a handpainted inscription *Joseph Little Wootten Basset 1826*, includes two views of the Hospital. One is the classic view from the Isle of Dogs; the other is a view from Greenwich Park, with cows in the foreground. It made a strangely peaceful setting for the last days of the sailor veterans, who, having survived bloody sea fights and storms at sea, could reflect, as Dibdin ended his song *The Greenwich Pensioner*:

Yet still am I enabled
To bring up in life's rear
Although I am disabled
And lie in Greenwich tier;
The king, God bless his royalty,
Who saved me from the main,
I'll praise with love and loyalty,
But ne'er to sea again.[21]

NOTES

1 *London Chronicle or Universal Evening Post* (18th March 1762) Vol XI no. 816 p263

2 Illustrated in Arthur Lane: *English Porcelain Figures of the 18th Century* (1961) plate 40. Ex Knoblock Collection.

3 This figure, sometimes catalogued as Tom Bowling, can be seen in Elizabeth Adams and David Redstone: *Bow Porcelain* (1981). Another slightly later version on a four-footed rococo scroll base is also known.

4 Jonas Hanway: *A Letter from a Member of the Marine Society* 4th edn (1757) and *Three Letters on the Subject of the Marine Society* (1758)

5 Reproduced in P D Gordon Pugh: *Naval Ceramics* (1971) plate 72

6 Queen Victoria: 'Journal written on board the *Victoria and Albert*, off St Helier's, Jersey' (Wednesday 2nd September 1846) quoted in Arthur Helps (ed.): *Leaves from the Journal of our Life in the Highlands 1848 to 1861 with additional extracts from the Queen's journal* (1868)

7 *Illustrated London News* (14th October 1848)

8 Ibid. (21st October 1882)

9 Ibid. (27th July 1895)

10 Patent nos 10774 and 12801 (Fulton's Military Handkerchief) and Fulton-Airey Patent no. 20771 (Naval Handkerchief). I am grateful to Ray Allen of the Imperial War Museum for the information on the military versions.

11 T Dibdin (ed.) *Songs of the Late Charles Dibdin* (1841) p1. The frontispiece is George Cruikshank's engraving of *Poor Jack*.

12 John Gay: *Poems and Fables* Vol II (1773)

13 See variation of verses in Lady Anne Lindsay: *Auld Robin Gray: A Ballad* (1825)

14 S M Riley (ed.) *A Trip to the Antipodes* (National Maritime Museum Monograph no. 45, 1980)

15 Elizabeth Linklater: *A Child Under Sail* (1949) pp217–18

16 Rev. G Goodenough RN: *The Handy Man Afloat and Ashore* (1901) p19

17 Elizabeth Linklater: op. cit. p168

18 A number of out-pensions were also granted to men not resident in the Hospital.

19 Public Record Office: ADM 6/322

20 T Dibdin: op. cit. p31

21 Ibid. p32

CHAPTER 5 Voyaging

The early voyages of discovery were marked by the production of engravings and the publication of illustrated journals, but seem to have been little celebrated in the popular decorative arts. In later periods some of the great explorers were commemorated in works of art by those who had the money to commission them, but little seems to have been produced for general sale.

A silver medallion map of the world by Michael Mercator of London commemorated Sir Francis Drake's (*c*1541–1596) voyage round the world in the *Golden Hind* 1577–80. Only nine of these medallions are known. The two sides of the thin circular silver plates are engraved with the eastern and western hemispheres showing Drake's course. Some important pieces of silver and sculpture were produced, including a terracotta bust of Sir Walter Ralegh (1552–1618), modelled in 1757 by the eminent sculptor John Michael Rysbrack from an engraving after an earlier painting of Ralegh with his son. This is one of a series of busts of notable figures made for Sir Edward Littleton. Ralegh is shown in a feathered hat, ruff and embroidered doublet (plate 110), and is a pair with a bust of Sir Francis Bacon (1561–1626). In a letter to his patron of 31st July 1756, Rysbrack wrote: *When I can possibly have an opportunity to begin the head of Sir Walter Raleigh I will take it in hand, but it is one of the most difficult in your whole list to make it do well.*[1]

Captain James Cook's (1728–1779) circumnavigational exploits were little celebrated in the decorative arts at the time of his voyages, apart from medallions and sculptures, but there are a few commemorative items at Greenwich, mostly from a later period, which celebrate the great explorer. On loan to the Museum is a pair of silver-gilt wine coasters by Paul Storr which commemorate Cook's voyages. Hallmarked 1800, the coasters are engraved inside with two world maps marking Cook's track. Outside are the twelve signs of the zodiac.

110 Terracotta bust of Sir Walter Ralegh, by John Michael Rysbrack, 1757.

Among the pieces of silver with a more direct Cook connection is a pair of candlesticks by John Parsons and Co. of Sheffield. The candlesticks have pedestal stems of square section, and stand on square moulded bases. The base is engraved with Captain Cook's crest: a raised arm holding a Union Flag. The crest is posthumous, however. Cook was killed in 1779 and the coat of arms was only granted to his family in 1785. The silver bears the hallmarks for 1784, and the provenance of the candlesticks and various other Cook relics can be traced back as far as Cook's widow, who outlived him by some fifty-six years.

Some ceramic items have also been produced in commemoration of Cook's voyages. There were two Wedgwood portrait medallions attributed to John Flaxman in 1779 and 1784. The first shows the subject facing half-front with his uniform coat open. This is taken from the engraving by J Basire after the portrait by William Hodges, which appeared as the frontispiece to James Cook's *Voyage towards the South Pole 1772–5*, published in 1777. Another portrait plaque of Cook was produced by Tassie after the painting by Nathaniel Dance. The subject must have proved popular, because in 1784 John Flaxman modelled another Cook portrait for Wedgwood, which again was issued as an oval jasper relief medallion. This version, which shows Cook in profile wearing his hair tied behind in a ribbon, was reissued by Wedgwood in the 1960s to commemorate the bicentenary of the voyages. This portrait, reversed, has much in common with the profile on the Royal Society medal of 1784 by Lewis Pingo.

In the mid-nineteenth century Cook was still attracting sufficient popular interest to be the subject of a Staffordshire earthenware figure (colour plate 111). Cook is shown seated in a chair with his right arm resting on a table, after the portrait of 1776 by Nathaniel Dance. Like the portrait, the figure is shown with some of his waistcoat buttons undone. More recently, in 1970 Royal Doulton produced a limited edition black basalt loving cup to commemorate the bicentenary of Cook's landing in Australia. In the last thirty years other ceramic souvenirs have commemorated the voyage to India in 1497 of Vasco da Gama (1469–1525), the sailing of the *Mayflower* in 1620, the birth of Matthew Flinders (1774–1814), and the departure of the First Fleet to Australia in 1787.

112 (right) 18th century Chinese porcelain plate painted with Dutch ships in Table Bay.

113 (below) Dutch tile picture with a whaling scene and the arms of the Dutch town of de Rijp.

Trade and voyages to the Orient are also reflected in the decorative arts of the eighteenth century. We have already seen how Chinese artists used European sources for decoration on ceramics intended for export. Both the shipbuilding bowl illustrated at the beginning of chapter 1 and the porcelain bowls commemorating the Battle of the Saints in 1782 are of this type. Other Chinese export pieces of the period were evidently intended for specific foreign markets. The collection at Greenwich includes an eighteenth century Chinese porcelain plate, painted in *famille rose* style, with a scene of Dutch merchant ships at anchor in Table Bay, Cape Town (plate 112). Coloured Dutch flags are shown on every mast as well as on shore, and there is an intricate black and gold border pattern. A number of very similar examples of this design are known, reflecting the importance of Cape Town in trade to the East.

Visitors to the East have always brought back exotic souvenirs. Among the earliest of these is a miniature Chinese garden at Greenwich said to have been given to Commodore Anson during his visit to the Canton River on his voyage round the world in 1740–44. The garden, mounted on a block of malachite on a rosewood and mother-of-pearl stand, is composed of trees made from coral, ivory and mother-of-pearl, with rocks of malachite and rose quartz, and ivory cranes, each element being symbolic.

Another early Oriental souvenir is the Chinese *ko'ssu* depicting the arrival of the Embassy from George III led by Lord George Macartney (1737–1806) at the Summer Palace of the Emperor of China in Peking. *Ko'ssu* means *cut silk*, and this silk tapestry picture shows the King's gift of large astronomical instruments arriving in Peking in September 1793. In fact, the designer of the picture has shown two items which had arrived earlier than Macartney's Embassy: the celestial globe of Ferdinand Verbiest of 1673 and a large armillary sundial, both from the Jesuit Observatory at Peking, rather than the astronomical planetarium and celestial globe actually delivered in 1793. He has also depicted the Europeans in sixteenth century costume.

In another direction, the English had been making whaling voyages to Nova Scotia since the late sixteenth century, and by the early seventeenth century they and the Dutch had become serious rivals at Spitzbergen. The Dutch became pre-eminent until the American whaling industry emerged, and English whaling did not revive until the early eighteenth century.

It is not common to find whaling subjects on items of decorative art other than those made by the whalemen themselves. However, there are a few fine exceptions to this rule, including a large late seventeenth century Dutch tile picture (plate 113). The tiles, set within a decorative blue tiled border are painted with a detailed whaling scene with whaleships in the ice, manned boats, two whales in the foreground and another alongside a ship. In the corner is the coat of arms of the small Dutch town of de Rijp, a shield with two crowned fish and lion supporters.

A later whaling memento, also at Greenwich, is a Leeds creamware teapot of *c*1776 (colour plate 114). The cylindrical body has double twist handles with flower and leaf terminals, a curved reeded spout and a floral knop on the lid. A three-masted whaleship with red ensign and jack is painted in colour on one side and there are three of the ships' boats in the water. On the other side is a coat of arms. Above the ship appears the name *Polar Star*, a vessel which was built in 1759 and appears in *Lloyd's Register* for only one year, 1775. In that year she was bound from Liverpool to Greenland, evidently on a whaling voyage, and her master was T Wilson. The Liverpool Museum also has a porcelain bowl painted in blue, with a ship, whaleboats and whales in the foreground, and inscribed *Success to the Polar Star Capt. Thos. Willson.*

The most specialised of the seamen's crafts was the *scrimshaw* produced by men on the whaleships from the by-products of their trade. Much has been written about the possible origins of the word, which also occurs as a family name, but basically scrimshaw was the decorating or carving of whalebone, whale teeth and baleen. The inscribed decoration might be the sailor's own ship, a scene inspired by a recent successful whalehunt, or motifs nostalgic of home. Sometimes old magazine engravings were copied, so that a fashion plate might appear incongruously on the reverse of a bloody whalehunting scene.

Times have changed people's attitudes and conceptions of our environment, and today few would encourage the decorative use of whale products, or regard an engraved tooth as a beautiful object to present to a loved one. But in the nineteenth century, when whale and hunter were more evenly matched than modern whaling methods allow, and the vulnerable whaleboats could be easily smashed and men lost in the hand-to-hand encounters, it was less surprising that whalemen should want to celebrate their part in the enterprise. To men of the time a captured whale represented a successful commercial operation to obtain the much-needed oil and other raw materials at considerable personal risk. Baleen was an important product of the whaling industry, being used for umbrellas, stay busks, bristle brushes, combs and sieves, while whalebone was used for a variety of useful and decorative items from fids (large tapered pins used for splicing rope) and belaying pins to necklets, teethers and napkin rings.

There are some good English examples of scrimshaw work, especially by men of the Hull whalers, but the majority of scrimshaw was made by American sailors, who were pre-eminent in the South Sea whale fisheries. Herman Melville's frequently quoted description in his classic whaling novel, *Moby-Dick*, first published in 1851, is worth repeating:

> *Throughout the Pacific, and also in Nantucket, and New Bedford, and Sag Harbor, you will come across lively sketches of whales and whaling scenes, graven by the fishermen themselves on Sperm whale-teeth, or ladies' busks wrought out of the Right Whale-bone, and other like scrimshander articles, as the whalemen call the numerous little ingenious contrivances they elaborately carve out of the rough material, in their hours of ocean leisure. Some of them have little boxes of dentistical-looking implements, specially intended for the scrimshandering business. But, in general, they toil with their jack-knives alone, and with that almost omnipotent tool of the sailor, they will turn you out anything you please, in the way of a mariner's fancy.*[2]

115 Scrimshawed whalebone stay busk with motifs reminding the whaleman of home. The other side is decorated with a whaling scene.

Often the whalemen carved or inscribed whalebone as a form of love token to be taken home to present to wives and lovers. The scrimshawed stay busk carved on a narrow strip of whalebone or baleen for the loved one to wear as a stiffener in a corset was perhaps the most intimate of these gifts. The motifs on one example at Greenwich include ships, a church, castle, black swan and cottage, with a heart and arrows and initials *AML* in the centre (plate 115), and on the other side a whaling scene with four whaleboats and captured whales. A very similar version can be seen in the Town Docks Museum in Hull.

Most popular of all were the decorated whalebone panels and sperm whale teeth. The teeth were naturally ribbed and needed careful rubbing down and polishing before they could be incised with a sharp knife or awl, and the resulting design clearly defined with lamp-black, ink, or occasionally a little colour. One fine example in the National Maritime Museum's collection is a large tooth engraved on one side with a young sailor climbing the ship's rigging (colour plate 116), and on the other side a theatrical portrait of the actress Eliza O'Neill (1791–1872) in the character of Belvidera. *The Sailor Boy* is accompanied by a Byron quotation:

> *Though the strained mast should quiver as a reed*
> *And the rent canvas fluttering strew the gale,*
> *Still must I on.*[3]

The illustration of the sailor boy, complete with ship cartouche from the 1839 frontispiece of *Shipwrecks and Disasters at Sea,* compiled by Charles Ellms, was first published in Philadelphia in 1836. The book was republished at least as late as 1860, and a very similar unsigned oil portrait is in the museum at Mystic Seaport, Connecticut, as well as another very close scrimshaw version on a whale's tooth.

Decorated whalebone panels were made from the lower jaw of the whale (plate 117). Sometimes they had an engraved border like a frame, and were often drilled with holes for suspension and generally decorated with scenes of the whalehunt. Unless there is an inscription, or some documentation exists, it is not usually possible to identify the ship represented or date the piece precisely. Very few whalemen signed their pieces, and even dates and ship names are rare. One tooth at Greenwich has a view on both sides relating to the same named ship. On one side is *Crew of the Japan killing a large Whale,* and on the other *Ship Japan cutting a large Whale.* This vessel, of 359 tons, built on the Thames and registered in London, is listed in *Lloyd's Register* for 1831 as being bound for the Southern Oceans. Another sperm whale tooth illustrates a damaged vessel reefed down in stormy seas, with the inscription *Ship Pacific off the Cape of Good Hope*, and on the other side the vessel is shown in calm seas under full sail.

Sometimes the subject of the engraving would be more domestic. One tooth in the Museum has a view of Reculver Church in Kent on one side and a farmyard scene on the other. Another has a sailor and lass in a farewell scene beneath a figure of Britannia. In recent years, with the increase in value of the original sailor-made pieces, there has been a deluge of fake scrimshaw onto the market. Some are easily-recognised pieces, mass-produced in resin, but other examples – where genuine old teeth have been enhanced by the addition of recent engraving – are more difficult to detect.

Carved whalebone objects made by the whalemen were sometimes more useful than ornamental. Homely items, such as pastry crimpers, knitting sheaths, and swifters for winding yarn, made suitable gifts. A more unusual memento of a whaling voyage is a garden seat made from whale ribs and vertebrae which is displayed at Hull Maritime Museum. Fids were sometimes carved from a suitable piece of whalebone. Presumably these were for the sailor's own use, as were the seam rubbers used to flatten the seams of canvas sails, which were often carved with initials, patterns or turk's head finials. Walking sticks were also popular items, sometimes being wooden sticks with carved whalebone handles, often shaped as elaborate turk's head knots. Other walking sticks were made from sharks' vertebrae, as described by John Youngs, chief engine room artificer of HMS *Goldfinch*, who wrote in his diary on 22nd September 1891:

117 Scrimshaw-decorated whales' teeth, pan-bone panel, stay busk and model whale.

Caught a shark after trying for a long time. It measured 7'6" long it was only a young one and had but one row of teeth. I have the back bone and am going to make a stick of it with a Whales tooth for a handle.[4]

Whalemen frequently brought back native work from the Arctic which they had obtained by bartering with tobacco, clothing or knives. Many such souvenirs – including model kayaks, a model bone igloo, animals and toys – were brought back by Hull whalers and are now in the Hull Maritime Museum. In the collection at Greenwich is a walrus tusk carved as a cribbage board which is almost certainly Inuit work. The base is carved with a map of the coastline from Cape Prince of Wales to St Michael, Alaska, with place names inscribed. The top surface, where the cribbage board is carved, also has a central line of three seals, a polar bear and a walrus head carved in relief.

The Arctic voyages of the nineteenth century created considerable public interest, and some of the explorers were handsomely rewarded for their discoveries. In 1984 a gold, silver and oak Freedom box presented to Captain W Edward Parry (1790–1855) by the City of Bath in 1821 was sold.[5] The honour marked his discoveries in the Arctic and his attempts to navigate the North-West Passage. The lid had a gold plaque with a scene of Parry's ships, *Hecla* and *Griper,* in the ice, and the box was made from the wood of the *Hecla.* Parry made four Arctic expeditions in the *Hecla,* and in 1827 got to within 453 miles of the North Pole.

On 27th August 1838 Captain Sir George Back RN (1796–1878) was presented with a silver Freedom box by a Birmingham maker, hallmarked 1836–7. The box, now at Greenwich, has a design on the lid depicting in relief a country house scene – evidently a stock piece rather than a special commission, as the design carries no reference to the recipient of the presentation. However, the inscription on the base reveals the reason for the gift:

Presented by the Master Pilots and Seamen of the Trinity House of Newcastle upon Tyne with the Freedom of their Corporation inclosed, to Captain Sir George Back RN as a testimony of their high approbation of the persevering and successful efforts in the cause of science and humanity displayed by him in the Polar Seas, 27 August 1838.

Back had earlier sailed with Sir John Franklin (1786–1847) and survived near-starvation on the Coppermine River expedition of 1819–22. In 1833 he led the Royal Geographical Society's expedition in relief of Captain Ross and, when news of Ross's arrival in England came through, he continued his expedition with a survey of the course of the Great Fish River. He survived a subsequent hazardous voyage to map the coastline further, and on his return received a knighthood, as well as the Royal Geographical Society's medals and a service of plate from the subscribers to the Arctic Land Expedition.

But perhaps the most famous Arctic explorer of the nineteenth century was Franklin, whose expedition of 1845 to navigate the North-West Passage, with his ships *Erebus* and *Terror*, ended in tragedy. He had already achieved fame for his Polar voyages, and was knighted in 1829. During the same year David d'Angers (1789–1856) sculpted a circular portrait plaque. The bronze relief profile of Franklin carries the inscription *Captain Franklin RN,* and is signed *David 1829.* Wax and plaster versions of this plaque are also known. A bronze bust was produced by A C Lecchesi, showing him wearing a fur coat over naval uniform, with the badge of the Royal Hanoverian Guelphic Order which he received in 1836. This badge, found later in the Arctic with other relics of the expedition, is now at Greenwich.

The *Erebus* and *Terror* overwintered in the Arctic at Beechey Island in 1845–6, and Franklin died in 1847. The crews were obliged to abandon ship in 1848 when they were beset in heavy ice, and tried to get back by way of the Great Fish River, but all perished. His wife, Lady Jane Franklin, refused to give up hope until the fate of her husband's expedition had been resolved. When the many official search expeditions ceased, a public subscription financed Captain Leopold McClintock's voyage in the *Fox,* 1857–9. This attempt recovered the last record of Franklin's expedition and many other relics which at last solved the mystery of his death.

Sir John and Lady Franklin were popularly commemorated by a pair of Staffordshire earthenware figures produced *c*1848 (at this period Franklin's fate was still unknown). He stands in naval uniform, holding a telescope, and the matching Lady Franklin wears a wreath of flowers in her hair (colour plate 118).

Arctic voyages of the early years of the

119 Dish from earthenware *Arctic Scenery* dinner service *c*1840. The Arctic scenes are derived from engravings in early 19th century published journals.

nineteenth century were brought to the public's notice through well-illustrated printed journals. Such engravings were also the inspiration for an interesting dinner service identified on the base as *Arctic Scenery* pattern. The designs on the various pieces of the service are taken from a number of published journals, sometimes incorporating elements from two or three different engravings in the same composite design. The National Maritime Museum has a good selection of the pieces in its collection. The service itself is earthenware, transfer-printed in blue, and dates from *c*1840. Although the main designs are taken from engravings of the Arctic, it is amusing that the border patterns are made up of tropical birds and beasts like lions, tigers, cheetahs and vultures, as well as European animals and panels of flowers.

It is worth examining in some detail the combinations of sources used in the design of the various pieces. The plates, for instance, are decorated with scenes of two ships overwintering in the ice, taken from an engraving by William Westall in W E Parry's *Journal of a Voyage for the Discovery of a N W Passage in HM Ships Hecla and Griper* (1821). In the foreground is a group of Inuit on a sledge being pulled by dogs, which is taken from an engraving by Edward Finden in W E Parry's *Journal of a 2nd Voyage in HM Ships Fury and Hecla* (1824).

The meat dishes of the service have a scene of Inuit dancing before a group of European sailors, with a ship in the ice in the background (plate 119). The Inuit are based on an engraving by Edward Finden, *Eskimaux children dancing, Igloolik 1823*, in Parry's *Journal* of 1824. The source of the sailors has not yet been identified, but they are somewhat inadequately dressed for the Arctic, so must be from some quite different source. The soup tureen has a scene of an Inuit family on each side, from an engraving by William Westall, *Esquimeaux of the inlet called the River Clyde, West Coast of Baffin's Bay,* in Parry's *Journal* of 1821. Ships and icebergs on the ends of the tureens are after another engraving from the same source. European animals in the border are after engravings by Thomas Bewick.

The sauce tureens, covers and stands have other Arctic views of a man fishing and two ships in the ice, and the stands have a canoeing scene on a lake. The scenes on the tureens are composite pictures based on two engravings in Parry's *Journal* of 1821. The canoeing scene on the stand is from an engraving by Edward Finden in Franklin's *Narrative of a Journey to the Shores of the Polar Sea* (1823) entitled *Expedition Crossing Lake Prosperous May 30, 1820.* The racoon, kangaroo and some of the other border animals are again from Thomas Bewick engravings.

Another scene on a tureen shows Europeans carrying a canoe and pulling small loads on sledges across a frozen lake, with icebergs in the background. The main scene is taken from an engraving by Edward Finden after a drawing by Lieutenant Back RN in Franklin's *Narrative* of 1823. The background has been changed from hills and cliffs to icebergs.

Although there are less commemorative pieces associated with the later Arctic voyages, some interesting relics have survived from the voyages themselves. Sir George Nares commanded the Arctic Expedition of 1875 in HMS *Discovery* and HMS *Alert.* Table services used on board these two ships were specially designed to incorporate the badge of the expedition: a motif of a polar bear within a garter inscribed *Arctic Expedition 1875.* All the pieces have an elaborate rope border design and the manufacturer's name, W T Copeland and Sons, printed on anchors beneath. The men used an earthenware service with separate sets printed in blue, black or brown, and another bone china set printed in black was presumably for the officers. On the base of each piece is printed the name of the ship in which it was used.

Similar services were made for use on later Polar expeditions. The *Discovery* Antarctic Expedition of 1901 had a service by Doulton of

Burslem. The simple design is a blue-printed motif of a penguin on an iceberg, within a garter inscribed *Discovery Antarctic Expedition 1901*, on a white ground, with blue borders and gold rims. In 1910 the British Antarctic Expedition had similar tableware by Dunn Bennet & Co. of Burslem, with a penguin on the South Pole region of the globe, inscribed *British Antarctic Expedition, Terra Nova RYS*. This was the expedition of 1910 led by Captain R F Scott (1868–1912), during which he and his companions died on their return from the South Pole in March 1912.

Another piece commemorating polar discovery is a silver statuette of a polar explorer hauling a sledge heavily laden with boxes, bags and various equipment, including a pair of skis (plate 120). This is mounted on a plinth made of *Discovery* oak which has a silver plaque inscribed: *Sir Clements Markham KCB FRS from the officers and men of the Discovery in commemoration of the Antarctic Expedition 1901–4.*

The geographer and explorer Sir Clements Robert Markham KCB (1830–1916) was chief sponsor of the *Discovery* expedition and the later *Morning* relief voyage. His brother, the Arctic explorer Sir Albert H Markham, recorded the presentation of the statuette at a reception at the Royal Geographical Society on 7th November 1904, following *Discovery*'s return from the National Antarctic Expedition of 1901–4:

> *Prior to the meeting, on arriving at the Albert Hall, Markham was taken into a small room in which all the officers of the two ships were assembled, when to his intense surprise, Captain Scott, in a very touching speech, presented him, on behalf of the officers of the expedition, with a beautifully wrought silver centrepiece representing a sledge being drawn by a man in sledging costume. It was a token of their esteem for all that he had done to create and organise the expedition, and of their gratitude for the interest that he took in its welfare and all those who served in it. He was quite taken aback at this wholly unexpected tribute of appreciation from the officers, and found it difficult to find words that would give appropriate expression to his feelings. It was a gift that in after-years he always valued as one of his most precious possessions.*[6]

The recipient recorded in his own diary not only the presentation but the fact that he was later photographed with the statuette. It also appears in

120 Silver statuette of a polar explorer presented to Sir Clements Markham in 1904.

the oil portrait of Markham by George Henry which hangs in the Royal Geographical Society, and is embossed in gold on the binding of the biography written in 1917 by his brother.

The nineteenth century was also the great age of passenger sea travel. In chapter 3 we saw some of the gifts of silver plate given to naval officers to mark heroism in battle. Silver cups and other items were also favourite presentation pieces to merchant ship captains following a successful voyage. Some of these gifts were given by the owners or Underwriters, and others by grateful passengers. A silver claret jug by Edward, John and William Barnard of London was presented to John Millar in 1832. The jug is decorated with fruiting vines, and the only maritime motif is a seashell knop on the lid. The body is inscribed: *Presented to Captain John Millar of the Brig Cherub by the Merchants of Quebec & Montreal: In testimony of their approbation of his successful attempt to perform in one season Three voyages from Greenock to Quebec 1831*. The jug was acquired with an oil painting of the brig *Cherub*. John Millar (1807–1884) later became harbour master at Greenock. A newspaper obituary referred particularly to his three Canadian voyages of 1831:

> *When it is remembered there were no steam tugs to assist sailing vessels at that time, the feat was a marvellous one. While in the Canadian trade, Captain Millar was recognised as as being one of the most efficient masters sailing out of the Clyde. His vessels were very popular with passengers, and frequently he carried out and home the Governors of Canada and their families.*

In the same year the editor of the newly-founded *Nautical Magazine* noted in his Nautical Miscellany column:

It is with great pleasure that we observe the commanders of our Quebec traders vying with each other in gaining the estimation of their passengers by that generous attention which characterises the British sailor. Mr J A Sharman, commanding the brig Venus, and Mr P Murphy, commanding the brig Recovery, have received letters expressive of the warmest thanks from their passengers; And Mr James Greig, commanding the ship Caroline, in addition to a similar letter, has been presented with a handsome silver cup, with the following inscription on it:– To James Greig, Esq. this is presented, as a memento of regard by his passengers, for his kind, liberal, and disinterested attention to them during their happy voyage to Quebec, on board the Caroline, in 1832. A cup of sufficient value could not be had at Quebec, and measures were taken for obtaining it in London.[7]

The early transatlantic steamships are commemorated in an interesting dinner service by James & Thomas Edwards of Kiln Croft Works, Burslem. The Boston Mail Series dates from 1841, and the pieces are printed with rare interior views of the first four Cunard ships: *Britannia, Columbia, Acadia* and *Caledonia.* Views include the Gentlemen's Cabin, Ladies' Cabin and Saloon. On 4th July 1840 *Britannia*, first ship of the Cunard Line, left Liverpool, and arrived in Boston two weeks later. The china services used on board were printed in four colours, black on a plain white ground, and brown, blue and lavender with decorative borders showing the four Cunard ships. Examples of each type are displayed at the Merseyside Maritime Museum, but the service is not yet represented at Greenwich.

Isambard Kingdom Brunel's (1806–1859) steamships the *Great Eastern* and *Great Britain,* are commemorated in specially-designed table services for use on board. The *Great Britain,* launched in 1843, later had a service from J Stonier of Liverpool. There are pieces of this service both at Bristol – where the ship was built and is now displayed as a museum ship – and at Greenwich. The National Maritime Museum has an ironstone soup plate and a pair of water carafes transfer-printed in blue with a distinctive knotted rope border design and the Victorian Royal coat of arms in the centre (plate 121). Above the arms is *Steam Ship Great Britain,* and the plate and one carafe also have *Saloon* below the coat of arms.

At Greenwich there is also a single plate for the *Great Eastern,* the third of Brunel's great ships, launched in 1858 (plate 121). It is printed in sepia with a small central motif of the *Great Eastern* at sea, with Britannia seated in the foreground with her lion, all within laurel sprays. The border is printed in yellow with stud-link chain cable, and the back of the plate is impressed *Great Ship Company Limited,* a company which was founded in 1858 and liquidated in 1863. The maker's mark for W H Kerr Binns & Co. of the Royal Porcelain Works, Worcester, is marked on the base. The Merseyside Maritime Museum has a *Great Eastern* meat dish of similar pattern, printed in blue. In the same museum there are a number of other mementoes of the ship, including a lustreware wall plaque and a printed cotton handkerchief with a picture of the *Great Eastern* as Lewis's Exhibition Ship in Liverpool in 1886. Sunderland Museum has a purple lustre bowl of about 1860 by Scotts Southwick Pottery, with a transfer of the *Great Eastern* overpainted in enamel colours.

Brunel's ships are also commemorated by carvings on nautilus shells. A number of these are known with overall decoration in slightly varying designs. One has the *Great Britain* and *Great Western* on one side (colour plate 122) and an extensive inscription giving details of the launch of the vessels and their dimensions, ending:

The whole of the embellishments on this beautiful NAUTILUS shell have been executed with nothing more than a common penknife and is a facsimile of the one generously accepted by her Majesty Queen Victoria Jany 1845.

The little Nautilus with purple pride
Expands its radiant wings
And dances o'er the tide.

Presented as a token of respect to — C H Wood.

121 Ironstone plate and carafe, marked J Stonier of Liverpool, for the SS *Great Britain*, and a Worcester porcelain plate for the SS *Great Eastern.*

C H Wood of High Street, Poplar, is known as a carver of shell and horn who produced many copies of the same design on nautilus and other shells, and is known to have sold examples on board the *Great Eastern* when she was at New York on her maiden voyage in 1860.[8]

The *Great Britain Times* of 4th November 1865 printed on board reported:

> *Sale by Auction. One of the passengers of gigantic stature, on Thursday last mounted the rostrum, and in stentorial tone, and seemingly professional ability, succeeded in disposing to the passengers some very handsome 'shells of the ocean' richly engraved with the figure of the Great Britain in full sail. There is no doubt many such little articles could thus be profitably and judiciously disposed of, to such persons as have neglected bringing with them some of the curiosities of Australia.*[9]

The *Great Eastern* also appears on engraved shells, usually on green turban shells, rather than the nautilus. On one example at Greenwich the outer surface is polished over three-quarters of its surface to reveal the mother-of-pearl, and in the polished area is engraved a portrait of the *Great Eastern* under sail with her six masts and five funnels (colour plate 122). The shell is inscribed *Steam Ship Leviathan. Designed by I K Brunel Esqr FRS.* and the dimensions of the ship. *Leviathan* was the original name of the *Great Eastern* during building, which was changed before launching. Another green turban shell in the collection has similar details but is inscribed *Great Eastern Steam Ship launched 31st Jan 1858.* A similar shell in a private collection is inscribed *Purchased on board the Great Eastern by — 15th Oct 1860.* This suggests that the buyer's name could be inserted after purchase.

Another nautilus shell is a dual-purpose commemorative for both the SS *Great Britain* and Nelson's victories. The shell is engraved with a view of the ship, a verse commemorating Nelson, and the inscription:

> *The Great Britain Iron Steam Ship. She is the largest ship in the world. She is built of iron and propelled by the screw instead of paddles.*
>
> *To the British Nation. This design represents Peace seated on the prow of a vessel pointing to the victories achieved by the immortal Nelson – Cape St Vincent, Mouth of the Nile, Copenhagen, Trafalgar.*

The engraving of nautilus shells as a craft was already well established by this time. The catalogue of Sir Ashton Lever's Museum, published in 1790 after the move from Leicester House to Blackfriars Road, describes *the great nautilus of Asia, ornamented with a Spanish coat of arms and other devices.* Another later nautilus shell at Greenwich is engraved with St George and the dragon, Britannia and the British lion, again commemorating Lord Nelson's victories. This example is mounted on a gilt twig stand and, according to the inscription, is the counterpart of the one exhibited in Class 30 of the Great Exhibition of 1851.

A major silver-gilt and silver dinner service was presented to Thomas Henry Ismay, founder and chairman of the White Star Line, by the shareholders of the company in 1885. The service, which for many years was on loan to the National Maritime Museum, is now in the Liverpool Museum. The large centrepiece is formed as a globe surmounted by a figure of Commerce, with figures of Jason, Columbus, Vasco da Gama and Captain Cook. Other pieces have emblematic figures of Navigation, figures of ancient navigators, a shipwright, an engineer, a captain and a seaman. There are also representations of the *Savannah* of 1818, first steamship to cross the Atlantic Ocean, and a White Star liner of 1880. The wine ewers are chased with scenes from Coleridge's *Ancient Mariner,* and the candelabra are supported by albatrosses. The salts are made as various coracles, canoes and other small boats.

Twentieth century liners are also celebrated by souvenirs, but many of them of a more ephemeral type. They are as yet little-represented in the collections of the National Maritime Museum, but there are some important private collections of such material and it is well-represented at the Merseyside Maritime Museum. One of the few commemorative liner items at Greenwich is a Minton bone china plate printed in colour with a view of the Cunard liner *Lusitania* at sea passing Sandy Hook Buoy. The border is decorated with scrolling foliage in yellow, blue and pink, and the Cunard crest appears at the top. The plate probably dates from soon after her launch in 1906. SS *Lusitania* was lost by enemy action off the Old Head of Kinsale on 7th May 1915.

Among the other twentieth century liner items at Greenwich are some attractive jigsaw puzzles depicting the Cunard liner *Queen Mary,* after a print of the ship showing how she would fit into

Trafalgar Square, and the *Aquitania*'s internal arrangements. There are also examples of the china services used by liner passengers, but much of this tableware is disappointingly devoid of maritime motifs. There are some White Star Line pieces which are plain white except for the company house flag or a monogram, P & O Line plates with the line's rising sun crest, and Orient Line pieces with anchors, compass roses and seashells. One distinctive Wedgwood service produced in a purple, black and grey abstract pattern was designed for the Orient Line in the 1950s by the artist Edward Bawden, who also painted mural decorations for liners.

NOTES

1 Mrs Arundell Esdaile: *The Art of John Michael Rysbrack in Terracotta* (1932)

2 Herman Melville: *Moby-Dick; or, the Whale* (1851) p303

3 Byron: 'Childe Harolde's Pilgrimage' Canto 3, ii in E H Coleridge (ed.): *The Poetical Works of Lord Byron* (1858) p185

4 Information made available by the Lynn Museum, Norfolk Museum Service.

5 Sotheby's, New York (21st June 1984) Lot 178

6 Admiral Sir A H Markham: *Life of Sir Clements R Markham* (1917) p338

7 *Nautical Magazine* Vol I (1832) pp337–8

8 For more information on his work, see Stuart M Frank: *Dictionary of Scrimshaw Artists* (1991).

9 George Ritchie (ed.): *The Great Britain Times* (1866). Compiled from the weekly newspaper printed on board during the passage from Melbourne to Liverpool 21st October to 22nd December 1865.

CHAPTER 6 Disaster at Sea

The commemoration of disaster at sea in three-dimensional form has a long history, and there are many monuments in churches carved with graphic representations of shipwrecks. The manufacture of objects to commemorate delivery from a near-tragedy is also a longstanding tradition. Such items frequently have a religious connotation, and early votive ship models and other objects made by seafarers in thanksgiving for escaping death are to be seen in many seaport churches, especially on the Continent.

The commemoration of such *dangers averted* goes back at least to the time of the Spanish Armada, when many medals were struck to commemorate the delivery from near-defeat. Many of the medals were struck in precious metals, setting a standard for the type of presentation piece produced later. Some show the Spanish fleet dispersed and wrecked, with the legend *Flavit et Dissipati* (He blew and they were scattered). Others have a portrait of Queen Elizabeth on the obverse and an Ark or bay tree, uninjured amid storm and waves, on the reverse.

In the eighteenth century it was not unusual for the Underwriters to present a gift of plate to a ship's captain who had saved his vessel with its valuable cargo from some marine disaster. Such gifts are normally inscribed in elaborate praise of the deed, but the most interesting may also have an engraved view of the ship involved. In the collection of the National Maritime Museum is a silver punch bowl engraved with a quarter view of the two-masted vessel *Earl of Bute* (plate 123). The inscription on the other side reads: *This piece of plate was presented by the private Assurers of London to Captain William Fullerton as a reward for his good Conduct in preserving the Snow Earl of Bute near Dunkirk the 19th March 1767.* The gallon-capacity bowl is by Thomas Whipham and Charles Wright of London, and was hallmarked in the year of presentation. The *Earl of Bute*, 150 tons, was built at Bath, Maine, probably in 1762, and in her first years was employed by her Glasgow owners in the Virginia trade. *Lloyd's List* for 24th April 1767 refers to the arrival of the vessel in Dunkirk from the Clyde. We do not know the full story behind the presentation, but the *Earl of Bute* is registered until 1776, when she is last recorded as bound for Rotterdam.

123 Silver punch bowl presented to Captain Fullerton of the *Earl of Bute*. By T Whipham and C Wright, 1767.

Also in the collection is a fine silver set of a punch bowl (plate 124), salver and two goblets presented by the Underwriters of London, Glasgow, Greenock and Newcastle to Captain Milne: *in honour of his sufferings and exemplary perseverance in conducting the Brunswick in the most perilous state from Fayal to Lisbon, 1795.* The separate pieces are by different makers: Charles Aldridge, Henry Chawner and John Hudson, all London silversmiths. The goblets were

124 (above) Silver punch bowl from a wine set presented to the captain of the *Brunswick*. By Charles Aldridge, 1795.

125 (right) Detail of engraving on the *Brunswick* bowl showing the ensign flying upside down as a sign of distress.

made in 1787 and later engraved, while the other two pieces were evidently made soon after the event.

The perilous state of the vessel is vividly portrayed in an engraved scene on the side of the bowl which shows the ship plunging in rough seas with only her foremast remaining, and flying her ensign upside down (plate 125). This signal of distress can occasionally be seen in marine paintings of the period, but is most unusual on a piece of silver. The *Brunswick* was a ship of 624 tons, built at Greenock in 1791. *Lloyd's List* for 24th April 1795 records the *Brunswick* arriving at Fayal in the Azores with 13 feet of water in her hold, having sprung a leak at sea. Being unable to unload her or heave her down, Captain Milne had proceeded to Lisbon with additional hands, and eventually reached Portsmouth in October.

Other presentations of silver record near-tragedies which took place rather nearer home. One such example is an ornate silver cup by E Terry of London, 1830, inscribed:

> *Presented to Mr Fitzjames R N of the Euphrates Expedition by his friends in Liverpool. A token of their admiration of his gallant heroism in saving a drowning man in the River Mersey on Sunday 1st Feb 1835, at the imminent hazard of his own life.*

The cup, which stands on a stem composed of three sailor figures leaning on anchors, is chased overall with shell motifs, and is decorated on one side with Neptune's chariot and on the other with two sailing cutters (colour plate 126). The recipient of the presentation was James Fitzjames, who later perished on the Franklin Expedition which set out in search of the North-West Passage in 1845. His medal of the Royal National (Lifeboat) Institution and his Royal Humane Society Citation awarded for the same heroic act are also in the Museum's collection.

Transatlantic passengers in the nineteenth century also risked the hazards of the elements during the long crossing. Most of their terrifying experiences have gone unrecorded, although there are some vivid accounts in private journals. One rough crossing, which was immortalised by the leading writer of the day, was that of the British and North American Royal Mail (Cunard) Steamship *Britannia* in January 1842. Her voyage from Liverpool to Boston was described in some detail by Charles Dickens in his *American Notes*, first published in 1842. The captain of the *Britannia*, John Hewitt, successfully completed the voyage despite the passengers' worst fears. In gratitude a collection was arranged, and the passengers presented a silver wine set. Dickens was one of the committee, and made the presentation speech in the Tremont Theatre, Boston, on 29th January 1842. He declared in the course of the speech:

> *In presenting Captain Hewitt with these slight and frail memorials, we are not following out a hollow custom, but are imperfectly expressing the warmest and most earnest feelings, being well assured that, with God's blessing, we owe our safety and preservation, under circumstances of unusual peril, to his ability, courage and skill. You will please to understand that these tokens on the table are an acknowledgment, not in themselves, but in the feeling which dictates their presentation, of many long and weary nights of watching and fatigue; of great exertion of body and much anxiety of mind; and of prompt and efficient discharge of arduous duties, such as do not often present themselves.*[1]

As a postscript to the story it is of interest to note that, although to modern eyes the presentation of the silver set appears to have been organised with remarkable speed following the arrival in Boston, Dickens in his speech still quibbled at the delay in completion of the order:

> *The ingenious artists who work in silver do not always, I find, keep their promises, even in Boston. I regret that instead of two Goblets which there should be here there is, at present, only one. This deficiency, however, will soon be supplied; and when it is our testimonial will be, so far, complete.*[2]

The silver wine set by Lows, Ball & Co of Boston, comprising a salver, ewer and a pair of goblets, all chased with flowers and foliage can now be seen at Greenwich (plate 127).

An earlier (presumably more tranquil) passage in the *Britannia* was marked by the presentation of another American silver ewer by Gale Wood and Hughes of New York, now in a private collection. The gift, which had been presented by the passengers the previous year to Captain Richard Cleland, is chased with a peaceful country cottage scene and inscribed: *as a testimonial of their high regard for his politeness and attention on the late passage from Liverpool to Boston, May 1841.*

What must surely be an unusual opportunity for heroism is commemorated by a two-handled silver cup presented to Captain Edward Freeman of the steamship *Roddam* in 1902. An inscription on one side of the cup records:

> *Presented by the British Government to Edward William Freeman, Master of the steamship Roddam of London, in acknowledgement of his gallantry and devotion to duty on the occasion of the destruction of the town of St Pierre, Martinique, by a volcanic eruption on the 8th May 1902.*

Following the eruption of Mt Pélée, Captain Freeman, with badly burned hands and face navigated his ship out of harbour with hot volcanic ash covering the decks. His narrative of the extraordinary escape appeared in *Pearson's Magazine* the same year under the title 'The Awful Doom of St Pierre'.

It is interesting that there almost seem to be more items commemorating escape from disaster and near-misses than memorials to actual losses. A few events, however, have gripped the imagination and led to the production of popular souvenirs rather than important presentation pieces.

127 American silver wine set presented to John Hewitt, captain of the Cunard Steamship *Britannia*, 1842.

One of the most unexpected naval losses of the eighteenth century is commemorated in William Cowper's poem *On the Loss of the Royal George*, written when news arrived in September 1782. The well-known verses begin:

> *Toll for the brave*
> *The brave! that are no more*
> *All sunk beneath the wave,*
> *Fast by their native shore.*
> *Eight hundred of the brave*
> *Whose courage well was tried,*
> *Had made the vessel heel*
> *And laid her on her side;*
> *A land-breeze shook the shrouds,*
> *And she was overset;*
> *Down went the Royal George,*
> *With all her crew complete.*

Cowper's explanation of the tragedy was not necessarily quite correct, but his verses give some idea of the public reaction to the event. On 29th August 1782, while preparing to sail as part of Admiral Howe's fleet to relieve besieged Gibraltar, HMS *Royal George* was heeled for minor repair at Spithead, when she suddenly filled with water and sank, with the loss of 900 lives. The disaster was never quite satisfactorily explained, but the court martial absolved the officers and ship's company of all blame.

Some of the most valuable materials and the guns were salvaged soon after the loss, but the wreck of the ship remained as a danger to other shipping at Spithead until it was finally blown up

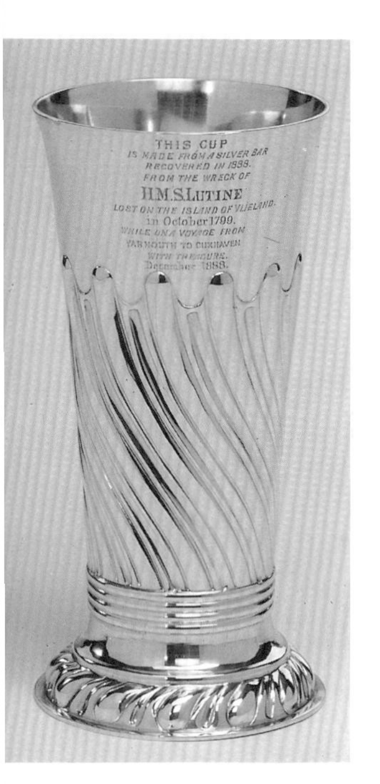

129 Silver beaker made in 1888 from a silver bar recovered from the wreck of HMS *Lutine*, lost off the Dutch coast in 1797.

by Colonel Charles Pasley's Royal Sappers and Miners between 1839 and 1843. These operations aroused extraordinary public enthusiasm, and it is interesting that we have recently seen similar popular interest inspired by the salvage of the *Mary Rose*, which was lost only a short distance from the *Royal George* site.

Many relics were raised as a result of the explosions, but in particular the operations produced a huge amount of timber and metal fittings from the ship, which became source material for a small souvenir industry. A contemporary history of the salvage records:

> *The pile of timber recovered between May 8th and October 28th, measured upwards of 120 feet long, 35 feet wide, and 7 feet high, contained 18,600 feet, or 372 loads of timber, a quantity sufficient to form innumerable relics of this far-famed wreck for years to come, has been, by order of the Lords of the Admiralty, publicly sold by auction.*[3]

The items produced ranged from walking sticks and snuff boxes to model guns and anchors, carving knives and miniature books containing a narrative of the loss of the *Royal George*. Some of these have a printed label which declares:

> *The publisher begs to inform the Public, that the Timber from which the covers of this Book were made, was purchased at H M Dockyard Portsmouth, and they may fully confide on its being a genuine Relic of the ill-fated Royal George.*[4]

Similar books, bound in wood salvaged from the timbers of the *Mary Rose* wreck, were also produced about this time to commemorate the sinking of that ship in 1545.

The most impressive use of *Royal George* salvaged timber, however, was the production of some unique items of furniture. The National Maritime Museum has a table and two armchairs made in 1842 from the wood recovered during the operations of 1839 to 1841. The designer was Henry Whitaker of Burley, near Otley, and the carpenter was Thomas Wood. The large octagonal table on a tripod base is decorated with parquetry designs and an inscription in wood veneer around the edge. An inscribed brass plate on the foot records that the table was made from a knee and part of the keelson of the *Royal George*. Accompanying the table are two chairs of bizarre design, each quite different (colour plate 128). One has a lower border of carved scallop shells and leaves, and rests not on legs but on two sea creatures with grotesque webbed feet at the front. The other highly-decorated chair has back legs formed from carved dolphins standing on their tails. The front legs are of zigzag form, which from one angle give an optical illusion of being straight.

Another shipping tragedy which is still famed today is that of HMS *Lutine*, lost with all hands in a gale off the island of Vlieland on the Dutch coast in October 1799 while on a voyage from Yarmouth to Cuxhaven. The ship's bell, salvaged in 1857, still hangs in the Lloyd's Building, where it is rung when important news is received. When she was lost the *Lutine* was carrying a large amount of specie and bullion, some of which was subsequently salvaged. At Greenwich there is a tall beaker made from one of the recovered silver bars (plate 129). The beaker, which was made in 1888, is decorated with spiral fluting, and in the base is set a Spanish coin of 1797.

In the next century a rare memorial ring is of particular interest as it relates to a death aboard a merchant vessel and has an unusually detailed reference to the incident. The bezel of the gold ring has a lock of plaited hair under glass, and an enamel surround lettered *Sacred to the Memory of. Ob 8 July 1817 Aet 20.* An inscription inside the bezel explains: *In memory of John Malcolm Stevens 2d Mate who in heaving the Log was knocked overboard by the Spanker Boom of the Ship Lord Cranstown. Jamaica to — Lat 46.10 N Long 30 W.*

The loss of the steamer *Forfarshire* on 7th September 1838 while bound from Hull to Dundee was made famous by the heroic exploits of Grace Darling (1815–1842), the lighthouse keeper's daughter from the Longstone – one of the Farne Islands. She rescued the survivors by rowing out to the wreck in a coble (a small local boat) and is much commemorated in ceramic souvenirs, as yet unrepresented at Greenwich. The Maritime Museum at Hull has a number of souvenirs, and mugs, jugs, ceramic cobles and Staffordshire figures of Grace Darling rowing are known. One Sunderland pink lustre jug is inscribed *William Darling and his daughter Grace Horsley Darling. The Forfarshire Steamer lost on Sept 7th 1838.* Another mug is printed in indigo with hand-colouring, with a view of Grace Darling rowing, and the words *Grace Darling the Northumbrian Heroine Born Nov 24, 1815. Died Oct 20 1842.* On the other side is a verse ending:

130 Earthenware plate used on board the steamer *Forfarshire* *c*1835. This vessel, then the largest ship to be launched on the Tay, was wrecked off the Farne Islands in 1838.

The maiden rows and courageously saves
Nine of the twelve from their watery graves.

At Hull and at Greenwich there are plates printed with a view of the *Forfarshire* and the name of the Dundee, Perth and London Shipping Company. An earthenware soup plate at Greenwich is printed in green with a view of a two-masted paddle steamer with name pennant flying and the words *Steamer Forfarshire* (plate 130). Another earthenware plaque is printed with a similar design.

On 24th March 1878 the cadets' training ship HMS *Eurydice* foundered off Sandown Bay in the Isle of Wight in a freak squall, and all but two of the crew of 300 were lost. Gerard Manley Hopkins wrote a poem, *The Loss of the Eurydice*, in April, and in September the vessel was recovered and brought into Portsmouth Dockyard. A memorial was erected in the Naval Cemetary at Haslar, Gosport. Some of the timber and copper was turned into memorial prayerbooks, vases, obelisks and other ornaments.

But perhaps the most famous shipping disaster is the loss of the liner *Titanic* in 1912. The recent discovery of the wreck, and the books and media coverage that this generated, have created considerable public interest. But even before this, in the eighty years since the ship went down, the name *Titanic* was constantly referred to, and few people can have heard nothing of the story. Particularly in America there are societies devoted to researching and keeping her memory alive, and the auction houses never seem to lack associated relics and commemorative bric à-brac.

However, the loss of the *Titanic* does not seem to have inspired the pottery manufacturers, and apart from medals there are relatively few mass-produced commemoratives. One unusual item at Greenwich is a silkwork picture depicting the liner, with a weeping angel in the foreground kneeling at a memorial which is draped with the British and American flags. A lifebelt bears the legend *To the heroes of the Titanic,* and on the memorial is inscribed: *In memory of those who perished at sea 15.4.1912 from Titanic. RIP.*

On 7th May 1915 the liner *Lusitania* was torpedoed and sunk by a German submarine 8 miles off the Old Head of Kinsale, Ireland. Of the 1,906 men, women and children on board, 1,142 were lost. The tragedy became part of a propaganda war between Germany and Britain, both nations producing medals to make their case. Among the more ephemeral mementoes of the incident is a crêpe paper napkin produced by the Palatine Press of Wigan, printed with a photograph of the *Lusitania* and details of the vessel's specifications and her fate, all within a flowered border.

In inshore waters lifeboatmen have been responsible for many selfless humanitarian acts over the years, and there are church memorials to record their deeds, and in some cases their tragic loss. A presentation piece made to honour a hard-working member of the Royal National Lifeboat Institution is at Greenwich. It is a modest silver salver of 1919, inscribed: *Presented to B Peart Esq by the crew of the Elizabeth Simpson in recognition of the untiring and valuable service he has rendered to the boat and her crew.* Names of thirty-seven crew members of the lifeboat are inscribed in the shape of a cross. The appearance of a number of repeated surnames, for instance six by the name of Woods, illustrates that often several members of a family would risk their lives serving in the local lifeboat.

There are a few nineteenth century pieces commemorating the early lifeboats, including a purple lustre quart mug of the 1820s, at Sunderland Museum, with a transfer print of the Sunderland lifeboat. A more modern illustration of the lifeboat service is a limited-edition silver and silver-gilt bowl commissioned by the Royal National Lifeboat Institution to commemorate their 150th Anniversary in 1974. The relief scene in the centre depicts the rescue of the crew and passengers of the Royal Mail Steamer *St George* off Douglas, Isle of Man, on 29th November 1830 by volunteers led by Sir William Hillary, founder of the institution.

We have seen in previous chapters some of the presentation pieces made to reward naval officers for gallantry in battle. Rather more unusual souvenirs of a close brush with death are the two pieces of silver plate which were kept until a few years ago by the descendants of Admiral Beatty. At the Battle of the Dogger Bank on 24th January 1915 a shell exploded in Beatty's cabin on board HMS *Lion*, and two pieces of silver were broken and buckled. Instead of being discarded, the two-branched candelabra and tea caddy were engraved with the story and kept by the family in their battle-worn condition. They are now a poignant relic of battle, kept with the more elegant presentations made to Beatty after the war.

The death of a hero in the hour of victory was the ultimate cause for popular commemoration, and as we have seen in earlier chapters, no victor has been accorded more acclaim than Vice Admiral Lord Nelson. We have already looked at some of the items produced to commemorate the victory at Trafalgar, but the pieces mourning his death in the battle were even more widely produced. The public interest in the story of his death has never waned, and memorial pieces have been produced ever since 1805, particularly in the 1840s and for the centenary of Trafalgar in 1905. The considerable collections at Greenwich relating to Nelson's death, funeral and subsequent hero worship are extraordinary enough to warrant devoting the remainder of this chapter to the subject.

131 Linen printed with a view of Nelson's funeral car and the procession nearing St Paul's Cathedral.

Nelson's funeral on 9th January 1806 was the greatest public spectacle seen in London during this period, incorporating as it did a river procession from Greenwich to Westminster and a procession with elaborate funeral carriage to St Paul's Cathedral. Afterwards the funeral car was displayed in the Painted Hall of Greenwich Hospital, until eventually it broke up. The only remaining pieces – which are now in the National Maritime Museum – are the figurehead in the form of a female figure of Victory holding aloft a laurel wreath, and two gilt letters *A* from the inscription. A print was published in which the entire procession is laid out in order in rows down the sheet, with the funeral carriage at the top. The engraving is known both as a print on paper and as a dissected picture, an early form of jigsaw puzzle.

The Old Sailor (pseudonym of Matthew Henry Barker, author of *Greenwich Hospital: Series of Naval Sketches* with George Cruikshank) wrote in his book *Tough Yarns* in 1835:

> *But who is there, your honor, that remembers Nelson now? Even the car that carried his body to its last moorings has been broken up as useless lumber, though I did hear that a gemman offered two thousand guineas for it. Some parts are down in the store rooms, and some has been burnt for fire-wood. There's his picture and his statue to be sure, but I think they should have spared the car.*[5]

Many prints and souvenirs of the time illustrate the funeral carriage. Sometimes the image was embroidered in silk or printed on textile, and there is one unusual printed linen square (plate 131) which shows the procession nearing St Paul's Cathedral, with crowds of spectators watching from the windows. Material was also sold by the yard for curtains or hangings, printed in brown, red and blue with a repeat pattern of four scenes of Nelson's death and funeral, showing Nelson collapsing on the deck of the *Victory*, the funeral barge, the funeral car, and Britannia mourning beneath an oak tree. The scenes are captioned and divided from each other by borders of oak leaves. The funeral scenes are taken from a series of aquatints published by Ackermann in January 1806. Another length of calico is printed in blue and brown with monuments, urns, obelisks and statues of Nelson amidst exotic foliage. On the base of one monument is written *To the memory of the hero of Aboukir, Copenhagen and Trafalgar*. This pattern appears as a sample in the stock sheets of John Bury of Lancashire for 1806, where it is described as the *Trafalgar Chintz*.

Another linen square is printed in dark red and black on a yellow background, with Britannia mourning before a Nelson monument shaped as a tall pyramid, and a portrait of the hero. A ribbon in the sky is inscribed *To the Memory of Lord Nelson*, and two sailors are at the foot of the side panels which list the ships of both fleets. The border is woven with the inscription *The Tars of Great Britain Humble the Pride of France*.

The funeral car is also engraved on the bowls of large glass rummers, which seem to have been particularly popular. Sometimes it appears on its own, but at other times is twinned with an engraving of HMS *Victory* under sail. One of these glasses, dating from *c*1810, shows the carriage being towed by a line of six sailors engraved right round the body of the glass, and is inscribed *In memory of Lord Nelson Jany 9 1806* (plate 132).

Another popular ornament at this period was the commemorative glass transfer print made by applying a soaked mezzotint engraving to the reverse of a treated sheet of crown glass and rubbing it down so that the paper pulp was removed and only the ink design remained. After varnishing and drying, oil paints were applied in layers to build up a translucent and colourful image. A number of Nelson subjects are known, among which is a view of the funeral car as displayed in the Painted Hall (colour plate 133). This picture, entitled *A Correct Representation of the Funeral Car which conveyed the Body of Lord Nelson from the Admiralty to St Pauls, Jany 9th 1806*, was published in February 1806 by W B Walker of Fox & Knot Court, Cow Lane, London. Other similar glass pictures show Nelson mortally wounded, the funeral barge on the Thames, Nelson in Neptune's chariot pulled through the waves by sea-horses, and Britannia lamenting Nelson's death as she leans against a monument bearing an oval portrait of the dead hero and the titles of his battles. The Britannia engraving, which was also published by W B Walker, is dated 5th December 1805, very soon after news of Trafalgar reached England, and the Neptune picture, by Stampa and Son of Leather Lane, is dated 14th March 1806.

Memorial rings were produced for Nelson's close friends and family to wear at the funeral. The gold rings with an enamelled bezel are decorated with a viscount's and a duke's coronet with the initials *N* and *B*, for Nelson and Bronte, and *Trafalgar* on a black enamel ground. The hoop of the ring is inscribed with Nelson's motto: *Palmam qui meruit ferat*. The rings were made by John Salter of the Strand, London: Nelson's jeweller. Lord Nelson's executors distributed the rings to at least fifty-eight recipients, including thirty-one of his relations.[6]

132 Two large rummers commemorating Nelson and his funeral.

The whereabouts of some twenty-eight rings are known today, four of them being in the National Maritime Museum (colour plate 134). One ring came to the collection from Earl Nelson, and was worn at the funeral by Thomas Bolton, who later became 2nd Earl Nelson. Although the ring resembles the usual Nelson memorial rings, the bezel is hinged on one side and opens to reveal plaited hair under the glass. The inside of the ring is inscribed *Lost to his Country 21 Octr 1805. Aged 47*. There is a family story that he lost the ring on the day after the funeral, and it was found by the gardener forty years later. Other rings containing the lock of hair are also known to exist. Another variation of the Nelson memorial ring at Greenwich is one worn at the funeral by Sir John Franklin.

Catherine Andras (1775–1860) of Pall Mall, London, modeller in wax to Queen Charlotte, modelled the head of a full-length effigy of Nelson after his death, dressed in garments which probably belonged to him, and a cocked hat which certainly did. The figure was added to the exhibition of funeral effigies in Westminster Abbey dating back as far as a wooden effigy of Edward III, and it can still be seen today in the crypt.

A pink wax profile portrait of Nelson in uniform was modelled by Catherine Andras from life in 1805 (colour plate 135). In a letter to M R Boulton in February 1806 Mr Tuffin writes that Lady Hamilton:

> *shewed me the inclosed Wax Profile which She declares is the most striking likeness that has been taken, and much more so than our little drawing or print by Mr da Costa . . . On asking Lady H: in what features the model so closely resembled Lord Nelson as she had declared, she said, in the direction and form of the nose, mouth and chin, that the general carriage of the body was exactly his, and that altogether the likeness was so great it was impossible for anybody, who had known him to doubt about or mistake it.*[7]

William Tassie's profile portrait of Nelson is based on this Andras wax. The white vitreous paste plaque is signed *Tassie F 1805,* and inscribed below the shoulder: *Admiral Lord Nelson died in the glorious Battle off Trafalgar Oct 21 1805.*[8]

The potteries, of course, marked Nelson's death by a vast production of commemorative wares of all types. Most pieces were transfer-printed, and many of the designs come directly from popular prints of the day which were first published on paper. A good example of this direct borrowing are the Newcastle creamware mugs decorated with a Nelson memorial bearing his profile portrait, after Simon de Koster, between two fasces, with flags and naval trophies above (plate 136). The memorial is supported in the manner of a coat of arms by a weeping sailor and a mourning marine on each side, who stand above the defeated French and Spanish flags. This design appears both as a black transfer print and also with additional hand-colouring, and similar engravings occur as glass pictures. The engraving on which this is based was published by Laurie and Whittle of Fleet Street, London, on 12th December 1805.

136 Newcastle creamware mug transfer-printed with a Nelson memorial after an engraving published on 12th December 1805.

Another creamware mug, probably made in Sunderland about 1806, is transfer-printed in black with a design of Britannia mourning and an inscription below: *Britannia leaning upon his Lordship's armorial ensigns, accompanied by her Lion, protecting the Union Shield and Spear, mourns for the loss of her illustrious Hero LORD NELSON.* A similarly decorated jug has additional hand-colouring in pink, red and green, with a merchant ship under sail on the other side, and the inscription *Success to Trade.*

Another series of jugs which appear in a variety of colours and types also depict a memorial to Nelson bearing his portrait, and surmounted by an urn, with a female mourner weeping as she leans on the monument (colour plate 137). Strangely the inscription on all these pieces is *Horatia Nelson.* Whether this was simply an error or whether there was some confusion with the name of Nelson's daughter is not known, but the dates of birth and death on the memorial are certainly Nelson's own, and the title of the illustration is *Britannia weeping o'er the ashes of her matchless hero Lord Nelson.*

Intricate cut paper-work pictures and paper fans were produced to commemorate Nelson's death. One fan, published by B Croker in November 1808, is printed in black with Nelson's monument, his bust crowned by Victory, a mourning Britannia, and a figure of Hope, who points to the inscription *He lives for ever* (plate 138). Another – which is inscribed *The New Trafalgar Fan* – was dedicated to Lady Collingwood, and the paper leaf is printed in black with a portrait of Nelson, naval trophies and warships, and verses which begin:

> *Again the loud ton'd trump of Fame*
> *Proclaims Britannia rules the main.*
> *Whilst sorrow whispers Nelson's name*
> *And mourns the gallant Victor slain*
> *Rule brave Britons rule the Main*
> *Avenge the Godlike hero slain.*

The patch box makers of Bilston, who decorated their enamel wares in celebration of the victory of Trafalgar, also produced many boxes mourning Nelson's death. The designs are many and varied, from Nelson falling on the deck of the *Victory* to scenes of Nelson's tomb with weeping female figures. One of these memorial scenes has a dejected figure of Hope seated beside an angel who holds a scroll inscribed *Nelsons Removed to the Armies above.* Another popular design showed a sailor standing beside a memorial surmounted by either an urn or a bust of Nelson. Usually he holds a banner, which might read *Glorious 21st October 1805* or *He lives in our Hearts.* Another simple blue and white design has a heart superimposed on an anchor with the words *He conquer'd and died.*

138 Printed fans commemorating Nelson's death at Trafalgar.

Nelson 1805. Other inscriptions on these boxes include:

> *Off Trafalgar the battle was Fought*
> *Nelson's Life the victory Bought.*

and:

> *Mourn England mourn grim Death*
> *As tore thy Darling Nelson away.*

The details of Nelson's death from his wound in the *Victory*'s cockpit were well known from Surgeon Beatty's published account, and the scene portrayed in an oil painting by Arthur Devis often appears on commemorative objects. There are examples of long-case clocks painted with Death of Nelson scenes on the arch above the dial. At Greenwich there is a mahogany clock dating from about 1820, by Young and Hedridge of Dundee, and another of the same date by Felmingham of Bungay which also has three brass finials on top with Nelson profiles. Tea trays were also popular, both in papier mâché and japanned tin, some with death scenes and others with Nelson portraits.

Many silkwork pictures commemorating Nelson's death are known. A typical example shows Britannia, Fame and Victory mourning at a memorial with a Nelson bust. The plinth of the monument is inscribed:

> *To express the deep regret of an admiring grateful nation and to implant in the minds of rising generations an ardent desire to emulate the bright example displayed in the skilful conduct and glorious death of the brave Lord Nelson.*

Commemorative metalwork was produced in every possible size and shape after the funeral, from figures and ornaments to doorstops. The many monuments and statues of Nelson erected in public places in the years following Trafalgar inspired many of the designs. Nelson's Column, with its statue by Baily, in Trafalgar Square was only completed in November 1843, and the bronze castings on the base were not all in position until 1854. The final parts of the design – Sir Edwin Landseer's lions – were only added in 1867. Models of the column have since been produced in silver, glass, pottery, marble, bronze and iron in every variety, from detailed copies to total travesties. Wedgwood produced an elegant set, complete with four lions in black basalt, and the Art Union of London was responsible for a bronze version. The four bronze panels at the base of Nelson's Column, each by a different sculptor, depict in relief scenes from Nelson's battles, and even these panels have been reproduced in miniature. One version in copper depicts Nelson being carried below by sailors during the Battle of Trafalgar and is inscribed with the Trafalgar signal.

Some of the other memorials to Nelson have also appeared in miniature versions. One of the first memorials to Nelson to be erected after Trafalgar was that at Birmingham, designed by Sir Richard Westmacott. The statue, which shows Nelson standing in front of the bow of a battle-damaged ship with a figurehead of Victory holding aloft a wreath, was unveiled on 25th October 1809. A cast brass doorstop based on this design was also produced for sale. Small trinkets appeared everywhere, from brass finials for clocks and furniture with hollow medal-shaped discs bearing Nelson's head in relief, to tiny brass watch guards. If the evidence is to be believed, everyone must have changed their drawer handles and door knobs after Trafalgar to new versions bearing a profile of the dead Nelson, or at least an inscription referring to Trafalgar.

Once Nelson's death ceased to be the latest news one might expect the flow of commemorative items to dwindle. In fact, in the middle years of the nineteenth century there was still a flourishing market for Nelson mementoes, doubtless encouraged by public interest in Trafalgar Square. Tinsel pictures were popular in the 1840s, and Nelson was an obvious subject. These pictures were coloured mezzotints decorated with embossed metal foil cut out and mounted on a coloured background, then framed. A typical tinsel picture showed Nelson standing full-length, holding a telescope, with a battle scene behind.

Much Nelson pottery continued to be produced in the mid-nineteenth century, and it is from this period that many of the Death of Nelson Staffordshire chimney groups (colour plate 139) and Nelson pottery figures date. These figures are of very varied quality, and were clearly made in the quickest and cheapest way possible. The colouring of many of the figures bears very little relationship to reality, and Nelson is to be found wearing pink, green or yellow breeches according to the whim or available materials of the painter.

Also dating from this period are the Doulton and Watts brown stoneware jugs modelled as a head and shoulders of Nelson in uniform, with his pigtail as the handle (colour plate 140). The jugs were made in at least three different sizes, and there was a large matching stoneware bottle. The original jugs were made in the 1840s and – for those whose interest was more historic than patriotic – a similar head of Napoleon could also be purchased. In 1905 the same firm produced copies of the Nelson jugs for the Trafalgar Centenary, complete with an impressed inscription on the base to avoid any danger of confusion with the originals.

There are also a number of small ivory statuettes of Nelson, carved full-length in uniform. One unusual example, inscribed *Nelson of Trafalgar*, shows him standing with a chart in his left hand and his empty right sleeve somewhat incongruously suspended in a sling. His chest is hinged, and opens in the centre to form a triptych carved with the dying admiral seated on a coil of rope, with two warships on the outer panels. Similar ivory figures of Napoleon are known, of nineteenth century French manufacture. Dieppe, which specialised in ivory carving, was a popular Continental holiday resort for English tourists in the later nineteenth century.

Commemoration of Nelson's death and Trafalgar continued longer after the event than for any other naval victory. A great opportunity for revival was the centenary of 1905, when exhibitions and celebrations inspired the souvenir manufacturers, and especially the potters, to start work again in celebration of Lord Nelson. Royal Doulton of Lambeth produced stoneware jugs depicting Nelson and his captains, as well as a set of glazed stoneware items in blue, green and brown with views of Nelson and the battle. In 1905 Copeland also produced three-handled loving cups printed in full colour with Nelson's portrait, Britannia, and ships spanning the centenary years.

The dishonest engraving of coronets and initials, coats of arms and crests, provided fakes which were eagerly bought by collectors. Even in the 1930s interest in Nelson was so strong that a series of notorious London sales included many fake items purporting to be relics of Nelson. This unprecedented popular enthusiasm for a man whose courage and achievements were remarkable, whose letters reveal a human, talented and vain individual, and whose private life contained romance and passion which have an everlasting appeal, accounts for the numerous large private accumulations of Nelson memorabilia and commemorative material, some of which have now passed into the Museum's collection. Mugs and jugs copied from the old designs are still being made today, and no doubt the year 2005 will see a major national celebration of the bicentenary of Trafalgar and Nelson's death.

NOTES

1 A broadsheet printed with Dickens's speech came with the silver. For the full text of the speech, see K J Fielding: *The Speeches of Charles Dickens* (1960) pp15–17.

2 Ibid.

3 *A Narrative of the Loss of the Royal George* (1843) p136

4 Ibid.

5 Matthew Barker (The Old Sailor): *Tough Yarns: A Series of Naval Tales and Sketches to please all Hands* (1835) p16

6 British Museum: Add Mss no. 34988; *Notes & Queries* 11th Series Vol XII (6th November 1915) pp361–2; George A Goulty: 'Nelson's Memorial Rings' (*Genealogist's Magazine* June 1990)

7 Quoted in E J Pyke: *A Biographical Dictionary of Wax Modellers* (1973) pp5–6

8 John M Gray: *James and William Tassie* (1894) pp70–1 and 132

CHAPTER 7 Boating for Pleasure

There is a long tradition of competitive sailing and rowing in Britain which no doubt goes back to the earliest days of waterborne activity. The Dutch invented sailing for pleasure on their *meers*, rivers and coasts. Yachting as such was only introduced into England from the Netherlands in 1660 with the gift of a Dutch yacht, the *Mary*, to Charles II on his Restoration. The King soon had another built by the shipbuilder Peter Pett, and by 1661 was able to race the two vessels, later adding several others to his fleet of pleasure boats. It is tempting to think that the early days of yachting might have been suitably commemorated by some engraved or handpainted decorative item. Unfortunately there is little to support the traditional belief that the small vessel painted on an attractive coloured delftware charger dated 1668 (now in the Nelson-Atkins Museum in Kansas City) represents the yacht *Mary*.

With the growth of yacht clubs after about 1720, yachting became an acceptable pastime for the wealthy. There must always have been rivalry and spontaneous racing but later on competitions were formalised, rules laid down and substantial prizes awarded. The trophies which were introduced later in the eighteenth century, although sometimes of considerable value in themselves, were primarily intended as symbols of honour worthy of competition by even the wealthy and noble.

The first recorded yacht race for more than two boats was held in 1749 on the Thames between Greenwich and the Nore. Among the earliest of the yachting trophies is the Cumberland Cup, presented by Henry Frederick, Duke of Cumberland, George III's younger brother, for a race between pleasure sailing craft on the Thames between Westminster and Putney. The cup was first competed for in 1775, and the Cumberland Fleet later became the Royal Thames Yacht Club. A new cup was presented each year, and the club now owns the second cup of 1776, made by John Wakelin and William Taylor of London. In that year there was also a yachting regatta at Cowes on the Isle of Wight, now home of the Royal Yacht Squadron.

The National Maritime Museum includes in its silver collections a small number of interesting yachting trophies. The earliest of these is the King's Cup awarded in 1830 by the Royal Yacht Club, forerunner of the Royal Yacht Squadron (colour plate 141). The trophy takes the form of a covered silver-gilt tankard by John Bridge of Rundell, Bridge and Rundell, London.[1] The tankard is decorated with friezes of oak sprays, anthemion, and putti rowing seashells, and an inset panel on the side depicts Neptune driving his sea-chariot. The hinged domed lid is surmounted by a Royal lion, and inside the lid is set a circular medallion of King William IV.

This, the third annual King's Cup Race, was won on 21st August 1830 at the Royal Yacht Club Regatta by Mr Joseph Weld of Lulworth in his cutter, *Alarm*, built by Inman of Lymington. At 193 tons and 80 feet length overall she was the largest racing cutter of her time, and this was the *Alarm*'s first major race. *The Times* reported on 23rd August 1830:

> *This day, being his Majesty's birthday, was fixed by the Yacht Club for the King's Cup to be sailed for, at Cowes, by yachts belonging to the club . . . The vessels which contested the prize were the* Alarm, *193 tons, belonging to Joseph Weld Esq; the* Scorpion, *110 tons, Lord Clonbrock; and the* Miranda, *164 tons, James Maxse Esq. . . . The vessels were limited to four sails – main, fore, jib and gafftop; but, in starting, the* Miranda *displayed a jib of monstrous dimensions, extending from the point of the boom to the foot of the mast. In a few minutes the* Alarm, *which is already distinguished in the prize annals here, took the lead in beautiful*

style, and soon left the others far astern. She kept ahead, till the vessels returned from the Nab; in passing Cowes, she was neared by Miranda, the Scorpion being sternmost; the Miranda had substituted a common-sized jib for her former fancy one, which was found not to answer.

About six o'clock, the Alarm reached the starting vessel, and won the cup, the Miranda being some distance astern. The day was extremely fine, and the race excellent. A good dinner took place at the club-house, and a splendid display of fireworks, and a ball closed the day. The yachts belonging to the club are numerous here, and as most of them followed the three vessels, the scene was very gay.

The *Alarm* went on to become one of the most outstanding racing yachts of her age, and Joseph Weld one of the most famous yachtsmen. Weld was a founder member of The Yacht Club in June 1815, which in 1820 – on George IV's accession – became the Royal Yacht Club, and finally in 1833 the Royal Yacht Squadron. He owned a number of other successful racing yachts of the period, including *Charlotte, Arrow, Lulworth* and *Meteor*. A painting at Greenwich by Nicholas Condy shows Joseph Weld seated on the deck of the *Alarm* in Plymouth Sound.

Similar tankards were presented annually between 1827 and 1839, and in 1990 the King's Cup won in 1831 was sold in a London saleroom.[2] The only difference between the King's Cups of 1830 and 1831 is the subject of the decoration on the applied plaque, which on the later presentation depicts Britannia and her attendants. Both trophies were made by Rundell, Bridge and Rundell in 1830. In 1834 the King's Cup was limited to vessels of 75 tons, which meant the *Alarm* could no longer compete in the race which she had won several times.

142 The first Queen's Trophy won at the Royal Yacht Squadron's Regatta of 1838 by the cutter *Alarm*. By Benjamin Preston, 1837.

Complementing the King's Cup is another trophy in the collection at Greenwich which was also won by the cutter *Alarm* (plate 142). This is the first Queen's Trophy for the Royal Yacht Squadron's Regatta of 1838, the year after Queen Victoria came to the throne. The trophy is a large silver-gilt shield by Benjamin Preston, decorated in relief with a central boss showing Britannia and a deep border of racing yachts under sail. At the bottom of the shield a cartouche, surmounted by the Royal Arms, is inscribed: *Royal Yacht Squadron, 1838. The Gift of Her Most Gracious Majesty Queen Victoria.* The view of the yachts is taken from a painting by Huggins owned by the Royal Yacht Squadron, and shows Lord Yarborough's 351-ton full-rigged ship, *Falcon*, and the squadron yachts *Alarm, Pearl* and *Waterwitch*. The race, which was open to yachts of all classes, took place on 17th August 1838, the Duchess of Kent's birthday. As an experiment the six entries were handicapped by a time allowance of 3 minutes for every 10 tons of difference, which in the calm conditions of that year's race had little effect on the result. Once again Joseph Weld triumphed in the *Alarm*, and won the first Queen's Trophy.

The yacht *Alarm* was seldom beaten, but in 1851 the new schooner *America* beat her to the Royal Yacht Squadron's 100 Guinea Cup in a race which was to be the forerunner of the America's Cup races, the first challenge being made in 1870. After her defeat by *America*, *Alarm* was lengthened by 20 feet and converted to schooner rig. She continued racing until 1867, and was only broken up in 1889.

Another yachting trophy in the Museum is a large silver two-handled cup and cover won by the Earl of Dunraven's yacht, *Valkyrie*, in 1891 (plate 143). The cup, made by Edgar Finley and Hugh Taylor of London in 1891, is surmounted by a figure of Neptune with his trident. One side is decorated with a scene of racing yachts, and on the other is a panel inscribed: *Presented by Her Majesty the Queen to the Royal Southern Yacht Club 1891. Won by Valkyrie.* The 56-ton cutter *Valkyrie*, the first of three notable racing yachts of that name, was designed by G L Watson and built in

126 Silver cup presented to James Fitzjames for saving a drowning man in the River Mersey in 1835.

128 Two chairs made from timber salvaged from the wreck of HMS *Royal George*. Designed by Henry Whitaker in 1842.

133 Glass picture showing Nelson's funeral car displayed in the Painted Hall at Greenwich.

137 (left) A selection of the many mugs and jugs produced *c*1806 to mourn the loss of the hero of Trafalgar.

134 (above) Gold and enamel memorial ring as worn by Lord Nelson's close friends and family after his death. The *N* and *B* stand for Nelson and Bronte.

135 (left) Wax profile portrait of Nelson modelled by Catherine Andras in 1805.

139 (far left) Mid-19th century Staffordshire earthenware group of the Death of Nelson.

140 (left) Doulton and Watts stoneware jugs representing Nelson, *c*1840. The factory produced replicas of these jugs in 1905 for the centenary of Trafalgar.

141 Silver-gilt King's Cup won in 1830 at the Royal Yacht Club Regatta by Joseph Weld in his cutter, *Alarm*. By John Bridge, 1830.

151 Services used on board the Victorian and Edwardian Royal Yachts.

152 Carved coat of arms of the South Sea Company *c*1711.

155 Nelson's personal porcelain: the shallow hot water dish and egg cup are from Worcester, the ice pail and plate with Nelson Arms and the fouled anchor plate and jug from the Baltic service are of Paris porcelain.

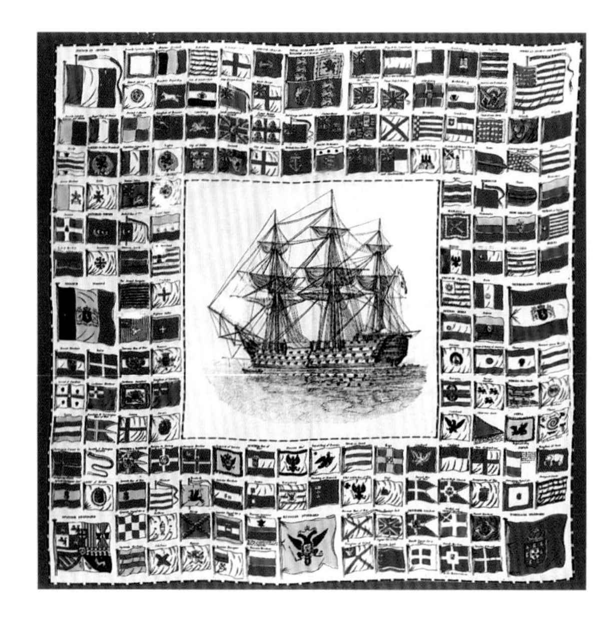

158 (right) Printed silk square with flags of all nations and the Victorian Royal Standard.

159 (far right) Liverpool creamware jug dated 1788, transfer-printed with the Liverpool lighthouse and Bidston Hill signal masts.

162 Admiral of the fleet's batons presented to John Jervis, Earl of St Vincent (top) and William, Duke of Clarence (bottom) in 1821.

163 Dish from the Flights of Worcester dinner service painted by James Pennington in 1792 for William, Duke of Clarence. Every piece depicts Hope with her anchor and a ship.

165 (above right) Liverpool creamware plate transfer-printed with a figure of Hope.

166 (above) Britannia on a painted porcelain jug by Flight and Barr of Worcester, and a printed Worcester pot-pourri vase, late 18th century.

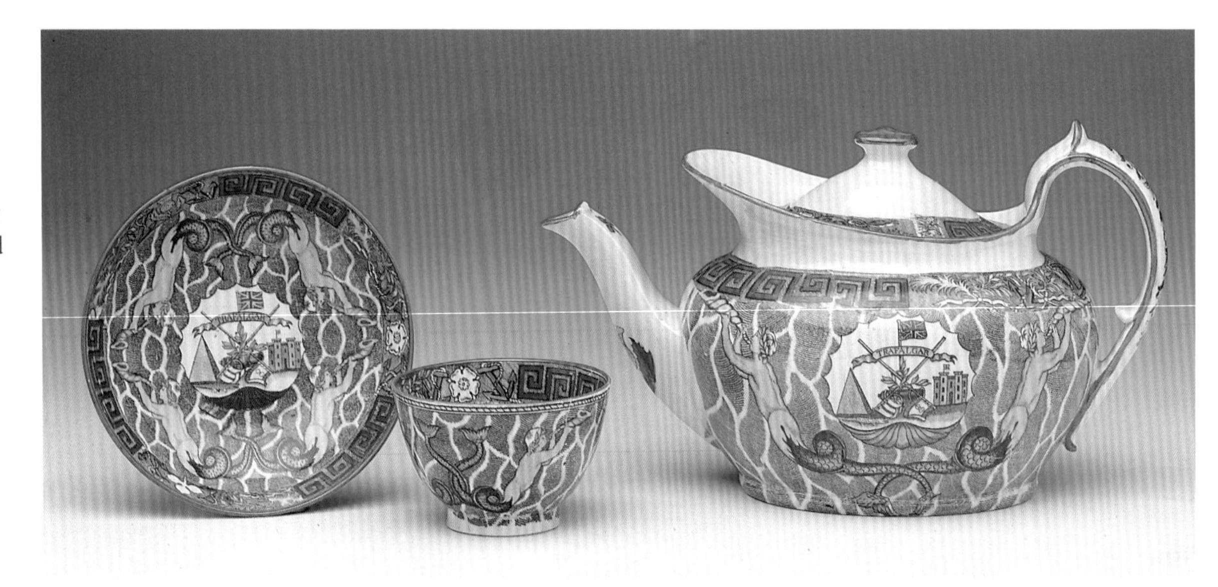

168 (right) Staffordshire earthenware teaset commemorating Trafalgar, printed with pairs of tritons.

1888 by J C Fay & Co. of Southampton. She was commissioned by the politician and yachtsman Windham Thomas Wyndham-Quin, Earl of Dunraven, originally as a challenger for the America's Cup. Although this challenge never took place, under Lord Dunraven's ownership *Valkyrie* was highly successful in the 1889, 1890 and 1891 yachting seasons, winning many prizes, with Tom Diaper of Itchen as her sailing master. Eventually she was sold to Archduke Karl Stephan of Austria. In 1893 and 1895 Lord Dunraven competed unsuccessfully for the America's Cup in *Valkyrie II* and *Valkyrie III*, both yachts being specially built for the challenge.

Silver prizes were also frequently awarded for rowing races. Sometimes these are in the form of arm badges, sometimes miniature oars or other small items, and sometimes more substantial cups. Perhaps the most interesting and historic prizes for rowing are the arm badges won in regattas and annual river races, which recall the brassards traditionally worn by Thames watermen. One of these watermen's circular badges, made in silvered copper, is in the collection at Greenwich. It carries in relief the shield of arms of the City of London and the arms of the Watermen's Company. The latter bears a rowing boat on waves below crossed oars and two cushions, and the supporters are dolphins. The badge is also engraved with a unique licence number and the words *Free Waterman. At command of our Superiors*, the motto of the Watermen's Company. Around the edge are five small holes for attachment to a sleeve.

A rare London delftware armorial caudle cup, dated 1682 and painted with the arms of the Watermen's Company, was sold recently from the Rous Lench collection,[3] and a London delftware plate with the same arms, dated 1770, is also known.[4] There also exist some rare examples of the Admiralty Barge Crew's badge – a large and elaborate silver-gilt brassard of 1736 by William Lukin – with a central Admiralty anchor surrounded by dolphins, navigation instruments and rococo decoration.

The Bow factory produced a porcelain figure of a Thames waterman *c*1750–54 (plate 144). The figure stands, wearing his distinctive full-skirted coat with a large brassard on his left sleeve, peaked cap, buttoned waistcoat, breeches and stockings. He half turns away, pointing with his left hand, and the well-modelled back view of the figure gives a good impression of the appearance

143 (left) Yachting trophy won by the Earl of Dunraven's yacht, *Valkyrie,* in 1891. By E Finley and H Taylor, 1891.

144 (below) Bow porcelain figure of a Thames waterman *c*1750–54.

of the costume from all angles. The Museum has a white porcelain version of this figure, which dates from the earliest period of figure production at the Bow factory. There are other, slightly later, coloured versions in other collections with a yellow or orange-trimmed coat and cap and a flowered waistcoat.[5] On some examples the arm badge bears an anchor cipher, on some three anchors, and on others the fouled-anchor badge of an Admiralty bargeman.

At Greenwich there is a small collection of silver brassards awarded as prizes for rowing. The best-known by far of the Thames rowing races is the annual Doggett's Race, with its prize coat and badge. Thomas Doggett (*c*1650–1721) was a comic actor and manager of the Drury Lane and Haymarket theatres. In the early eighteenth century the Thames watermen provided everyday transport for Londoners, and in 1716 Thomas Doggett, a staunch Whig, decided to mark the anniversary of King George I's accession with a prize rowing race for watermen. A notice was posted on London Bridge on 1st August 1716:

> *This being the day of his Majesty's happy accession to the throne, there will be given by Mr Doggett an orange colour livery with a badge representing liberty to be rowed for by six watermen that are out of their time within the year past. They are to row from London Bridge to Chelsea. It will be continued annually on the same day forever.*[6]

Doggett's will provided £5 annually for a silver badge of about 12 ounces, and the race still continues today, the trust being administered by the Fishmongers' Company.

There are four of these silver badges at Greenwich, dating between 1836 and 1920 (plate 145). The design of all the badges is similar. In relief is the galloping white horse of Hanover from the Hanoverian Arms, a scroll with *Liberty* and the name of the winner and *The Gift of Mr Thos. Doggett the famous Comedian.* Over the years the treatment of these essential elements has altered subtly to reflect the fashion of the time.

145 (right) Silver arm badges won at the annual Doggett's Race in 1836 and 1920.

146 (below) Brassards awarded for rowing. Left: won at the Seamen's Hospital Society Greenwich Regatta 1834. Centre: Deptford Regatta 1830. Right: Deptford Apprentices Annual Regatta 1862.

The 1836 badge, won by James Morriss, was made by Charles Reily and George Storer of London. Another badge, made by Charles Favell of Sheffield in 1875, was won by William Phelps. Two of the badges are still complete with the original red coat with silver buttons. The earlier of these was won by Henry Cole in 1886, and the silver badge was also made in Sheffield. Henry Cole (born *c*1865) was also twice winner of the Veteran's Race in the Seamen's Hospital Regatta, and he died in 1943 in the Dreadnought Seamen's Hospital. The most recent Doggett's coat and badge in the collection at Greenwich was won by Harry Hayes in August 1920, and this silver badge was also made in Sheffield. It was still inscribed: *The gift of Mr Thomas Doggett, the late famous Comedian. In commemoration of King George's happy accession to the throne of Great Britain, 1714.*

Other rowing prizes at Greenwich (plate 146) include an oval badge by Richard Atkins and William Somersall of London, dated 1827, bearing in relief a figure of blind Justice holding sword and scales, with a small figure below rowing a skiff, and inscribed: *Success to the Subscribers of the Deptford Regatta, 1830.* Another later badge, won by R J Cornish on 21st July 1862 at the Deptford Apprentices' Annual Regatta, is by W Mann of London. It bears the coat of arms of the Watermen's Company. Three years later William Taylor won a coat and badge in the Royal Regatta to commemorate the coming of age of Prince Alfred on 7th August 1865. The arm badge is decorated in relief with a portrait of Prince Alfred, Duke of Edinburgh (1844–1900), Queen Victoria's second son.

Another coat and badge with a Royal association is that won by M J Mears at the Eastern Thames Regatta in 1902. Winners on this occasion were given prize coats and gold medals instead of money, to mark the coronation of King Edward VII. The badge represents the crowned head of the King superimposed on crossed oars and a crossed Union Flag and Royal Standard in coloured enamel. In 1934 A E Gobbett won a coat with an oval silver-gilt badge at the Seamen's Hospital Society Greenwich Regatta. This, the fifth Dreadnought coat and badge, was decorated with crossed oars and a fouled anchor and the letters *SHS* for Seamen's Hospital Society.

Thames regattas were also commemorated by decorated backboards from winning skiffs. One of these, from the skiff *Jennie* which won a race at the Greenwich Annual Town Regatta in 1888, is painted with a detailed view of Greenwich Hospital. Another example, won by William Prince, came from a winning skiff in the Royal Victoria and Albert Docks Regatta of August 1886.

In its collection of boat race trophies the National Maritime Museum has a large urn-shaped cup and cover made in Birmingham in 1934. In 1920 Mr T B F Davis of Durban had founded the South African Training Ship *General Botha*, to be run on similar lines to the merchant service cadets' training ships, *Worcester* and *Conway*. The cup is engraved on one side:

> *Howard Davis Challenge Cup presented by T B F Davis in memory of his son Howard who was a Worcester Cadet and gave his life for his King at the Battle of the Somme in the great War.*
>
> *For competition between the Cadets serving on the Training Ships Worcester, Conway and General Botha. The race to be in cutters of twelve oars the winner to retain the Cup. Challenger to give three months notice. Holders of the cup to select waters for the race. First race to be held in London 1935 in commemoration of the Silver Jubilee of His Majesty King George V.*

Also engraved on the side is a scene of the three cutters racing. The cup was originally silver-gilt and was surmounted by a finial shaped as a cutter, with the crew holding aloft the oars in salute, but this is no longer with the cup. The first race was held in the Royal Albert Dock on 29th June 1935 over a distance of 1 mile, and the *Worcester* crew won by 2 lengths, with *General Botha* coming second.

The earlier trophies presented for *Worcester/Conway* cutter races are also at Greenwich. One is a challenge shield surmounted by the Merchant Navy badge. This was first rowed for in 1897, and crews from the *Worcester* and *Conway* competed annually in six-oared whalers, alternately in the Thames and Medway. The winning teams up to 1939 are recorded on nineteen small plaques. Over this period *Worcester* won fourteen times, *Conway* five times and there was a dead heat in 1905.

The other *Worcester/Conway* boat race trophy is a double-handled cup of shallow bowl shape made in Birmingham in 1926, which, according to a plaque on the base, was won by *Worcester* every year from 1929 to 1939, and again in 1959. Opposite sides of the cup are inscribed:

> *Pull, Worcester, pull, until the truth be seen*
> *Whether the Thames or Mersey be the Queen.*

and:

> *Come, Brother Conways, come and lift your boat*
> *A length ahead of everything afloat.*

Tankards, napkin rings and miniature silver oars were popular prizes for pulling races. At Greenwich the earliest example of the silver oars is a set of two in a presentation case, won for racing in galley and skiff, from the battleship HMS *Majestic* in 1898. A set of three oars was won in the China Fleet Annual Pulling Regatta at Wei-Hai-Wei. Another set of four silver oars was won by Robert, later Vice Admiral Elkins, while serving in HMS *Queen Elizabeth*, HMS *Valiant* and HMS *Cumberland* between 1925 and 1938. The blades of the oars are inscribed with the names of the crews of the officers' gigs, and Robert Elkins's name and ship is engraved on the looms.

Another unusual award is a wooden model of a 27-foot Montague whaler, complete with two hallmarked silver oars. The model, which is only some 9 inches long, was presented by HRH the Prince of Wales (later King Edward VIII) to Mr R H Curram as cox of the winning boat in the Royal Naval Volunteer Reserve Inter-Port Whaler races of 1931. His name is engraved on one of the silver oars.

A Wedgwood punch bowl at Greenwich celebrates the University Boat Race of 1938. The bowl and a matching vase were designed by the artist Eric Ravilious and produced in Queen's Ware. Views of the race and the London scene on the day are printed in black and colour inside and outside the bowl.

There are relatively few examples of fine ceramics and silver, other than racing trophies, which depict sailing and rowing events. Until television made it possible to watch yacht racing in close-up, sailing tended to be a participator sport, which may explain the scarcity of popular souvenirs; yacht races were observed by the masses from afar. However, important regattas and races such as the America's Cup series have always inspired

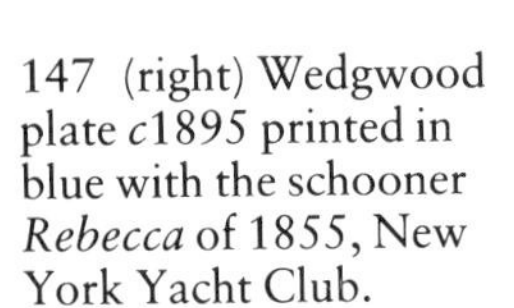

147 (right) Wedgwood plate *c*1895 printed in blue with the schooner *Rebecca* of 1855, New York Yacht Club.

148 (far right) Royal Worcester plate *c*1880 for the steam yacht *Lancashire Witch,* Royal Yacht Squadron, built in 1878.

some commemorative pieces, but they have tended to be rather ephemeral. Souvenir programmes of regattas are not unusual, and there is a good example at Greenwich, printed on satin, for the Torbay Royal Regatta of 28–29th August 1883. The illustration on the cover is a view of Torquay Harbour from Park Hill, and two gaff cutters racing. There are some good private collections of these souvenirs, and there is now increasing interest in exhibiting such collections to tie in with current sporting events.

Some interesting items on loan to Greenwich were produced to commemorate the America's Cup race of 1895. A white-glazed earthenware jug of unmarked ware is printed in brown and hand-coloured with the American yacht, *Defender,* on one side and the Earl of Dunraven's new boat, *Valkyrie III,* on the other. There is also a lapel button for *Defender*, the yacht which succeeded in retaining the cup for America that year. For the next America's Cup race of 1899 there is a handkerchief printed in green commemorating Sir Thomas Lipton's challenger, *Shamrock*. The challenge failed and the American *Columbia*, skippered by Charlie Barr, won all three races. There is also a printed biscuit tin depicting *Columbia* and *Shamrock,* and listing the winners between 1851 and 1895.

In 1895 Wedgwood produced a fine set of yachting plates commemorating yachts of the New York Yacht Club, some of which are also on loan to the Museum from a private collector. The plates are printed in various colours and all have floral borders. The subjects are *The Fanny on the Port Tack* (a sloop of 1874), the *Intrepid*, *The Lillie off Telegraph Hill*, the *Rebecca* (a schooner of 1855) and a line of yachts *Running in from the Light Ship*. The *Rebecca* plate also appears as a larger version with a more elaborate passion-flower border (plate 147).

Gentlemen yacht-owners of the late nineteenth and early twentieth century sometimes commissioned their own dinner services for a particular vessel, often incorporating the boat's name and a reference to the yacht club. A fine pair of such plates by Royal Worcester is on loan to the Museum (plate 148). The plates, which date from about 1880, are printed in blue on a white ground with attractive designs of fish and seaweed. On the rim is the name *Lancashire Witch,* with *RYS* in monogram, for the Royal Yacht Squadron. The vessel was a large screw steam yacht of 306 tons, built at Greenock in 1878 and owned by Sir T G F Hesketh Bt.

Another set of vegetable dishes printed in blue was made by Cauldon of Hanley in *c*1905–10 for *Island Home*, Royal Thames Yacht Club. She was a yawl of 33 tons and 64 feet length, built at Wivenhoe in 1871. The yacht was owned by Lieutenant Colonel Travers, and registered at Colchester, disappearing from *Lloyd's Yacht Register* after 1910. Also made by Cauldon, a soup plate with a floral border printed in dark blue bears in the centre the burgee of the Royal Mersey Yacht

Club with its liver bird motif and the name *Whisper RMYC*.

Among the several silver models at Greenwich is one of the schooner yacht *Mavourneen*, by Francis Meli of Malta, *c*1902. The yacht was built in 1871 at Gosport by Camper and Nicholson, and was bought by the Admiralty in 1900. She served at Malta as the yacht of Lord Fisher, Commander-in-Chief, Mediterranean, until 1910.

Jewellery with a nautical flavour was sometimes commissioned by wealthy yacht-owners. Sir Thomas Lipton ordered an emerald and diamond brooch representing the pennant of the Royal Ulster Yacht Club and the pennant of his yacht, *Shamrock III,* for presentation to the Countess of Shaftesbury, when she launched the yacht in 1903. In the collection at Greenwich there is a gold tie pin enamelled with the racing flag of the Royal racing cutter *Britannia*, given by King George V to the Rt Hon. Walter Runciman on board *Britannia* in the Solent in August 1935.

There is a long tradition of the Sovereign participating in cruising and racing in luxury yachts. Many members of the Royal Family have also been serving naval officers. At Greenwich there is a collection of items commemorating these Royal sailors and depicting them in naval uniform, the earliest representing William Henry, Duke of Clarence, later William IV (1765–1837). A Liverpool creamware jug dated 1789 (plate 149) is transfer-printed in black with a portrait of the duke in captain's uniform, and a battle scene on the other side. The inscription is:

The Royal British Tar
He's Royal, he's Noble, he's chosen to be
The Guard of our Island and Prince of the Sea.

Another earthenware mug, made for the coronation of the duke as William IV, also shows him wearing flag officer's full dress uniform.

There were several souvenirs of Prince Alfred, Duke of Edinburgh, who after an active naval career became admiral of the fleet. One is a pottery plate printed in purple with a full-length figure of the Prince in midshipman's uniform. He stands amid tropical trees, with his ship, HMS *Euryalus,* in the background. The rim of the plate is decorated with anchors on rope swags, oak leaves and acorns, and the plate is inscribed *Welcome Prince Alfred 1861*. It was produced to celebrate Prince Alfred's return to England in August 1861 after a cruise to the Mediterranean, South Africa and the West Indies. He entered the Navy in August 1858 and was appointed to HMS *Euryalus*. He pursued a successful naval career, becoming admiral of the fleet in 1893.

149 Liverpool creamware jug of 1789 with portrait of William Henry, Duke of Clarence, and a mug of 1830 for the duke's coronation as William IV.

A Staffordshire flatback figure was produced showing Prince Alfred standing beside a chair, dressed in naval uniform and holding a straw hat. Another figure of about 1858 shows him wearing a blue jacket, white shirt and trousers with a red sash, black scarf and straw hat, and resting his right arm on a capstan. A more elegant figure of the Prince is a small plaster model, probably for a bronze or marble figure. He stands in the undress uniform of a captain Royal Navy of 1866–78 pattern, wearing a round jacket, cap, and carrying a telescope. The figure is by Count Gleichen RN, who was a cousin of the Prince and became an admiral himself in 1887. A Stevengraph woven silk picture of the naval Prince was also produced.

Edward VII (1841–1910) was another popular figure on pottery and other souvenirs. As the young Prince of Wales he was depicted wearing a sailor suit, appearing as a pottery figure in about 1852, as a bronze statuette and on earthenware jugs and mugs, both in relief and as a coloured print. The same figure appears in relief on a silver christening mug by J C Edington in 1849. In one version of the figure he wears white trousers, a blue-spotted white shirt with sailor collar, black neckerchief and a sennit hat. The figure appears both as a crisply moulded figure and in a small, cruder version. Later he appears in admiral of the

150 Services used on board the Victorian and Edwardian Royal Yachts.

fleet's uniform as King Edward VII on a Coalport porcelain plate commemorating the opening of the Royal Edward Dock at Avonmouth on 9th July 1908. The plate is printed in blue, with the King in the centre surrounded by an inscription, and a border with an elaborate decoration of the arms of countries of the Empire surmounted by the Royal monogram.

The Royal Yachts, above all, are associated with luxury at sea. Sunderland made plates decorated with a transfer of the second *Victoria and Albert* paddle yacht of 1855. Large porcelain services were ordered for the yachts, and since they frequently incorporated a Royal monogram, the services were changed on the accession of a new monarch. In about 1815 Spode made a service for George IV, when he was Prince Regent, which included an anchor in the design and was probably used aboard the Royal Yacht. At Greenwich there are examples of Royal Yacht porcelain and glass dating back to Queen Victoria's time. The earliest pieces had little maritime decoration and were probably no different to the services used in the Royal palaces, although they are well-authenticated as being in use on board the Royal Yacht *Alberta*. However, a teaset from the second *Victoria and Albert* is of white porcelain printed in blue, with a design of looped rope round the borders (plate 150). This service was made by the Worcester Royal Porcelain Company between 1873 and 1880.

There is also a Minton plate from 1876 with the Prince of Wales's crest above an anchor, and the inscription *Royal Yacht Osborne*. This was the second yacht of the name, launched in 1868 and first commissioned in 1874. A terracotta water jug from the same yacht has a similar motif below the lip (plate 150), and Derby Crown Porcelain and Minton pieces are also inscribed with the name of the Royal Yacht *Osborne*.

A Coalport service with Queen Victoria's cipher, dating from about 1891, is painted with brightly coloured flowers and has an inscription *J Whitman Cowes Royal Yacht* (colour plate 151). Other Copeland pieces in blue and white have *Her Majesty's Yacht* within a garter. Copeland also produced a green-bordered porcelain service with a gilt interlaced rope pattern, anchors, and the cipher of Edward VII, as well as garter badges and the inscription *The Royal Yacht*. From *c*1909 there is a service by Copeland, with blue and gold decoration and the Royal Yacht cipher, which was made for the Royal Yacht *Victoria and Albert* and known to have been used in the wardroom.

NOTES

1 After 1805 the firm of Rundell and Bridge, of Ludgate Hill, became Rundell, Bridge and Rundell, until 1833, when the style changed again to Rundell, Bridge and Co.

2 Christie's (24th October 1990) Lot 118

3 Christie's (29th/30th May 1990) Lot 9

4 Louis Lipski and Michael Archer: *Dated English Delftware* (1984) no. 660

5 Elizabeth Adams and David Redstone: *Bow Porcelain* (1981) plate 127

6 T Cook and G Nichalls: *Thomas Doggett Deceased* (1908) p5

CHAPTER 8 Symbolism of the Sea

It would be surprising if an island race did not adopt nautical motifs as part of its national symbolism. Sometimes such designs celebrate specific ships, people or events with maritime associations, but almost as frequently they have been used as attractive decoration in their own right.

Ships, anchors, compass roses, rope and chain cable, naval crowns and other heraldic devices, tridents and ensigns all make their appearance in many guises, ranging from exact depictions to stylised symbolic representations. Variations of these symbols may be printed or painted on ceramics, or engraved on silver and glass, and can be found carved or inlaid in furniture or formed into pieces of jewellery or other trinkets. Trophies of naval weapons and equipment are often seen incorporated in engravings, printed on pottery or carved on picture frames.

These motifs also frequently occur as part of nautical heraldry. They are found in the corporate arms of towns and institutions with maritime associations, and in personal coats of arms. This is a tradition which goes back to medieval times. In fact the frequent appearance of ships on town seals provides some of the most valuable information on the development of early vessels. The designs are shown in sufficient detail to allow us to discern features which can provide important evidence on the date of introduction of various developments. The Brindley Collection of seal casts at the National Maritime Museum is a large and historically valuable collection representing the seals of towns dating back as far as the thirteenth century. The typical medieval ship seal shows a single-masted vessel, perhaps depicted with some artistic licence to fit it into the circular shape of the seal. The town name is generally inscribed around the outside. In addition to the ship and features like reef points, rudders and shrouds, other interesting equipment is often visible, ranging from anchors, lanterns and ship's boats to flags and trumpets.[1]

There are some interesting carved coats of arms in the Museum's collection. One is a carved and painted version of the South Sea Company Arms dating from 1711 or 1712, which was removed from the company's London offices in Threadneedle Street in 1855 and is now on loan to Greenwich (colour plate 152). The South Sea Company was founded in 1711 and suffered a spectacular crash in 1720, made famous as the South Sea Bubble. The shield of arms has as its supporters figures of Britannia and a fisherman. Britannia holds a small posy composed of a rose, thistle and shamrock, and the fisherman carries a net. The arms are surmounted by a ship crest, in this case a three-dimensional ship model. The arms are believed to have been the work of Richard Jones, who carved the Royal Arms of William III which appear in the Painted Hall at Greenwich.

A porcelain plate on loan to the collection is painted in colour with the coat of arms of the East India Company. The plate, by Spode, dates from *c*1824 and has floral sprays on the border, a moulded rim and a large coat of arms in the centre with lion supporters, a lion crest and the motto *Auspicio Regis et Senatus Angliae*. On the bottom of the plate, *The London* refers to the name of the East India Company ship on which it was used.

Noble families which had earned maritime honours were often granted naval crowns, ships, anchors and other nautical symbols as crests or augmentations to the family coat of arms. Nelson's coat of arms is a particularly interesting example, illustrating as it does the development of his personal heraldry throughout his naval career. Subsequent battles resulted in an accumulation of honours and changes to his coat of arms. Originally he bore the family arms *Or, a cross flory sable, over all a bend, gules*. After the Battle of Cape St

153 The silver sauce tureens and plate with Nelson's Arms are part of the service purchased by Nelson with money granted by Lloyd's after the Battle of Copenhagen. Plate by Timothy Renou, 1801, tureens by Daniel Pontifex, 1801. The chamber candlestick by William Bennett, 1798, also has Nelson's Arms, and the hot water jug by Paul Storr, 1799, has his brother, Earl Nelson's, arms.

Vincent in 1797 he was created a Knight of the Bath and chose his own crest and supporters: a sailor with a broad pennant, and a lion tearing the Spanish flag. His crest was the stern of the *San Josef*, the ship he had captured in the battle.

Following the Battle of the Nile in 1798 he received augmentations to his arms: a chief to the shield, with a palm tree, disabled ship and a ruined fort. The sailor supporter acquired a palm branch, and the lion a palm and an additional French flag. At the same time he took the motto *Palmam qui meruit ferat* (Let him bear the palm who deserves it). Another crest was added, the *chelengk*, rising from a naval crown, as a reference to the diamond aigrette presented to him by Selim III, the Sultan of Turkey, after the Battle of the Nile. When the heraldic painters first got to work they had very little idea of the design of this Turkish honour, so their representations were rather inaccurate.

After the battle of Trafalgar, Nelson's brother, William, became 1st Earl Nelson and retained his brother's coat of arms, with the augmentation of *Trafalgar* on the bend. This difference, together with the earl's coronet, enables us to distinguish between the arms of Admiral Nelson and his brother, Earl Nelson. At Greenwich there are many pieces of silver bearing Nelson's coat of arms, and one or two fine pieces with the Earl Nelson Arms, including a hot water jug by Paul Storr, hallmarked 1799, which is engraved with the arms with the Trafalgar augmentation (plate 153).

Nelson's personal seal, used after the Battle of Copenhagen to seal the truce document, is also at Greenwich (plate 154). The oval silver seal is set on an ivory handle and bears Nelson's coat of arms as a baron, with the *San Josef* and *chelengk* crests. The Nelson Arms appear not only on silver, but on some of his personal porcelain services. In August 1802 Nelson, with Sir William and Lady Hamilton, visited the Royal Porcelain Factory at Worcester. One of the workmen there described the appearance in the painting shop of *a very battered looking gentleman*, and it was reported that Nelson:

> *on inspection of the superb assortment of china at the shop in the High Street, honoured Messrs Chamberlain by declaring that, although possessed of the finest porcelain the Courts of Dresden and Naples could afford, he had seen none equal to the productions of their manufactory, in testimony of which, he left a very large order for china, to be decorated with his arms, insignia etc. Sir William and Lady Hamilton also favoured the proprietors with liberal purchases.*[2]

He ordered a large dinner and breakfast service, and the record of the original order is still at Worcester. Only the breakfast service was completed before his death (colour plate 155). The design he chose was a standard Worcester pattern in a Japan style, but the coat of arms was also to appear on some of the major pieces. The *San Josef* and *chelengk* crests appeared on all other pieces, replacing panels of fretwork in the original design. Various erroneous traditions grew up around this service, such as that the two small green birds in the design were intended to represent the 'love-birds', Nelson and Emma. As the birds were simply part of the original Worcester design this was clearly untrue. None of the pieces of this service at Greenwich have the full arms, but plates and a teapot are known in other collections.

The full Nelson Arms appear on another important Nelson service: a large service decorated with oak leaf borders, with swags bearing the names and dates of his actions – 14th February for the Battle of Cape St Vincent in 1797, 1st August for the Battle of the Nile in 1798, and 2nd April for the Battle of Copenhagen in 1801. The name *Nelson* also appears on every piece. The coat of arms – complete with both the *San Josef* and *chelengk* crests and the viscount's and his Sicilian ducal coronets, with the naval gold medal below – appears on all the plates and larger items, such as the urn-shaped ice pails (colour plate 155).

This service is made up of porcelain items from the Coalport and Paris factories; the latter may have been obtained as blank porcelain for decorating in England. A number of later copies are also known and some, probably by Sampson of Paris, are very close to the originals. Other copies have an incorrect date – 22 April instead of 2nd April – and very unrealistic oak leaves, and other errors in the heraldry. Nelson's motto, *Palmam qui meruit ferat*, appears as *Palmam out meruit ferat*, and the family motto, *Faith and Works*, is transmuted to *Faith and Word*. There is another service of Paris porcelain which is related to the oak leaf service and has the same oak leaf border and blue swags with the names and dates of Nelson's battles, but in the centre, in place of the coat of arms, is a fouled anchor with laurel sprays and the words *Nelson 2nd April Baltic*. The same pattern is also found in a creamware body by Wilson of Hanley.

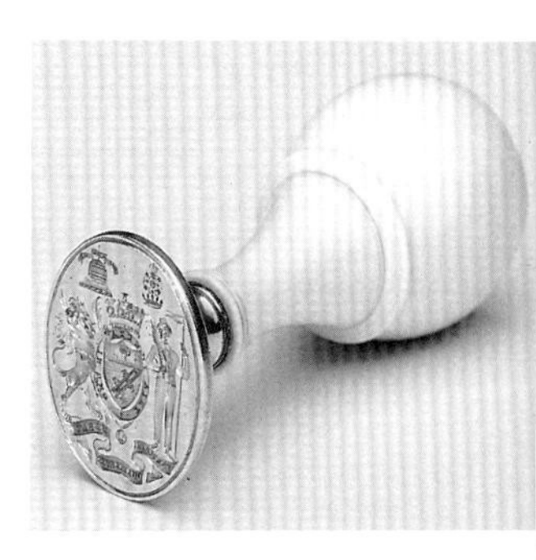

154 Nelson's personal seal used after the Battle of Copenhagen, 1801.

Later commemorative pieces also frequently employed the Nelson coat of arms. The arms appear on items such as inlaid wooden marquetry tea trays, mirrors, chests and writing boxes.

Many other naval families included nautical references in their arms. Admiral Adam Duncan's coat of arms had as supporters Hope with her anchor and a palm branch on the dexter side, and on the sinister *a sailor, habited and armed proper; his left hand supporting a staff, thereon hoisted a flag azure; the Dutch colours wreathed about the middle of the staff.* One of the charges on his arms was a naval crown with a naval gold medal and the name *Camperdown*, and his crest was *A first rate Ship of War, with masts broken, rigging torn and in disorder, floating on the sea all proper.* These arms appear on silver and on fob seals.

Another coat of arms with a sailor supporter holding a pennant is that of Sir John Duckworth (1748–1817). The sailor figure is a pair to a figure of Hercules with his club, and the shield of the arms includes an anchor among the charges. The arms are engraved on a silver tea kettle of 1805 at Greenwich. The arms of Admiral of the Fleet Sir Edward, later Lord, Hawke (1705–1781) included Neptune and a sea-horse as supporters. Anson had a sea-horse and a sea-lion as supporters, and Hood had a merman with a trident and a mermaid with a mirror.

Anchors, naval crowns and other nautical devices frequently appear in the coats of arms of institutions with maritime associations. The Greenwich Hospital coat of arms, for instance, is a shield charged with four anchors, supported by a merman and a sea-lion (a half-lion with a fish tail). The crest is a naval crown with two Union Flags. The crest appeared on much of the equipment used at the Royal Hospital, including the dinner plates made by Davenport (plate 156). The Greenwich Hospital School, formerly housed in the

156 Davenport plate for Greenwich Hospital, *c*1850.

buildings of the present National Maritime Museum, used the same crest. A sealed Admiralty pattern bedspread of the type used in the school dormitories is woven in red and navy blue with the arms of Greenwich Hospital as a large central device and crossed anchors and tridents in the four corners.

Ships have always carried an element of symbolism – religious, heraldic or decorative – in their carving, painting and flags. From the days of sail the figurehead was regarded with particular affection. Until the mid-eighteenth century a lion figurehead was usual on warships, although there were many exceptions. Later, naval vessels tended to have figureheads which referred to their names, and merchant vessels often had female figureheads or a figure representing the owner. With the changes in ship design the figurehead fell out of use, and the desire for a symbolic identity for a ship was reborn in the form of ship badges. These badges first appeared in the second half of the nineteenth century, when they were designed largely at the whim of individual commanding officers for use on the bows of ships' boats. In a squadron or fleet it was necessary to identify your ship's boat among many gathered together. These early badges were frequently no more than the initial letter of the ship's name, but a few interesting designs are known, such as the black flying Angel of Death with flaming sword and trumpet which was adopted by HMS *Devastation*, a turret ship built at Portsmouth Dockyard in 1871 and sold in 1908.

At the end of World War I these designs were regularised and a Ships' Badge Committee was set up to decide on the form of individual designs. The designs of the cast brass badges usually relate to the name of a ship or to her battle honours, and there is often a heraldic element, which may be derived from family or town arms. The ship's badge of HMS *Nelson*, for instance, carries the lion supporter and the palm frond from Lord Nelson's coat of arms. The badge of HMS *St Vincent* is *a winged horse silver, mane and hooves gold, wings blue charged with a fleur de lys gold*, which is derived from the crest of the Earl of St Vincent. Sometimes, in the best heraldic tradition, there were punning allusions. The badge of HMS *Delphinium*, for instance, depicted not the flower but a dolphin.

The large badges carried prominently on the fore part of a ship's bridge usually have the name of the ship in a plaque at the top and are surmounted by a naval crown. The origins of the naval crown (made up of alternate sterns and topsails) are classical, deriving from the gold naval and rostral crowns given to officers in the ancient Greek and Roman navies. The badges are painted in full colour according to the official pattern. Smaller badges without the name and naval crown are used on the ships' boats and in other locations. A variation of the design is used on the circular tompions which are fitted into the muzzles of guns while not in use.

At first the shape of the badges was significant, circular denoting battleships and battlecruisers, pentagonal for cruisers, shield-shaped for destroyers, and diamond-shaped for other vessels. After 1940 badges for all seagoing ships became circular, and shore establishments diamond-shaped. The badges of Royal Fleet Auxiliaries are pentagonal. Modern warships still carry ships' badges, and the official design for an individual ship is used as a logo for many purposes. In fact, the tradition of the badge appearing on ships' stationery goes back to the 1870s, and by the end of the century sufficient examples had appeared to be mounted in crest albums by collectors of ephemera.

Ships' badges are usually associated with the Royal Navy, but some merchant vessels have also carried crests and badges with the device of the shipping company. The P & O Company's rising sun crest and the motto *Quis Separabit* appear on a circular cast brass boat badge of 1904 (plate 157).

In this example the background to the rising sun above the waves is painted red and the name *Macedonia* is cast in large letters at the top. The brass badge is mounted on a circular wooden backboard with a rope border. Badges of this type can be seen in photographs of the ships' boats of the *Macedonia*, the P & O twin-screw steamer built by Harland and Wolff of Belfast in 1904. She was designed primarily for the Indian Service, but was employed on both the Australian and Bombay services. During World War I she was commissioned as an auxiliary cruiser, and in 1921 resumed her merchant service to India, Australia and the Far East, until she was sold to Japanese shipbreakers in 1931. P & O badges of another design are also known: they have the field divided into four quarters with views of Britannia, an Indian elephant, Chinese pagodas and the pyramids, with a central ship and rising sun crest, and the company motto.

157 Brass boat badge of the P & O Company's ship *Macedonia,* built at Belfast in 1904.

Flags are among the most colourful and interesting of all the forms of symbolism associated with ships and the sea. Over the centuries flags have provided a language of their own, and have been used to represent the nationality of a ship, the squadron to which a naval vessel belonged, and to indicate whether she carried a senior officer – a flag officer – and was therefore a flagship. In the merchant service, house flags have served to indicate the company owning the ship, and code flags to identify the individual vessel. To convey more detailed messages complex naval and commercial flag signal codes were developed to communicate between vessels at sea and between ship and shore. These codes were constantly amended and improved over the years until the advent of radio communication rendered them largely obsolete. In pleasure boating, yacht ensigns and burgees serve to identify the owner's yacht club.

For researchers today the evidence provided by depictions of flags – if they have been portrayed accurately by the artist – can be invaluable for identifying and dating paintings and other items. Flags were included in paintings and on commemorative objects not only for their patriotic significance but for their innate colourful and attractive qualities. In sailors' woolwork pictures, for instance, ships are often shown dressed overall with signal flags, in order to enliven the scene rather than to indicate any particular event.

In the eighteenth and early nineteenth centuries flag charts were issued on paper sheets or in instructional booklets displaying maritime flags of all nations. These charts also appear as very attractive silk squares printed in full colour. Sometimes the flags are combined with ship illustrations and Royal coats of arms, and these, together with the evidence of the flags themselves, enable approximate dates to be assigned to the textiles.

The earliest of the silk flag squares at Greenwich date from 1817–29, according to the flags. The Royal Standard at the top is the Hanoverian Arms of 1817–37, and the Royal Yacht Club flag is shown as a red flag with a gold crown over a fouled anchor, a flag not used after 1829. Sailing ships sometimes appear in eight panels around the borders of these squares. This design was also updated to replace the earlier Royal Standard by the Victorian version used after 1837. The Victorian Royal Standard also appears on a red-bordered silk square which has the coloured flags arranged round a central black-printed three-decker (colour plate 158). In other versions the Royal Standard appears in the centre of the other flags in varying sizes, and one example has the date 1840 printed below the standard.

One Liverpool creamware jug is transfer-printed with a ship on one side and on the other a view of *Liverpool Light House & Signals on Bidston Hill 1788* (colour plate 159). Hand-coloured flags on the row of signal masts are identified by numbers, 1–44, which link with a key to the merchant shipowners listed below the transfer. The jug illustrates the system set up in Liverpool by local shipowners, who used these flagpoles to signal the arrival of their ships in port. Bidston Hill commands a good view of approaches to the Mersey. Other signals indicated a ship reported to be lost or in distress. The lighthouse was built in 1771, and the semaphore signalling system used between Holyhead and Liverpool operated efficiently well into the nineteenth century. This jug has the earliest of the Bidston Hill pottery transfers, and the same version appears on earthenware beakers and a very rare black-printed opaque glass beaker. The transfer was later updated to accommodate changes in signals and shipowners. A jug dated 1789 has 47 poles, and the Victoria & Albert Museum, Merseyside Maritime Museum and other collections have later examples, including undated jugs which list 50, 58 and 75 flag signals. The Herculaneum factory at Liverpool was still producing Bidston Hill jugs between 1810 and 1820 with 75 poles listed.[3]

While naval uniforms, with their long and fascinating history of marks of rank, are outside the scope of this book, there are certain symbols of authority which *do* come within our province as they are decorative or precious objects in their own right which are not, strictly speaking, uniform items. The first of these is the boatswain's call. A whistle of precious metal is an ancient naval symbol, and a gold whistle is known to have been the mark of office of the Lord High Admiral in the sixteenth century. The more humble boatswain's call probably has an even longer history. Its typical shape, with a roughly spherical buoy at the end, a narrow curved pipe and a flat keel below the pipe, goes back to whistles of medieval times, and pewter and base-metal examples have been found on the banks of the Thames. There are thirteenth and fourteenth century references to the use of the whistle at sea, and *An Act for the Reformacyon of Excesse in Apparayle* of Henry VIII of 1532 authorises: *Maisters of the Shipps or other Vessails and maryners to wear whistells of Silver, with the cheyne of Silver to hange the same uppon.*[4] There is one medieval pewter call at Greenwich, but the earliest silver example in the collection dates from 1761.

Boatswains' calls were personal items of equipment rather than official issue, so were often made of silver and personally engraved to the taste of the owner. Many survive intact with their original long chains. Among the many interesting boatswains' calls at Greenwich is one by Hester Bateman of London, made in 1788 (plate 160). This call was used on board HMS *Monarch* the day after the Battle of Camperdown in 1797 to signal the three cheers for Duncan on board the *Venerable*, which were taken up by every ship in the fleet. The buoy has the early rosette design on the ends, which was later replaced by a fouled anchor in line with the development of naval uniform buttons.

Another early call in the collection is by Henry and Richard Croswell of London (plate 160). It has a medallion incorporated in the chain which bears a crest of a ship's stern and the inscription: *Blockade of Toulon. Presented to the Fund for Gallant Conduct to Arthur Taylor Boatswain HMS Superb 21st March 1804.* After 1812, when naval buttons changed to a crown and anchor design, the boatswain's call tended to follow the same pattern. When a call bears no hallmark this is sometimes the only guidance to its date other than the general decorative finish. The earliest buoys are spherical, later becoming barrel-shaped, and then in more modern times spherical again. In essence, however, a modern boatswain's call is little different in shape from the very earliest calls.

The call, however, is more than simply a symbol of office, for it has a very practical purpose. Its high-pitched or trilling notes could be heard above the sound of wind and waves, and its

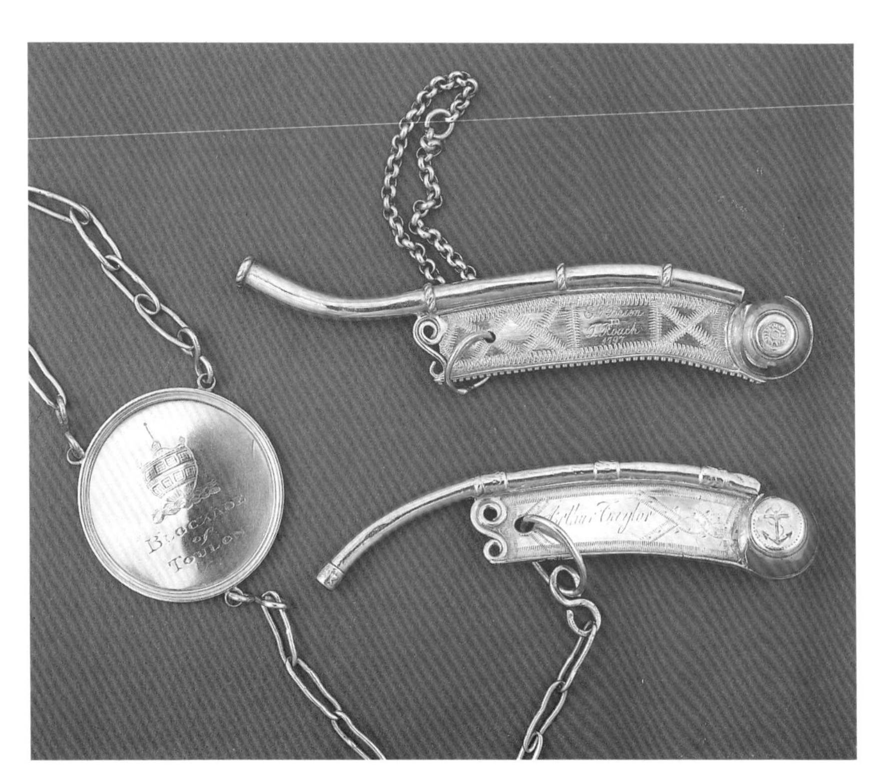

160 Two silver boatswains' calls. Top: used after the Battle of Camperdown, 1797. Bottom: presented to the boatswain of HMS *Superb*, 1804.

repertoire of signals was used to convey many orders at sea. Today the call is seldom heard other than in 'piping the side' – the traditional salute given when the captain or a senior officer is boarding or leaving a ship – and knowledge of the intriguing variety of signals relating back to the sailing Navy is dying out.

A baton has long been a symbol of office for senior commanders, generals or admirals, and many sixteenth and seventeenth century portraits of admirals show the subject holding a plain baton, which might be mistaken for a telescope! It was not until 1821 that the first admiral of the fleet's batons appeared. In all but colour the appearance was identical to the red velvet-covered field marshals' batons. The admiral of the fleet's batons were originally covered in navy blue velvet with gold terminals, and at the top a figure of St George and the Dragon. The bottom terminals are engraved with presentation inscriptions and the baton is mounted with small gold lions passant along its length.[5]

The first two batons to be presented are both in the Museum's collection. One is to William, Duke of Clarence (plate 161), and the other to John Jervis, Earl of St Vincent (colour plate 162). They were made by John Northam of London for Rundell, Bridge and Rundell, and the presentation inscription on one runs: *From his Majesty George IV King of the United Kingdom of Great Britain and Ireland to first Admiral of the Fleet, his Royal Highness William Henry Duke of Clarence. KG 1821.* In 1830 the Duke of Clarence gave his own baton to Admiral of the Fleet William Williams-Freeman. Only four such batons were ever made, and they were given by the Sovereign as a personal honour. One went to James, Lord Gambier in 1832, and in 1897 Queen Victoria presented a baton to her son, Prince Alfred, Duke of Saxe-Coburg and Gotha and Duke of Edinburgh. This example is now in the Museum in Coburg.

Throughout the present survey of maritime commemorative objects, various allegorical figures have been a recurring theme in decoration. In celebration of battle, figures of Fame, Victory and Hope are often seen printed on popular pottery and painted on expensive porcelain, engraved on silver, and featured on enamels, painted lockets and other jewellery.

Hope, with her attribute, an anchor, was inevitably a particularly popular symbol. Among her more elegant appearances in the eighteenth century is the famous *Hope* dinner service made by the Royal Porcelain Works at Worcester in 1792 for the Duke of Clarence, later King William IV. This service has often been erroneously described as depicting Lady Hamilton, and being presented by the nation to Lord Nelson.

The true story is given in a contemporary report in the *Reading Mercury* of 21st March 1791:

> *The manufacturers of Worcester China are now busily employed in a double set for his Royal Highness the Duke of Clarence. There are near 500 pieces and the price is to be 800 guineas. The ground is very antique and upon every piece there is painted a figure of Hope and in each drawing the attitude is varied. Besides this there is a view of a ship in full sail.*

This design was entirely appropriate to the Duke of Clarence's naval career. Each piece has a different variation of the subject painted in monochrome, and all have a dark blue rim with elaborate gold decoration divided into panels by gold rosettes (colour plate 163). The painting is by James Pennington, who came from Wedgwood to become chief artist at Flight and Barr, the Royal Porcelain Works, Worcester, where this was his first work.[6]

There is an interesting contemporary reference to the dinner service being viewed by Catherine Matcham (Lord Nelson's sister) and her husband, George, at the china manufactory at Worcester, where they saw *a dinner sett for the Duke of Clarence; the figure of Hope in different attitudes in the middle, a very rich border of purple and gold.*[7]

Another pair of large baluster-shaped porcelain vases are painted in purple with a figure of Hope (plate 164). On one side she stands on the seashore, with left hand raised, beside an anchor on the ground. On the other she leans with one elbow on an upright anchor. Around the neck of the vase is a pattern of anchors linked by a gilt ribbon. The vases are said to have been made for Lady Hamilton, but the figures have much in common with those on the *Hope* service. They are unmarked, but are of typical Worcester shape, and are similar to a vase in the Dyson Perrins Museum at Worcester which is painted with a study of Britannia with a lion. All these vases have the unusual feature that the pattern extends only part-way round the neck until it is just out of sight.

161 Detail of Duke of Clarence's baton as admiral of the fleet.

164 Worcester porcelain vases painted with figures of Hope with her attribute, an anchor, 1790–1805.

It is possible that they may have been samples produced prior to a large commission. They date from 1790–1805, and are thought to have been painted either by James Pennington or by Thomas Baxter, who visited and sketched at Merton in 1802–3.

At the other end of the market are the cheap transfer-printed plates with versions of the Hope figure. One Liverpool creamware plate, also dating from about 1790, has a hand-coloured transfer showing a figure of Hope seated with an anchor and wearing a red tartan dress (colour plate 165). To her right is a stern view of a ship, and the border is decorated with six bird vignettes. She is also to be seen as one of the transfer prints on the outside of creamware punch bowls. The *Molly* ship bowl at Greenwich, for instance, has four good quality transfers of Hope, Neptune's chariot, a church and a shore scene. Hope is seen leaning nonchalantly on a large anchor, resting her folded arms on the stock while her hair blows in the breeze.

Hope also appears as a Staffordshire earthenware figure. One variation shows her standing on a square base, wearing a white dress decorated with flower sprigs and a purple sash, sandals and an orange-edged yellow mantle. Her left arm is raised to her head and she leans on a large anchor, gazing into the distance. Elsewhere she is on the outer case of a verge watch by Mary Bradley of London, under a clear tortoiseshell covering. Painted lockets were popular in the early nineteenth century, and two examples at Greenwich have miniature paintings of Hope on a seashore, supporting a large anchor, with a departing warship in the background. The paintings are on circles of ivory set in gold mounts with suspension rings. Both lockets have an empty compartment at the back to take a lock of hair.

We have seen that the enamellers of Bilston produced patch boxes and other small items to commemorate every victory at the end of the eighteenth century. Some of the boxes were decorated with allegorical figures, especially Hope, Victory, Fame and Britannia. One such coloured box shows Hope leaning on her anchor, while behind her Fame blows a trumpet, all against a background of a naval battle, probably intended to be the Battle of the Nile. The inscription around the rim is:

Hope stands beholding their Actions most Glorious
Fame with her trumpet sounds Nelson Victorious.

On another box, winged Fame appears in the sky above a naval battle, blowing her trumpet and holding a banner with the words *Britons Rule.* Fame also features in a miniature painted on ivory which was made to commemorate Admiral Duncan's victory at Camperdown in 1797. In the centre is a cameo portrait of Duncan, and behind him stands Fame with trumpet extended. The fleet is shown in the background, and in the foreground are guns and shot, an anchor and Union Flag. Two putti in the sky hold out a banner inscribed *Duncan's Victory.*

Not surprisingly, Britannia also features prominently on these patch boxes. One box shows a figure of Britannia seated beside a rock with her lion, while a female figure of Peace hands her an olive branch. The inscription is *Peace rewarding Britannia.* Another patch box is printed with Britannia weeping at a memorial to Nelson. A more animated version of Britannia shows her pointing to a ship at sea, with the inscription *Britannia triumphant,* and in another there is an eye and nimbus above her head, and the words *Britannia rules the Waves.*

Britannia also frequently appears on late eighteenth century ceramics, glass pictures and engravings. Sometimes she is the main subject, complete with shield, lion and ship in the background, but more often she appears as one component of a scene of mourning, or in commemoration of a national victory.

A porcelain jug at Greenwich by Flight and Barr of Worcester, dating from 1793–1807, is decorated *en grisaille* with a painting of Britannia leaning on an oval shield and holding a spear surmounted by a cap of liberty, with a cornucopia beside her and a brig in the background (colour plate 166). The design on a late eighteenth century bat-printed pot-pourri vase at Greenwich and a bough pot at Monmouth is described by R W Binns in his history of the Worcester Royal Porcelain Works:

> *One of the best engraved figure subjects in this style was a group designed in honour of Nelson. 'Neptune' and 'Britannia' are seated in a car, drawn by six horses, advancing towards the spectator: Neptune holds a shield, on which a portrait of the Admiral is engraved; and a Cupid, representing 'Fame' stands on the front of the car, sounding a trumpet.*[8]

An important Coalport porcelain plate signed by Thomas Baxter and dated 1806 shows Lady Hamilton as Britannia crowning a bust of Nelson, with four panels on the border depicting his battles and death. Baxter's drawing had been engraved in stipple by A R Burt, and published on 5th December 1805. This plate, which is in the collection of the Victoria & Albert Museum, appears clearly in the foreground of Baxter's watercolour of his father's porcelain-decorating studio, exhibited at the Royal Academy in 1809.[9]

William Duesbury of Derby produced a Britannia figure in *c*1770, showing her standing, wearing a flowered dress and plumed helmet, with a sword and trumpet at her feet. Staffordshire figures of Britannia were also made. In one large example she is shown seated on a grassy mound holding a trident in her right hand, her left hand on a shield, and a lion reclining at her feet. She is dressed in an orange skirt with a floral design in blue and gold, a blue tunic fastened on her shoulders with chain mail, and a white plumed helmet.

Britannia can also be found on eighteenth century embroidered silkwork pictures. On one she leans on a monument which bears a portrait of Nelson, while her grim-faced lion lies at the base of the monument alongside an anchor. A number of variations of the design are known. She also appears on commemorative japanned tin teatrays, standing beside a Nelson monument, with Fame crowning his bust with a laurel wreath. On another tray she stands over the fallen hero, who lies with his arm over her lion while a naval officer presents him with a sword.

167 Liverpool creamware ship bowl *c*1787, transfer-printed with Neptune in his sea-chariot.

Since antiquity, mythical sea monsters and dolphins have been popular decorative devices. Strange creatures from the deep appear on charts, on engraved silver, and most often as part of Neptune's retinue. The creatures might be grotesque fish, combinations of land and sea beasts, or half-man and half-fish. Tritons (mermen) and mermaids, as well as every variation of combined creatures from sea mythology, appear in heraldry. As we have seen, bowls and jugs with ship subjects, both painted and printed creamware, were often decorated with additional Liverpool transfer prints. Neptune was frequently to be found in company with the *Sailor's Farewell and Return* and various drinking and rural subjects. One of these bowls has Neptune standing in his chariot, using his trident to urge along his sea-horses while a triton precedes him blowing on a conch (plate 167). On the other side is another scene of the Birth of Venus, complete with sea creatures and dolphins.

The Derby factory produced a porcelain figure of Neptune *c*1770, naked but for a flowered cloak, and holding aloft a trident, with a dolphin beside him. The figure, which stands on a rococo scroll base decorated with shells, is part of a set of *The Four Elements*. At Greenwich a triton appears on an enamel patch box. The cherubic figure sits astride a dolphin blowing a conch and holding a laurel wreath, and the rim carries the inscription:

> *Victorious Nelson Immortal be his NAME*
> *The Triton with his shell resounds his FAME.*

There is also an earthenware teaset, probably by Thomas Harley of Lane End, Staffordshire, which commemorates Trafalgar. The teapot and other pieces are transfer-printed with pairs of tritons with entwined tails (colour plate 168). The set was made in brown background colour with hand-coloured pink tritons, as well as in dark green transfer with additional hand-colouring, and in plain blue. From the late nineteenth century there is a blue and white transfer-printed soup plate with a scene of Neptune in his chariot pulled by sea-horses and other sea creatures, including a boy riding a dolphin. Four profile heads on the border between trophies of arms are intended to represent Nelson.

Carved wooden pipe cases of the late seventeenth or early eighteenth century were sometimes carved as mermaids. The hardwood case is intended as a travelling case for a clay pipe, and has a sliding shutter at the base and a silver end. In the example at Greenwich the long curling hair of the mermaid merges with a twisted fish tail, below which the pipe case is carved with flowers, scallop shells and foliage.[10] A curved silver whistle of the same period, made in the form of a mermaid blowing a shell, is also known. It is thought to be Spanish, and was probably intended as a child's rattle.

Dolphins have also long been a subject for popular mythology, and in more recent centuries they can be found in various decorative forms as supporters in coats of arms, on silver presentation pieces, as devices on ships' badges, brass tiller yokes, as supports for furniture, brass stands for compass binnacles, and candlesticks. The famous Fish furniture which is now displayed at the Royal Pavilion, Brighton, has dolphins entwined on every one of the gilded pieces. The suite was made in 1815 by William Collins of Tothill Fields, and was a gift of John Fish Esq., to the memory of Lord Nelson. Originally designed for the governor of Greenwich Hospital, after 1869 it went to Admiralty House, and was later transferred to Brighton.[11]

Josiah Wedgwood (1730–1795) produced ceramic candlesticks in the form of dolphins with their heads and bodies resting on a plinth decorated with scallop shells, their upturned tails forming the candleholder. These candlesticks were produced in a variety of ceramic bodies, including creamware, black basalt, and green-glazed earthenware. The black basalt example illustrated (plate 169) is one of a pair dating from *c*1830, but very similar dolphin candlesticks are still being made at the factory today. Their continuing popularity through the years is perhaps symbolic of our national enthusiasm for celebrating all aspects of the sea.

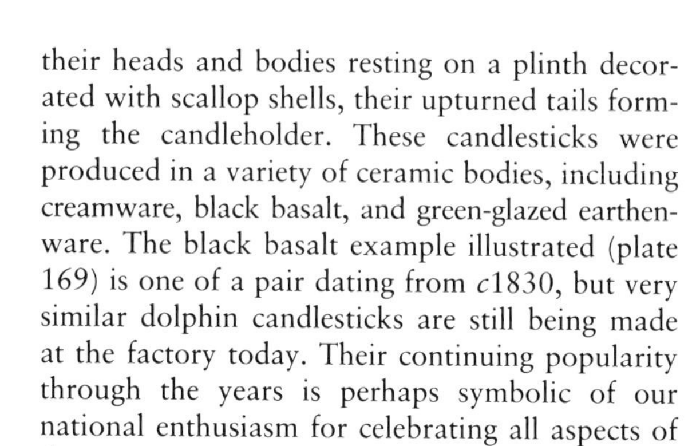

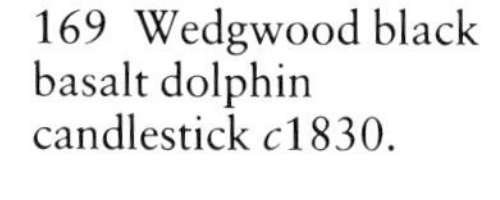

169 Wedgwood black basalt dolphin candlestick *c*1830.

NOTES

1 H H Brindley: *Impressions and Casts of Seals, Coins, Tokens, Medals* (1938)

2 R W Binns: *A Century of Potting in the City of Worcester* (1865) p144

3 A C Wardle: 'Liverpool Merchant Signals & House Flags' (*Mariner's Mirror* Vol 34 no. 3, 1948) pp161–8; K Boney: 'Bidston Hill in Pottery Decoration' (*Apollo* 1961 pp37–9)

4 *Mariner's Mirror* Vol IX no. 11 (1923) p342

5 W E May: 'Admirals of the Fleet and their Batons' (*Mariner's Mirror* Vol 66 no. 3, 1980) pp225–32

6 R W Binns: op. cit. pp107–8

7 E Eyre Matcham: *The Nelsons of Burnham Thorpe* (1911)

8 R W Binns: op. cit. p115

9 John Sandon: 'Nelson's China' (*Antique Dealer & Collector's Guide* March 1989)

10 See Edward H Pinto: *Treen and Other Wooden Bygones* (1969) plate 354C and p335

11 Illustrated in Viscount Cilcennin: *Admiralty House* (1960) pp13–17, 20, 22–3

Select Bibliography

Ayres, James: *British Folk Art* (1977)

Baker, John C: *Sunderland Pottery* (1984)

Banks, Steven: *The Handicrafts of the Sailor* (1974)

Benjamin, Susan: *English Enamel Boxes from the 18th to 20th Century* (1978)

Bicketon, L M: *An Illustrated Guide to 18th Century English Drinking Glasses* (1971)

Binns, R W: *A Century of Potting in the City of Worcester* (1865)

Blair, Claude: *Three Presentation Swords* (1972)

Brindley, H H: *Impressions & Casts of Seals, Coins, Tokens, Medals* (1938)

Britton, Frank: *English Delftware in the Bristol Collection* (1982)

Costa, Giancarlo: *Figureheads* (1981)

Dawson, Warren R: *The Nelson Collection at Lloyds* (1932)

Dibdin, T (ed.): *Songs of the Late Charles Dibdin* (1841)

Dickens, Gerald: *The Dress of the British Sailor* (1977)

Drakard, David: *Printed English Pottery: History and Humour in the reign of George III 1760–1820* (1992)

Ellenbogen, Eileen: *English Vinaigrettes* (1956)

English Ceramic Circle: *Transactions*

Field, June: *Collecting Georgian and Victorian Crafts* (1973)

Flayderman, E Norman: *Scrimshaw and Scrimshanders: Whales and Whalemen* (1972)

Frank, Stuart M: *Dictionary of Scrimshaw Artists* (1991)

Freeston, Ewart C: *Prisoner-of-War Ship Models 1775–1825* (1973)

Frere-Cook, Gervis (ed.): *The Decorative Arts of the Mariner* (1966)

Garner, F H and Archer, Michael: *English Delftware* (1972)

Glanville, Philippa: *Silver in England* (1987)

Godden, Geoffrey A: *Oriental Export Market Porcelain* (1979)

Goodall, Lamb & Heighway Ltd: *Nelson's Flagship the Foudroyant* (1899)

Gray, John M: *James and William Tassie.* (1894)

Grimwade, Arthur: *London Goldsmiths 1697–1837: Their Marks and Lives* (1976)

Gunnis, Rupert: *Dictionary of British Sculptors 1660–1851* (1964)

Hajdamach, Charles R: *British Glass 1800–1914* (1991)

Halfpenny, Pat: *English Earthenware Figures 1740–1840* (1991)

Hansen, Hans Jurgen Hansen (ed.): *Art and the Seafarer* (1968)

Hardwick, Paula: *Discovering Horn* (1981)

Hughes, G Bernard: *English Pottery and Porcelain Figures* (1964)

Jarrett, Dudley: *British Naval Dress* (1960)

Klamkin, Marian: *Marine Antiques* (1975)

Kranz, Jacqueline L: *American Nautical Art and Antiques* (1975)

Lane, Arthur: *English Porcelain Figures of the 18th Century* (1961)

Lewis, John and Griselda: *Pratt Ware 1780–1840* (1984)

Malley, Richard C: *Graven by the fishermen themselves: Scrimshaw in Mystic Seaport Museum* (1983)

Mariner's Mirror, Journal of the Society for Nautical Research

May, J and J: *Commemorative Pottery 1780–1900* (1972)

May, W E: *The Dress of Naval Officers* (1966)

May, W E and Annis, P G W: *Swords for Sea Service* 2 Vols (1970)

Milford Haven, Marquess of: *British Naval Medals* (1919)

Norton, Peter: *Ships' Figureheads* (1976)

Oliver, Anthony: *The Victorian Staffordshire Figure* (1971)

Penzer, N M: *Paul Storr 1771–1844 Silversmith and Goldsmith (1971)*

Pinto, Edward H: *Treen and Other Wooden Bygones* (1969)

Pugh, P D Gordon: *Naval Ceramics* (1971)

Pugh, P D Gordon: *Staffordshire Portrait Figures* (1971)

Pyke, E J: *A Biographical Dictionary of Wax Modellers* (1973) and Supplement (1981)

Rackham, Bernard: *Catalogue of the Schreiber Collection* 3 Vols (1924–30)

Randier, Jean: *Nautical Antiques for the Collector* (1976)

Reilly, Robin and Savage, George: *Wedgwood, the Portrait Medallions* (1973)

Reilly, Robin and Savage, George: *The Dictionary of Wedgwood* (1980)

Robinson, C N: *The British Tar in Fact and Fiction* (1909)

Royal Naval Exhibition, Chelsea, *Catalogue* (1891)

Rudolph, Wolfgang: *Seefahrer-Souvenirs* (1982)

Schiffer, Peter, Nancy and Herbert: *The Brass Book* (1978)

Silver Society Journal.

Smith, Alan: *Liverpool Herculaneum Pottery 1796–1840* (1970)

Towner, Donald: *Creamware* (1978)

Twitchett, John: *Derby Porcelain* (1980)

Weightman, Alfred E: *Heraldry in the Royal Navy: Crests and Badges of HM Ships* (1957)

Williams-Wood, Cyril: *English Transfer-printed Pottery and Porcelain* (1981)

Wilson, Timothy: *Flags at Sea* (1986)

Winton, John: *Hurrah for the Life of a Sailor* (1977)

Index

Ship names appear in *italics*, with the date of launch, where known. In other cases the date is that of the action recorded. References to illustrations and their captions appear at the end of each entry, with the plate number in *italics*. A 'c' following the reference indicates that the plate is in colour.